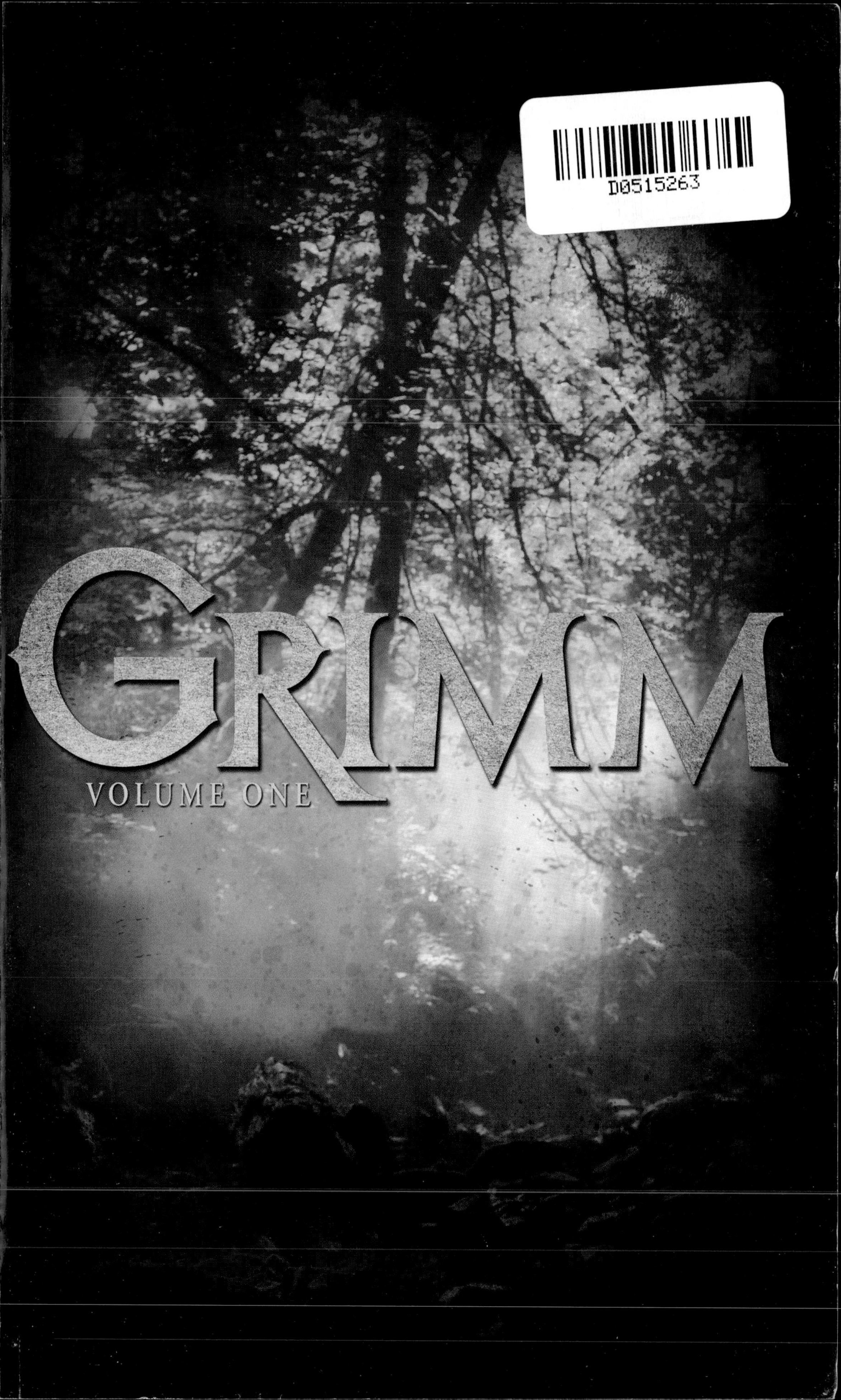
GRIMM
VOLUME ONE

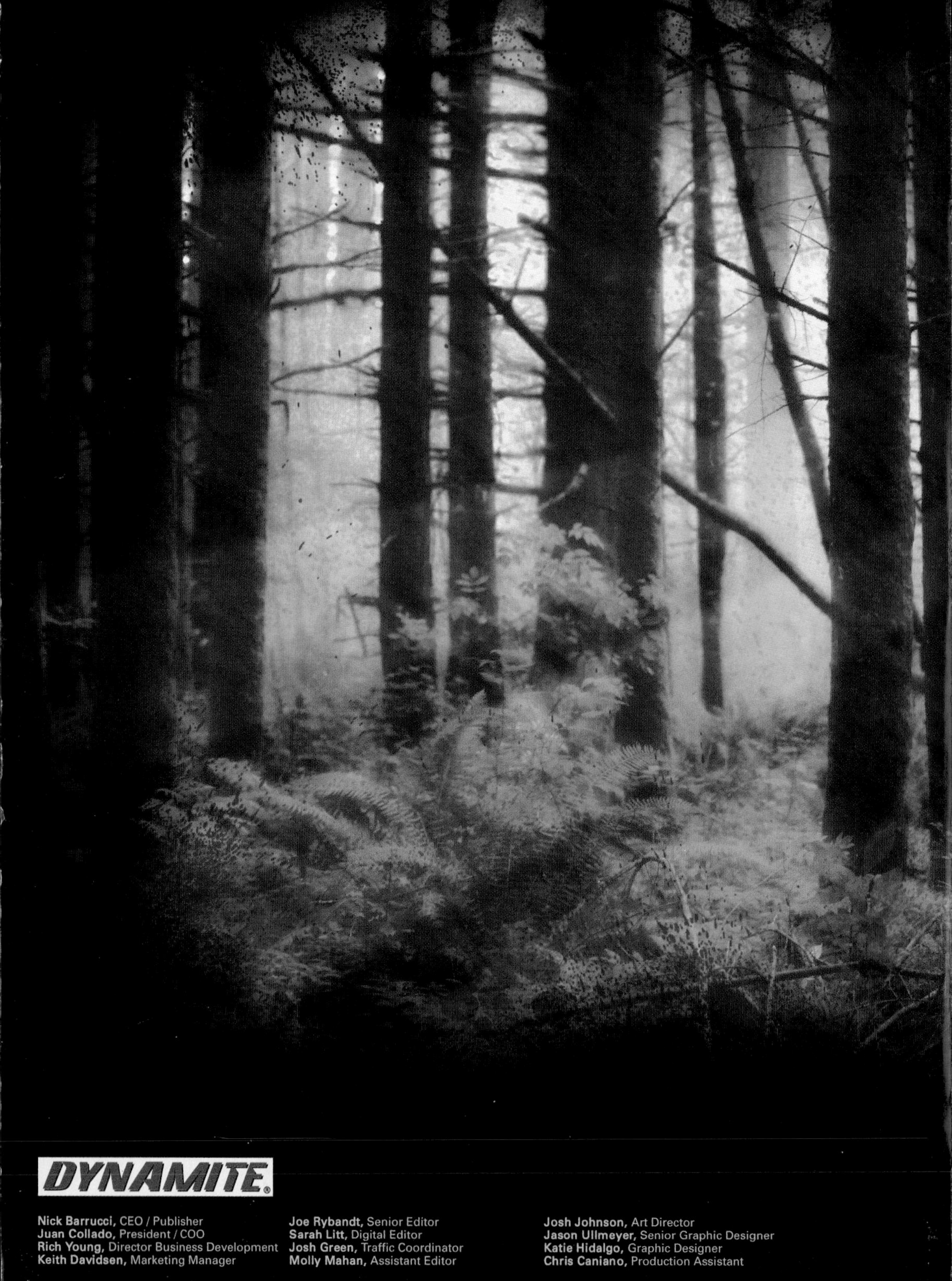

DYNAMITE®

Nick Barrucci, CEO / Publisher
Juan Collado, President / COO
Rich Young, Director Business Development
Keith Davidsen, Marketing Manager

Joe Rybandt, Senior Editor
Sarah Litt, Digital Editor
Josh Green, Traffic Coordinator
Molly Mahan, Assistant Editor

Josh Johnson, Art Director
Jason Ullmeyer, Senior Graphic Designer
Katie Hidalgo, Graphic Designer
Chris Caniano, Production Assistant

GRIMM

VOLUME ONE

Plot by
JIM KOUF & DAVID GREENWALT

Script by
MARC GAFFEN & KYLE McVEY

Art by
JOSÉ MALAGA

Colors by
THIAGO DAL BELLO

Letters by
MARSHALL DILLON

Collection design by JOSH JOHNSON

Special thanks to
CHRIS LUCERO, LYNN KOUF, KIM NIEMI & ED PRINCE

Based on the NBC Television series "Grimm."

ISBN-10: 1-60690-450-7   ISBN-13: 978-1-60690-450-3
First Printing   10 9 8 7 6 5 4 3 2 1

Visit us online at **www.DYNAMITE.com**
Follow us on Twitter **@dynamitecomics**
Like us on Facebook **/Dynamitecomics**
Watch us on YouTube **/Dynamitecomics**

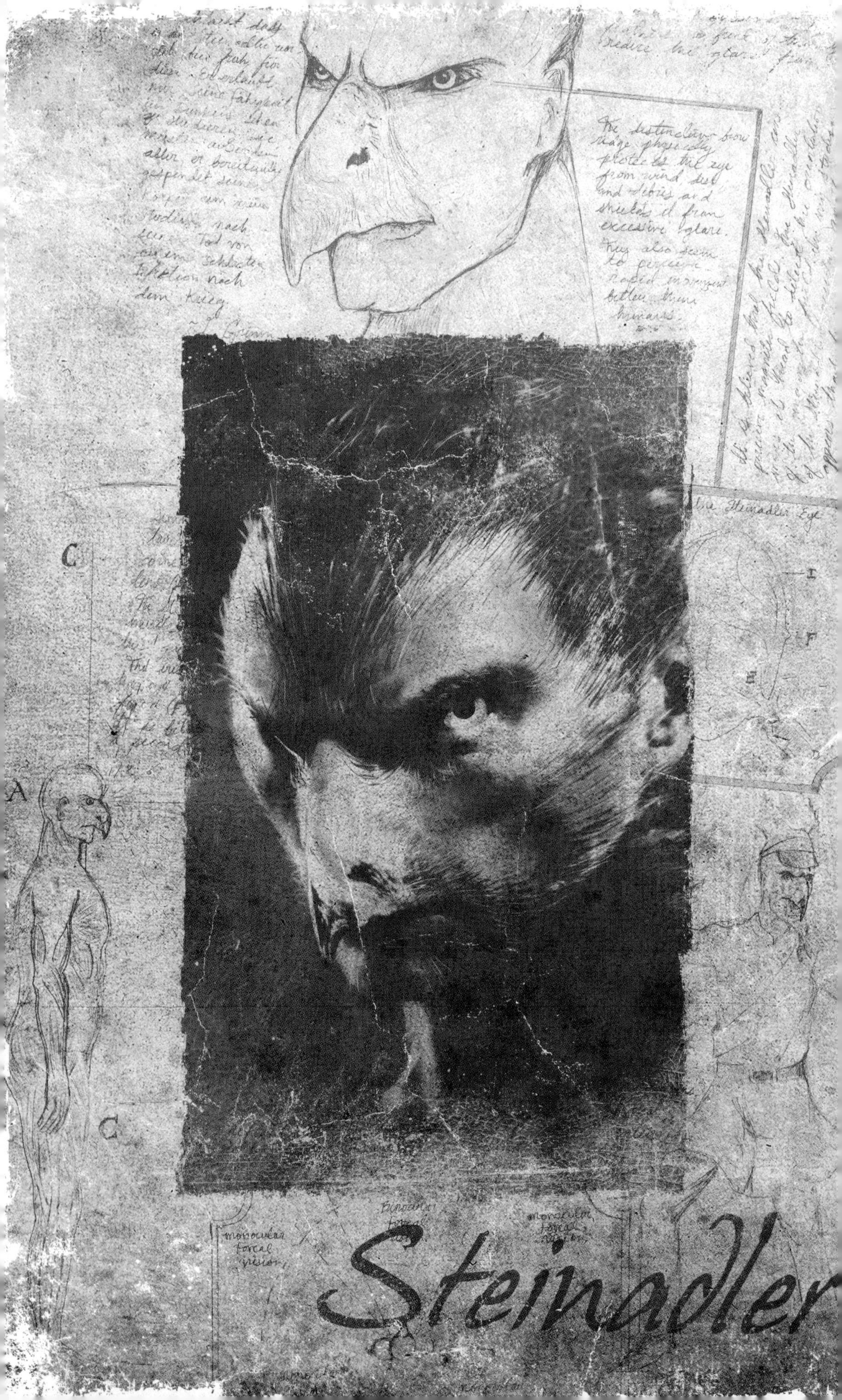
Steinadler

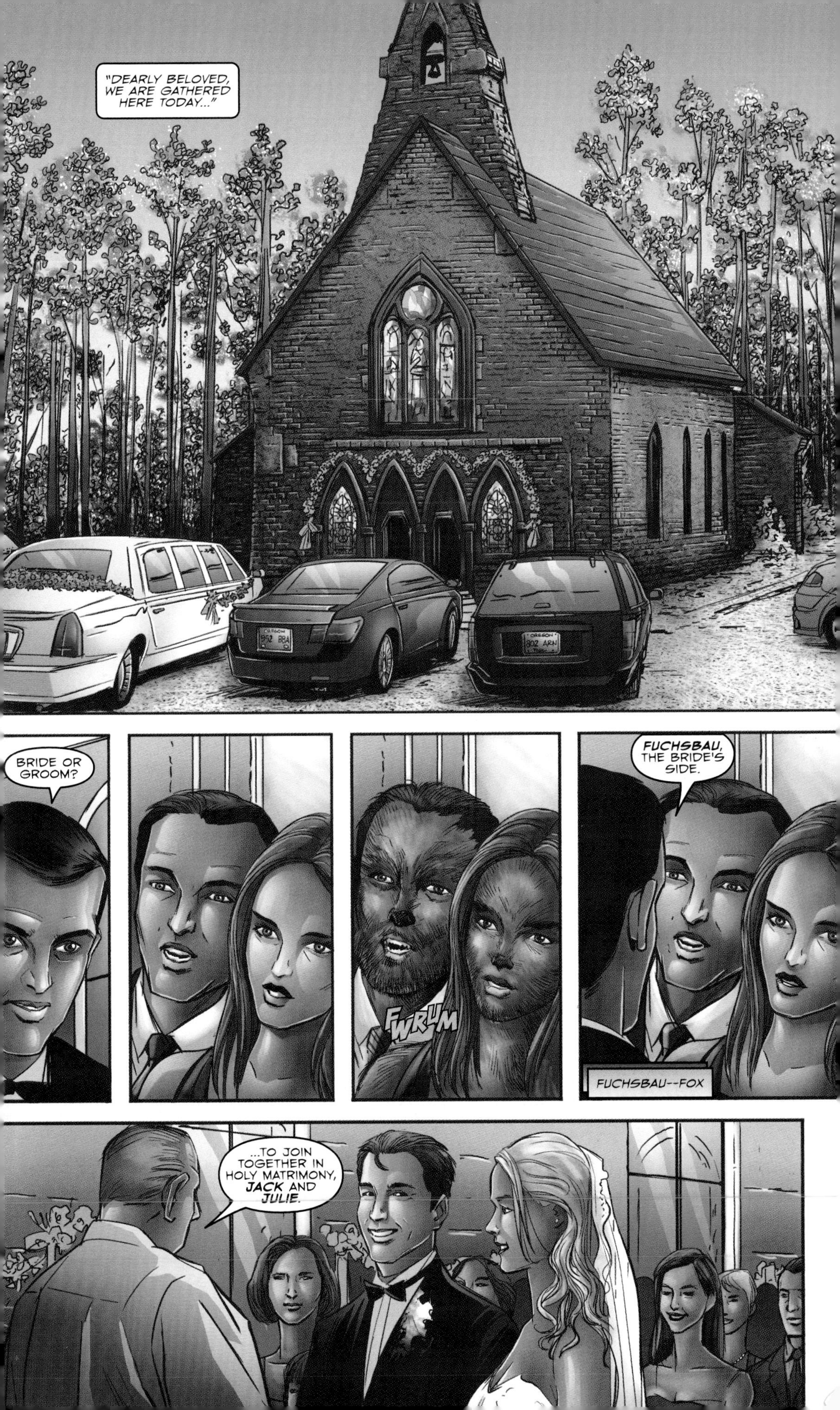
"DEARLY BELOVED, WE ARE GATHERED HERE TODAY..."
BRIDE OR GROOM?
FWRUM
FUCHSBAU, THE BRIDE'S SIDE.
FUCHSBAU--FOX
...TO JOIN TOGETHER IN HOLY MATRIMONY, JACK AND JULIE.

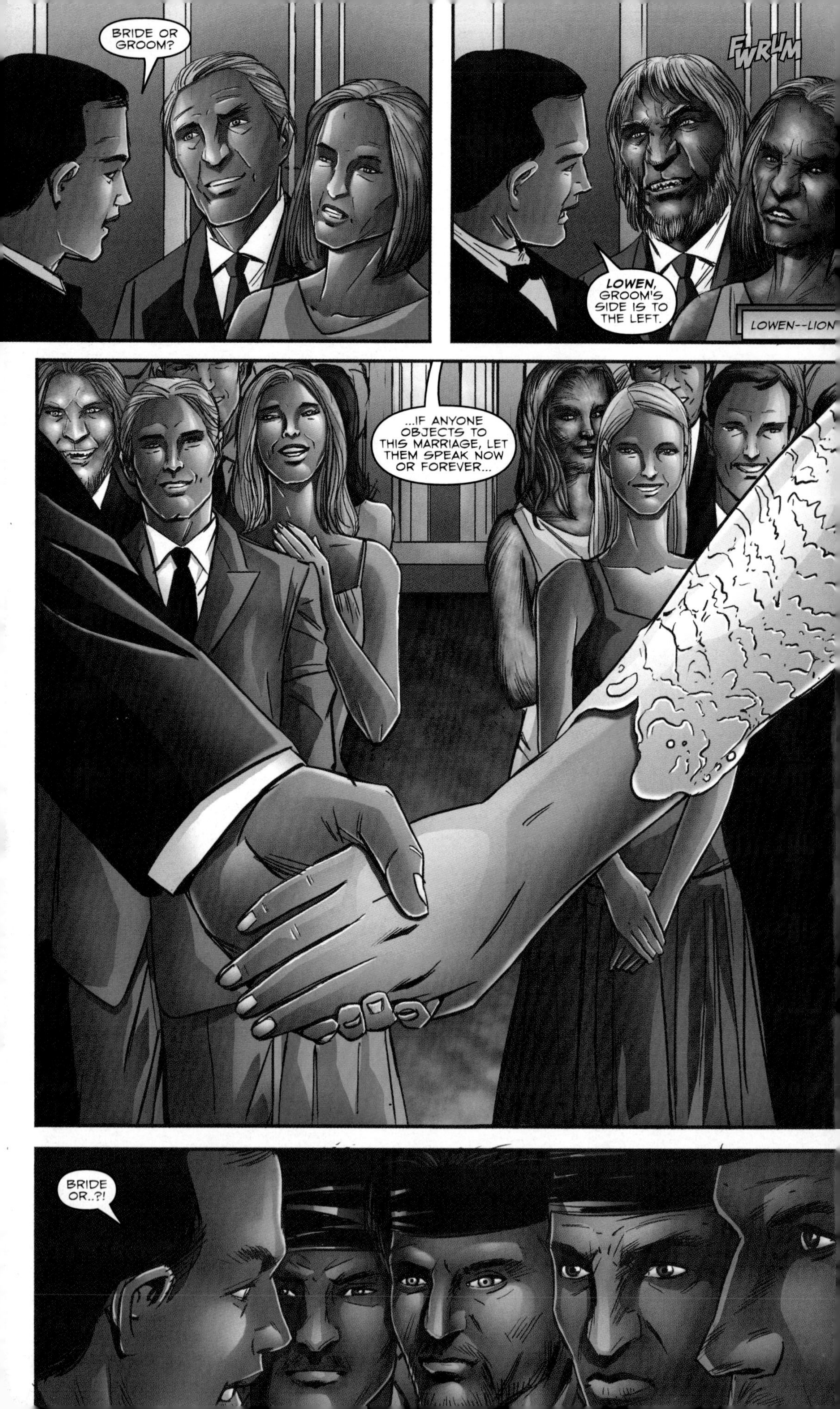
BRIDE OR GROOM?
FWRUM
LOWEN, GROOM'S SIDE IS TO THE LEFT.
LOWEN--LION
...IF ANYONE OBJECTS TO THIS MARRIAGE, LET THEM SPEAK NOW OR FOREVER...
BRIDE OR..?!

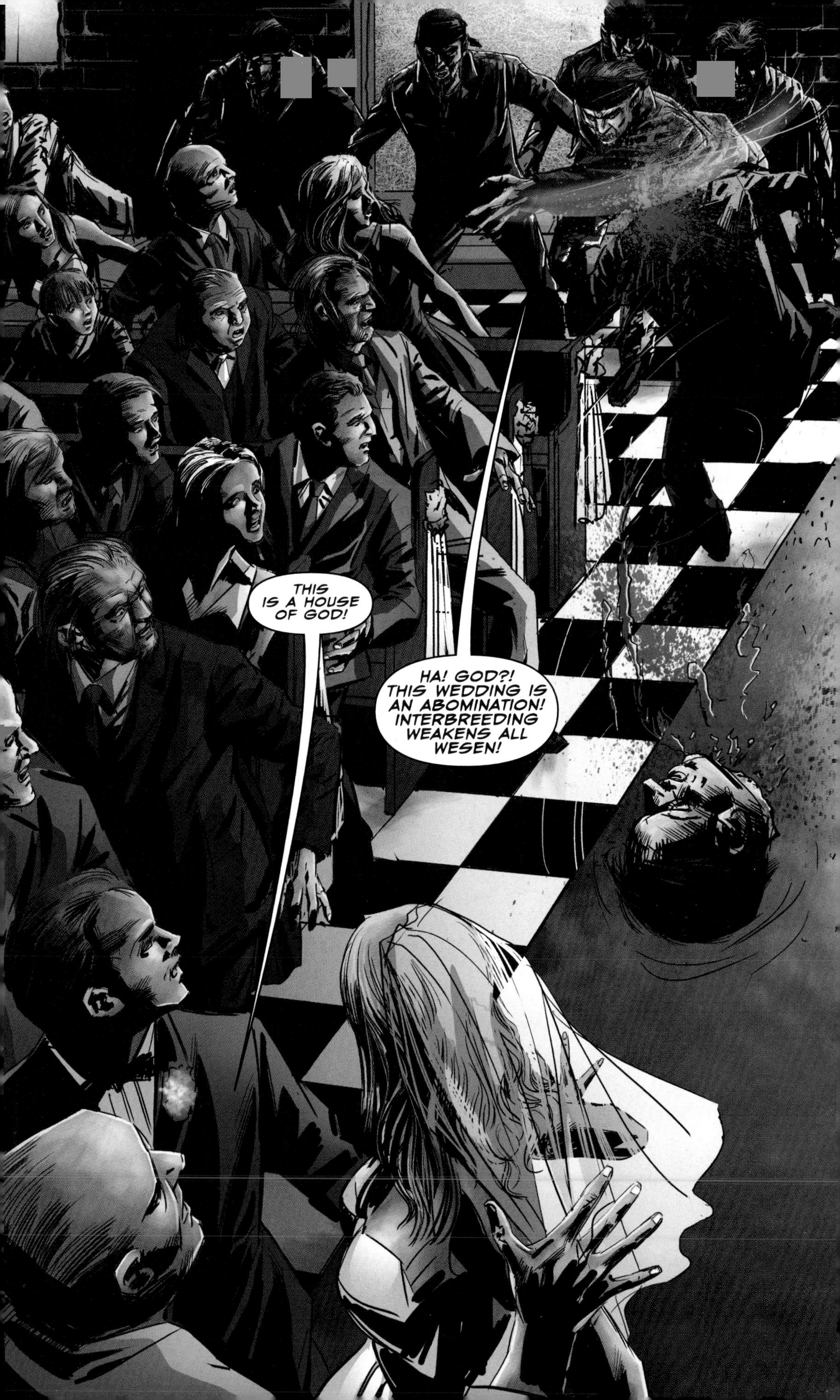
THIS IS A HOUSE OF GOD!
HA! GOD?! THIS WEDDING IS AN ABOMINATION! INTERBREEDING WEAKENS ALL WESEN!

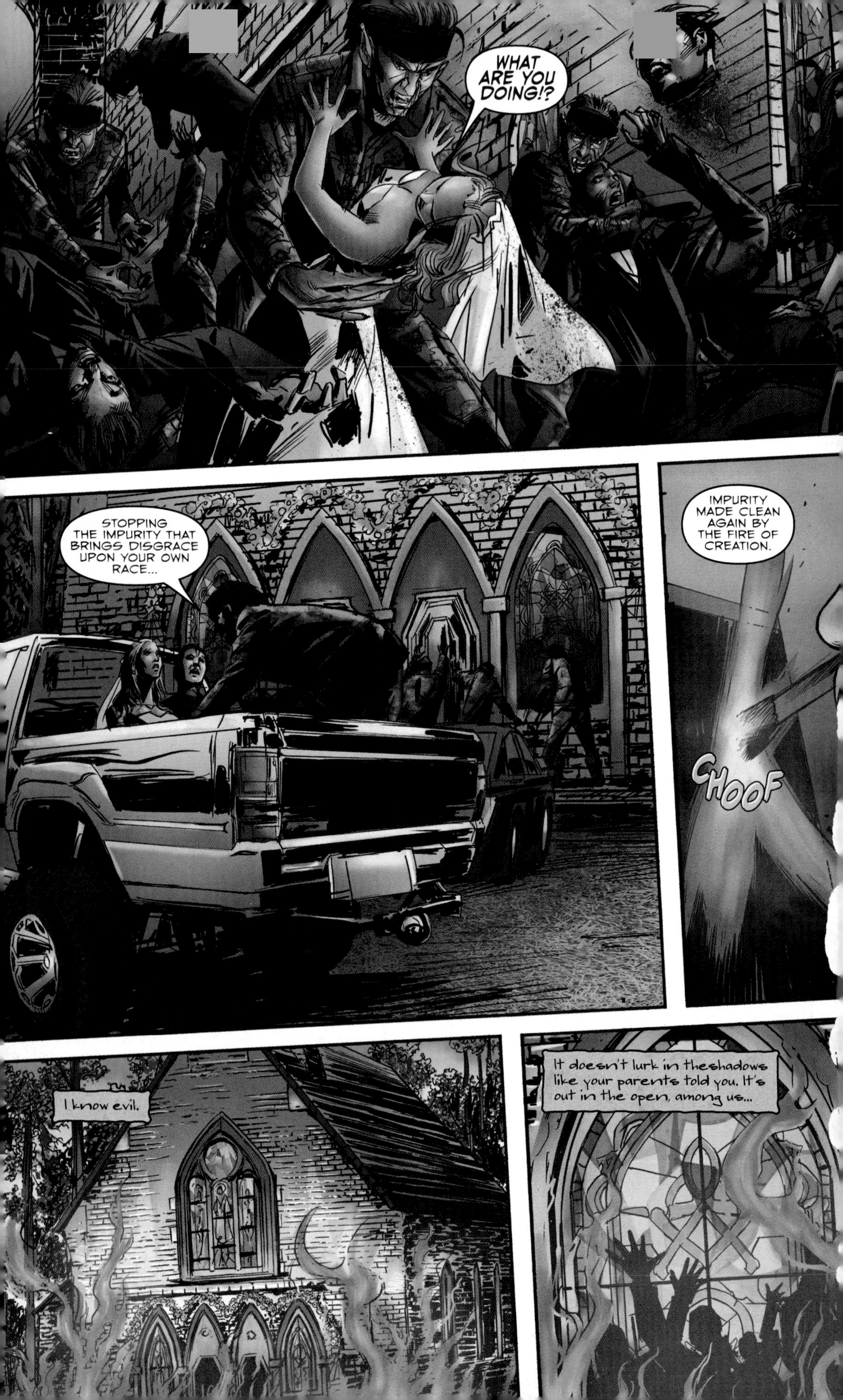
WHAT ARE YOU DOING!?
STOPPING THE IMPURITY THAT BRINGS DISGRACE UPON YOUR OWN RACE...
IMPURITY MADE CLEAN AGAIN BY THE FIRE OF CREATION.
CHOOF
I know evil.
It doesn't lurk in theshadows like your parents told you. It's out in the open, among us...

...You just need to know what you're looking for.
UNBELIEVABLE. THIS IS DISGUSTING.
I SPECIFICALLY TOLD THEM NO ONIONS.
My name is Nick Burkhardt. I'm a Detective in the Portland PD. And a Grimm.
WOULD YOU LIKE TO FILE A POLICE REPORT?
WHAT'S THE POINT, POLICE NEVER HELP.
NOT ON AN EMPTY STOMACH.
DETECTIVE GRIFFIN, YOU'RE MY HERO.
Yea, like those old children's fairy tales.
Turns out they're true. Monsters are hiding among us. And I can see them when they don't want to be seen.
It's a secret burden my family has carried for centuries. My Aunt was one. My Mom is. Now me.
Few people know my secret. My partner Hank Griffin and my Captain among them.
MURDER AND MAYHEM AT PINE HILL CHURCH. AND NICK... IT WAS A MIXED MARRIAGE.
I know it sounds glamorous. Secret life. Creatures of the night trying to kill you. But I'm no super hero. Hell. I can't even get a sandwich without onions on it.

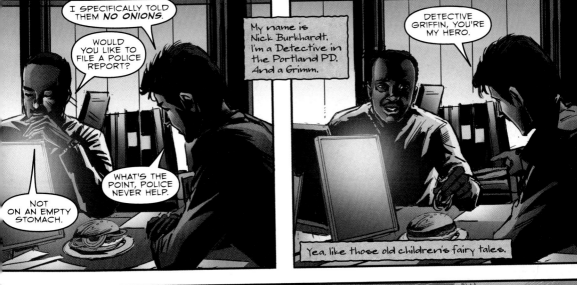

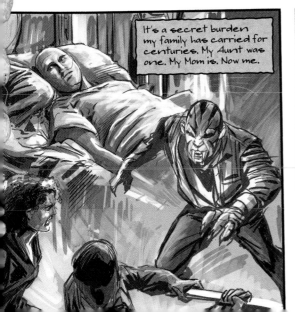

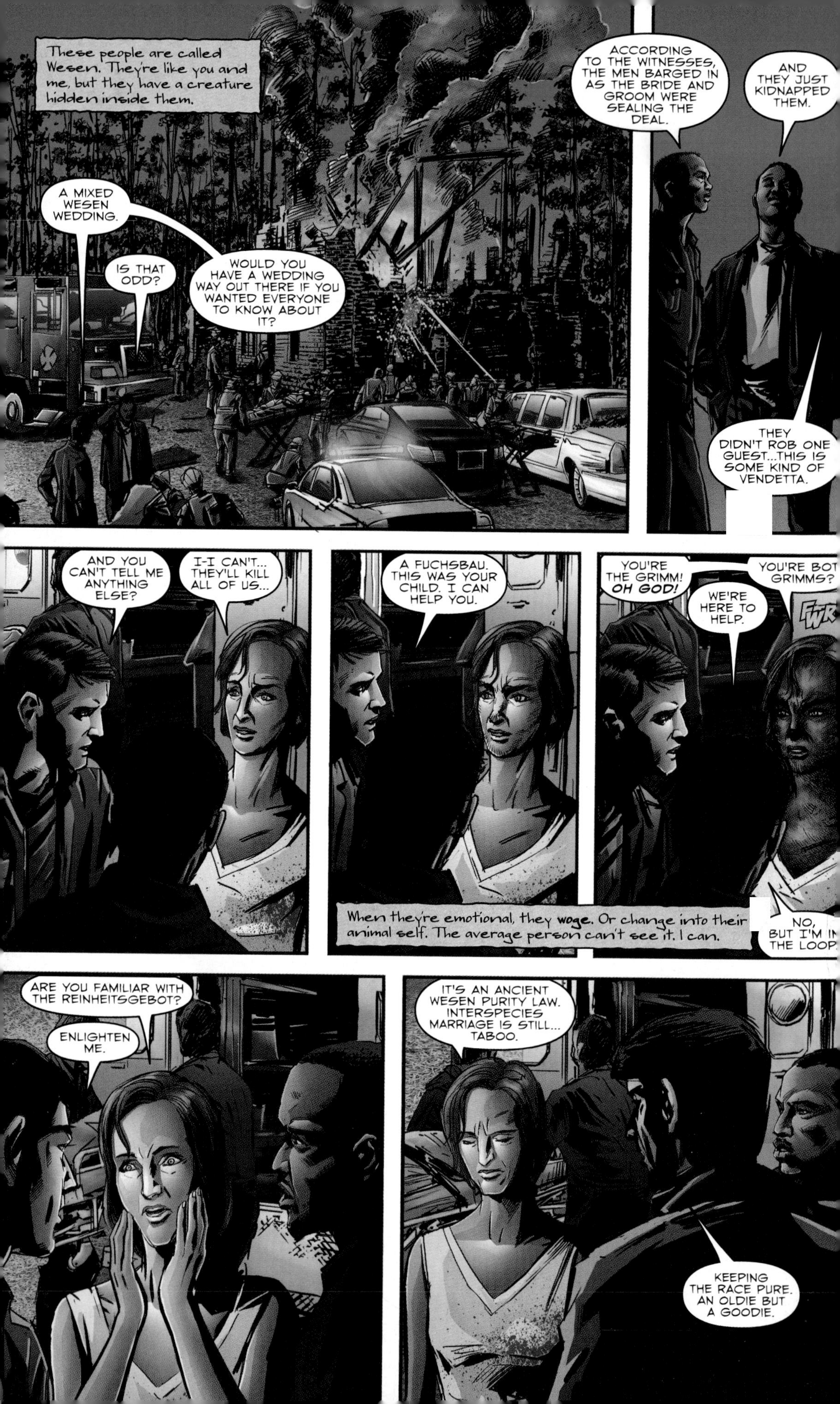
These people are called Wesen. They're like you and me, but they have a creature hidden inside them.
A MIXED WESEN WEDDING.
IS THAT ODD?
WOULD YOU HAVE A WEDDING WAY OUT THERE IF YOU WANTED EVERYONE TO KNOW ABOUT IT?
ACCORDING TO THE WITNESSES, THE MEN BARGED IN AS THE BRIDE AND GROOM WERE SEALING THE DEAL.
AND THEY JUST KIDNAPPED THEM.
THEY DIDN'T ROB ONE GUEST...THIS IS SOME KIND OF VENDETTA.
AND YOU CAN'T TELL ME ANYTHING ELSE?
I-I CAN'T... THEY'LL KILL ALL OF US...
A FUCHSBAU. THIS WAS YOUR CHILD. I CAN HELP YOU.
YOU'RE THE GRIMM! OH GOD!
WE'RE HERE TO HELP.
YOU'RE BOT GRIMMS?
FWR
When they're emotional, they woge. Or change into their animal self. The average person can't see it. I can.
NO, BUT I'M IN THE LOOP.
ARE YOU FAMILIAR WITH THE REINHEITSGEBOT?
ENLIGHTEN ME.
IT'S AN ANCIENT WESEN PURITY LAW. INTERSPECIES MARRIAGE IS STILL... TABOO.
KEEPING THE RACE PURE. AN OLDIE BUT A GOODIE.

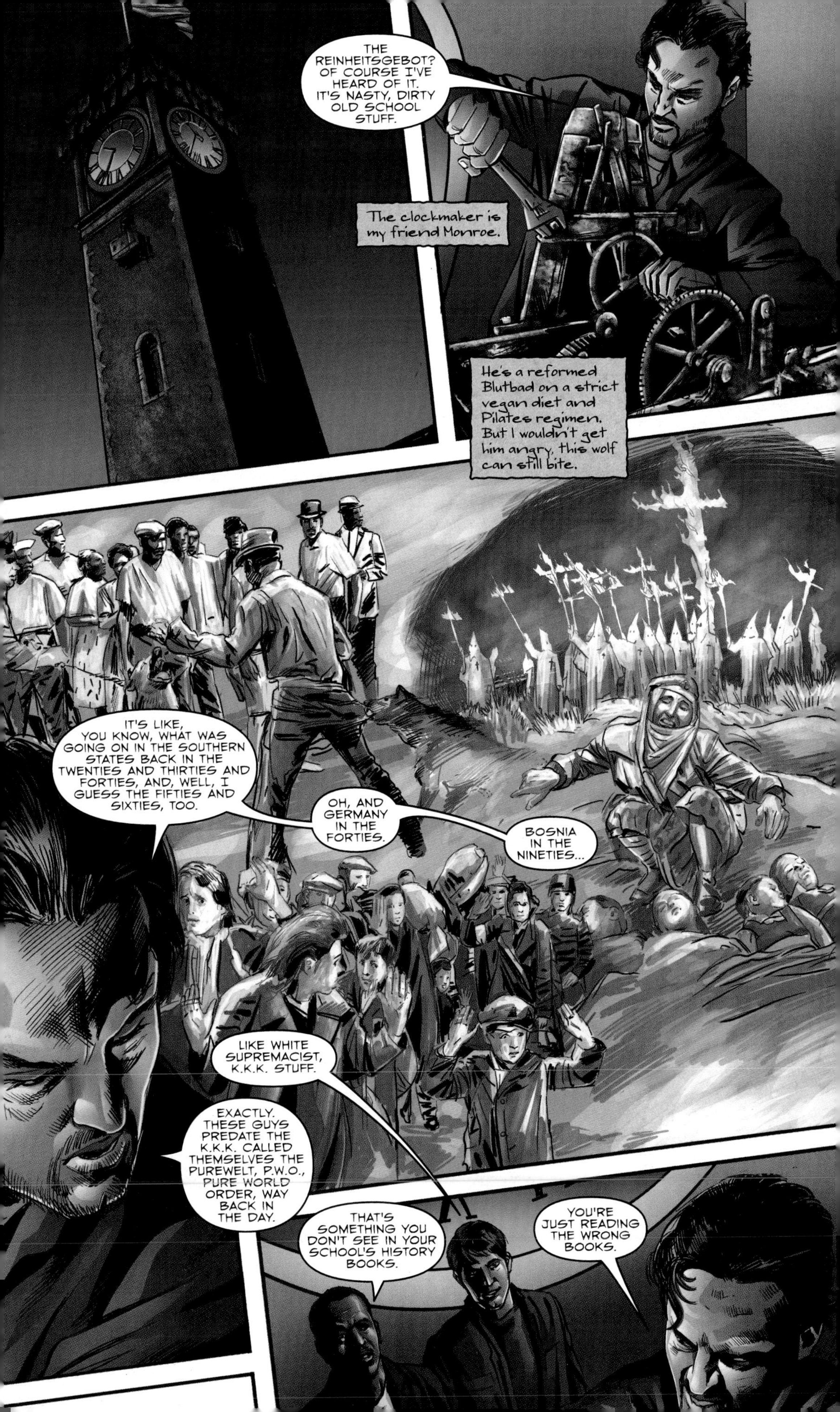
THE REINHEITSGEBOT? OF COURSE I'VE HEARD OF IT. IT'S NASTY, DIRTY OLD SCHOOL STUFF.
The clockmaker is my friend Monroe.
He's a reformed Blutbad on a strict vegan diet and Pilates regimen. But I wouldn't get him angry, this wolf can still bite.
IT'S LIKE, YOU KNOW, WHAT WAS GOING ON IN THE SOUTHERN STATES BACK IN THE TWENTIES AND THIRTIES AND FORTIES, AND, WELL, I GUESS THE FIFTIES AND SIXTIES, TOO.
OH, AND GERMANY IN THE FORTIES.
BOSNIA IN THE NINETIES...
LIKE WHITE SUPREMACIST, K.K.K. STUFF.
EXACTLY. THESE GUYS PREDATE THE K.K.K. CALLED THEMSELVES THE PUREWELT, P.W.O., PURE WORLD ORDER, WAY BACK IN THE DAY.
THAT'S SOMETHING YOU DON'T SEE IN YOUR SCHOOL'S HISTORY BOOKS.
YOU'RE JUST READING THE WRONG BOOKS.

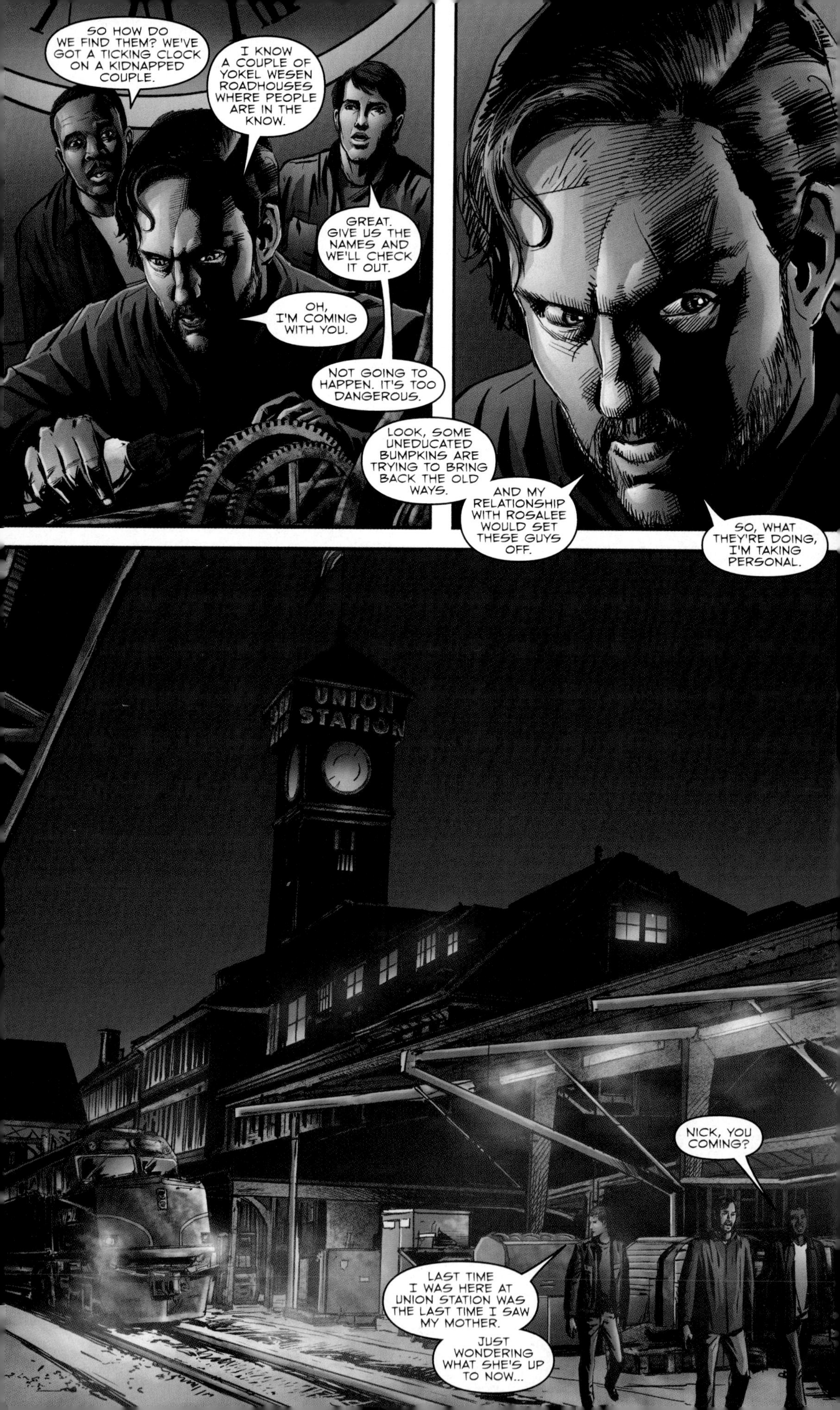
SO HOW DO WE FIND THEM? WE'VE GOT A TICKING CLOCK ON A KIDNAPPED COUPLE.
I KNOW A COUPLE OF YOKEL WESEN ROADHOUSES WHERE PEOPLE ARE IN THE KNOW.
GREAT. GIVE US THE NAMES AND WE'LL CHECK IT OUT.
OH, I'M COMING WITH YOU.
NOT GOING TO HAPPEN. IT'S TOO DANGEROUS.
LOOK, SOME UNEDUCATED BUMPKINS ARE TRYING TO BRING BACK THE OLD WAYS.
AND MY RELATIONSHIP WITH ROSALEE WOULD SET THESE GUYS OFF.
SO, WHAT THEY'RE DOING, I'M TAKING PERSONAL.
UNION STATION
NICK, YOU COMING?
LAST TIME I WAS HERE AT UNION STATION WAS THE LAST TIME I SAW MY MOTHER.
JUST WONDERING WHAT SHE'S UP TO NOW...

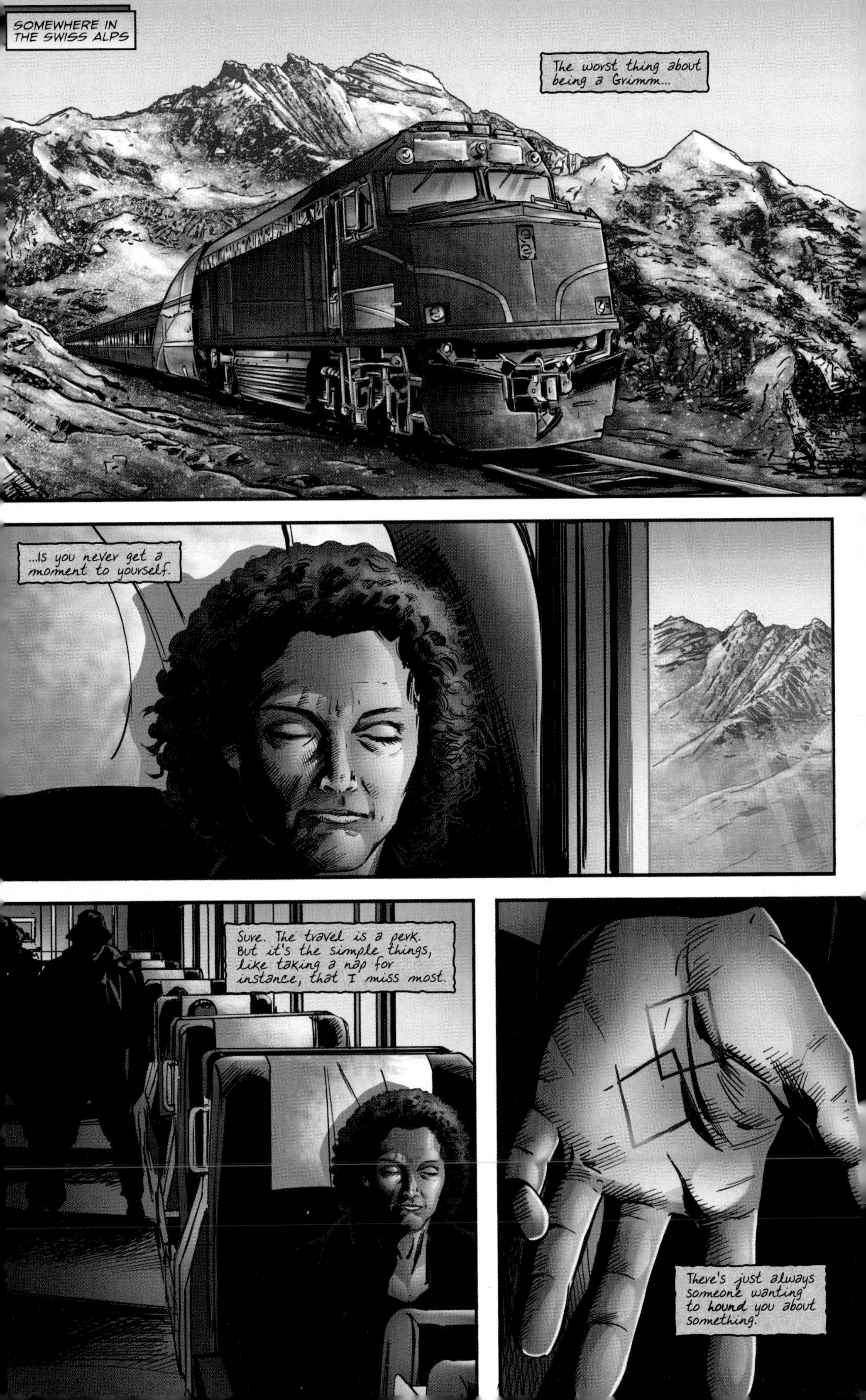
SOMEWHERE IN THE SWISS ALPS
The worst thing about being a Grimm...
...Is you never get a moment to yourself.
Sure. The travel is a perk. But it's the simple things, like taking a nap for instance, that I miss most.
There's just always someone wanting to hound you about something.

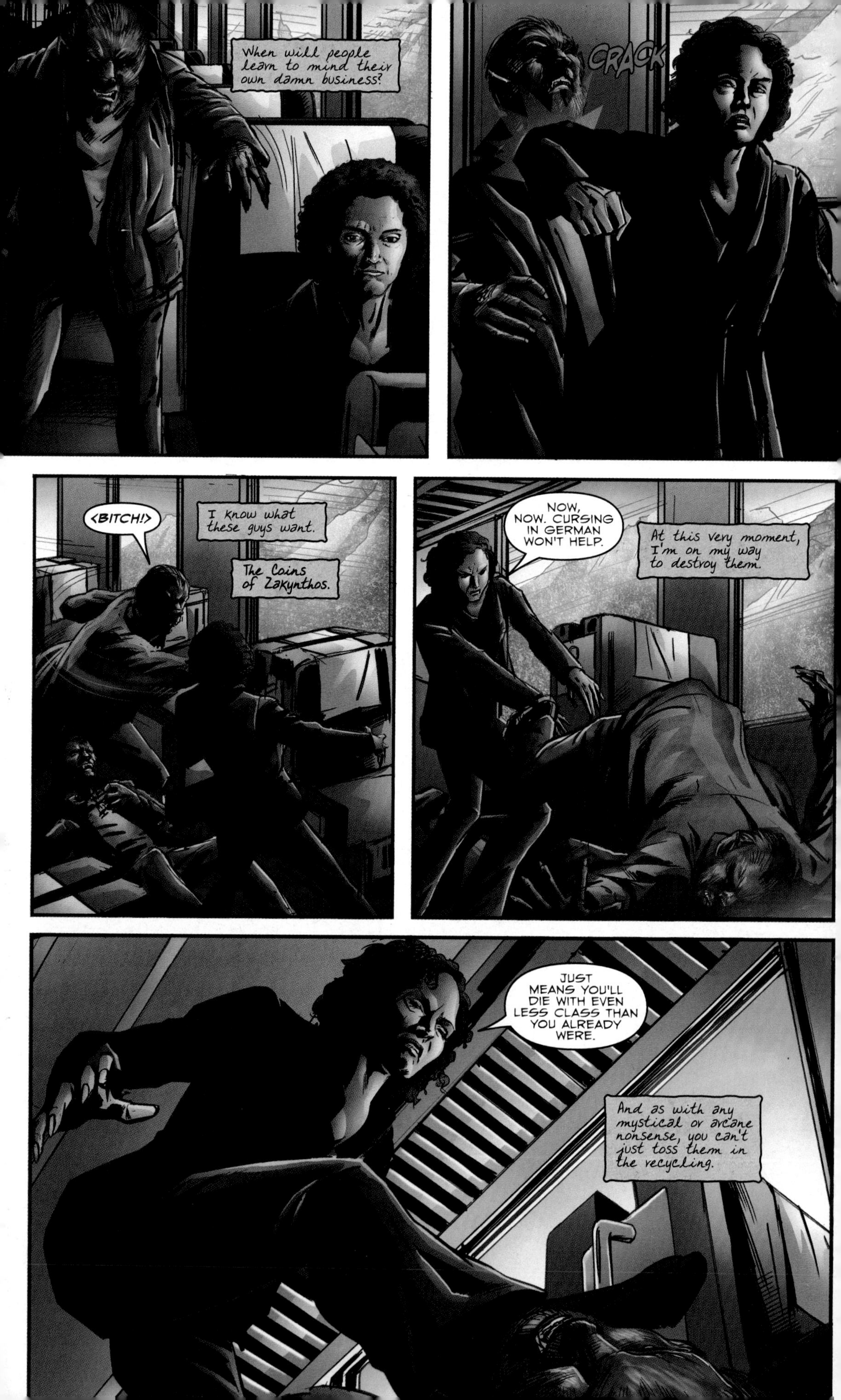
When will people learn to mind their own damn business?
CRACK
<BITCH!>
I know what these guys want.
The Coins of Zakynthos.
NOW, NOW. CURSING IN GERMAN WON'T HELP.
At this very moment, I'm on my way to destroy them.
JUST MEANS YOU'LL DIE WITH EVEN LESS CLASS THAN YOU ALREADY WERE.
And as with any mystical or arcane nonsense, you can't just toss them in the recycling.

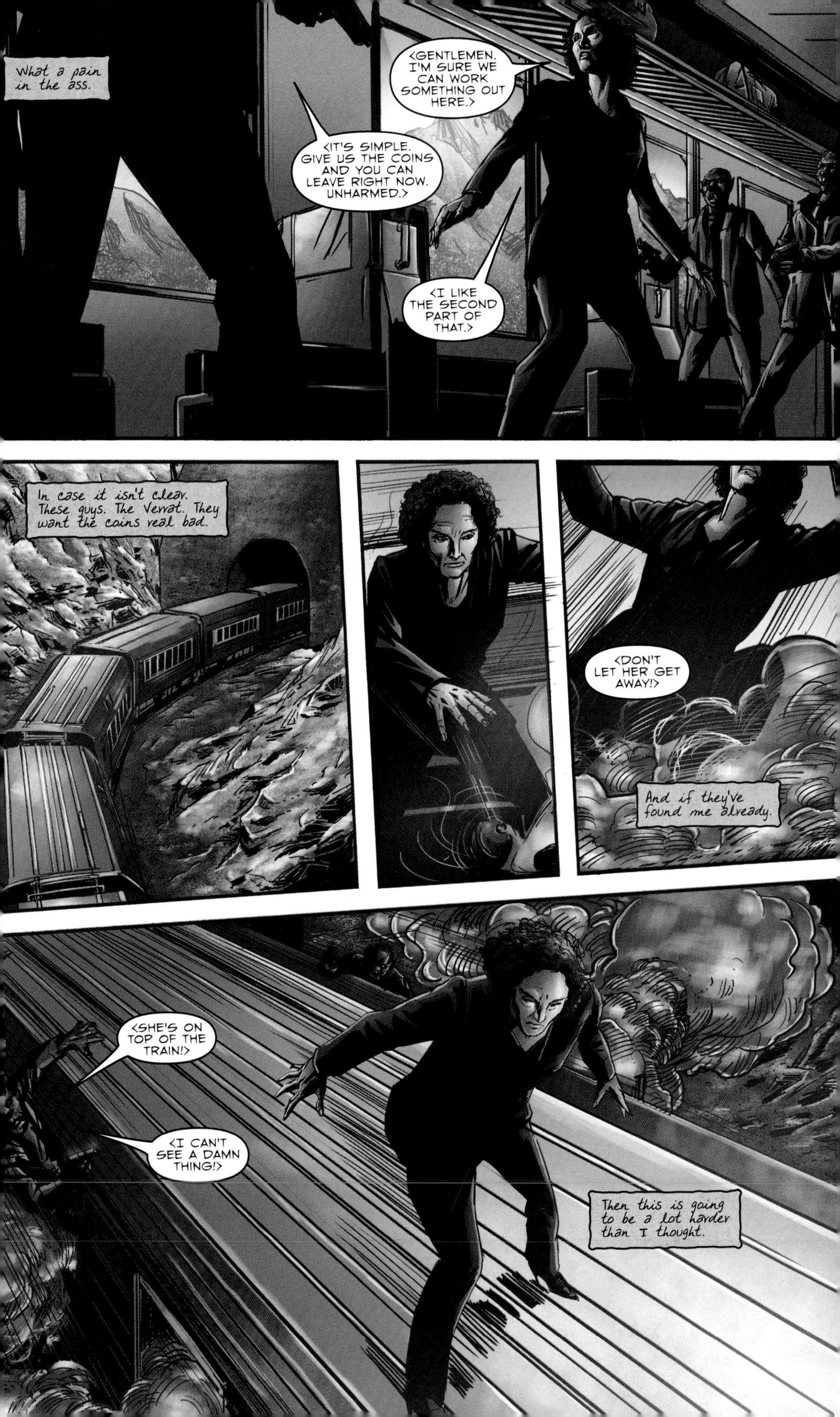
What a pain in the ass.
<GENTLEMEN. I'M SURE WE CAN WORK SOMETHING OUT HERE.>
<IT'S SIMPLE. GIVE US THE COINS AND YOU CAN LEAVE RIGHT NOW. UNHARMED.>
<I LIKE THE SECOND PART OF THAT.>
In case it isn't clear. These guys. The Verrat. They want the coins real bad.
<DON'T LET HER GET AWAY!>
And if they've found me already.
<SHE'S ON TOP OF THE TRAIN!>
<I CAN'T SEE A DAMN THING!>
Then this is going to be a lot harder than I thought.

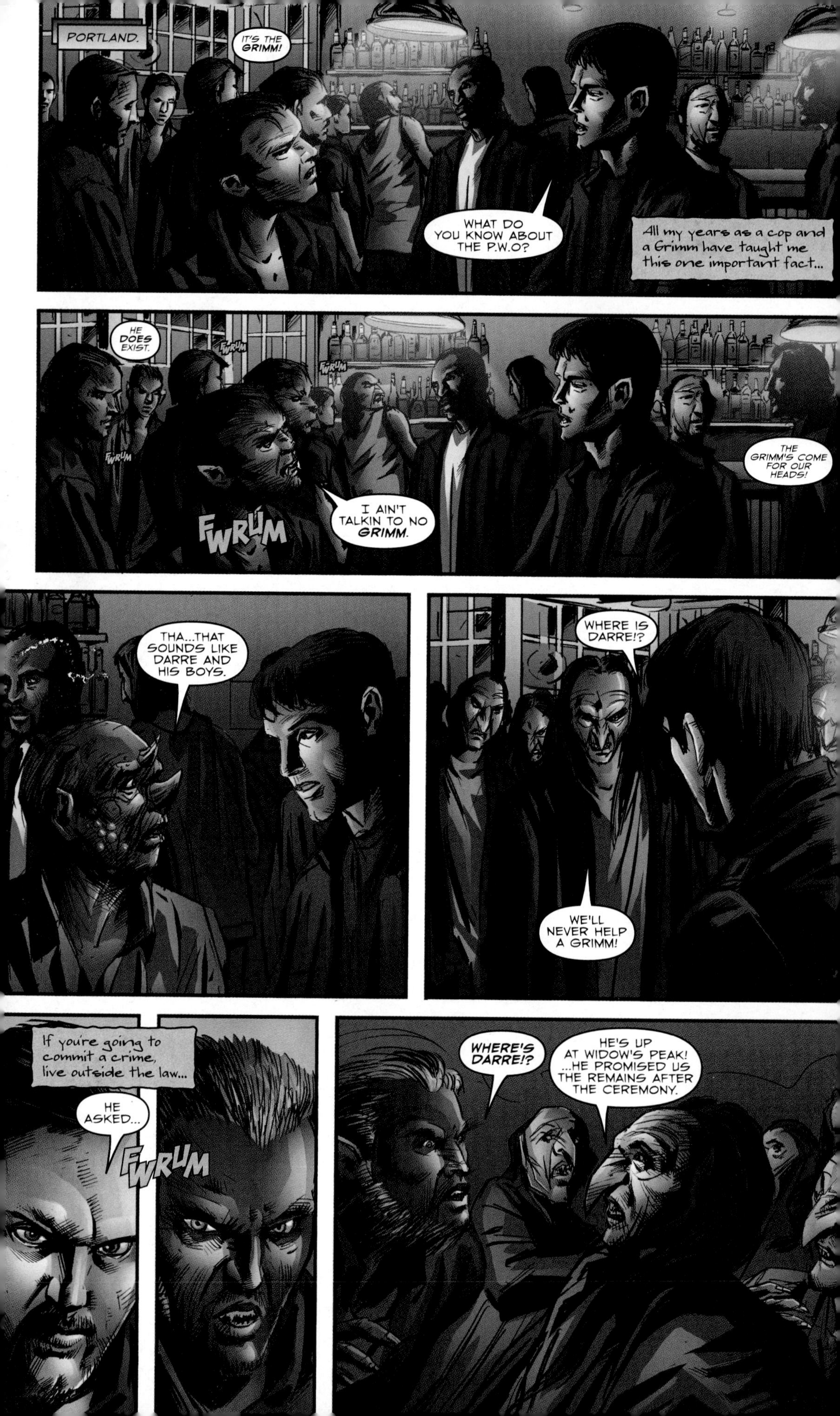
PORTLAND.
IT'S THE GRIMM!
WHAT DO YOU KNOW ABOUT THE P.W.O?
All my years as a cop and a Grimm have taught me this one important fact...
HE DOES EXIST.
FWRUM
FWRUM
FWRUM
THE GRIMM'S COME FOR OUR HEADS!
I AIN'T TALKIN TO NO GRIMM.
FWRUM
THA...THAT SOUNDS LIKE DARRE AND HIS BOYS.
WHERE IS DARRE!?
WE'LL NEVER HELP A GRIMM!
If you're going to commit a crime, live outside the law...
HE ASKED...
FWRUM
WHERE'S DARRE!?
HE'S UP AT WIDOW'S PEAK! ...HE PROMISED US THE REMAINS AFTER THE CEREMONY.

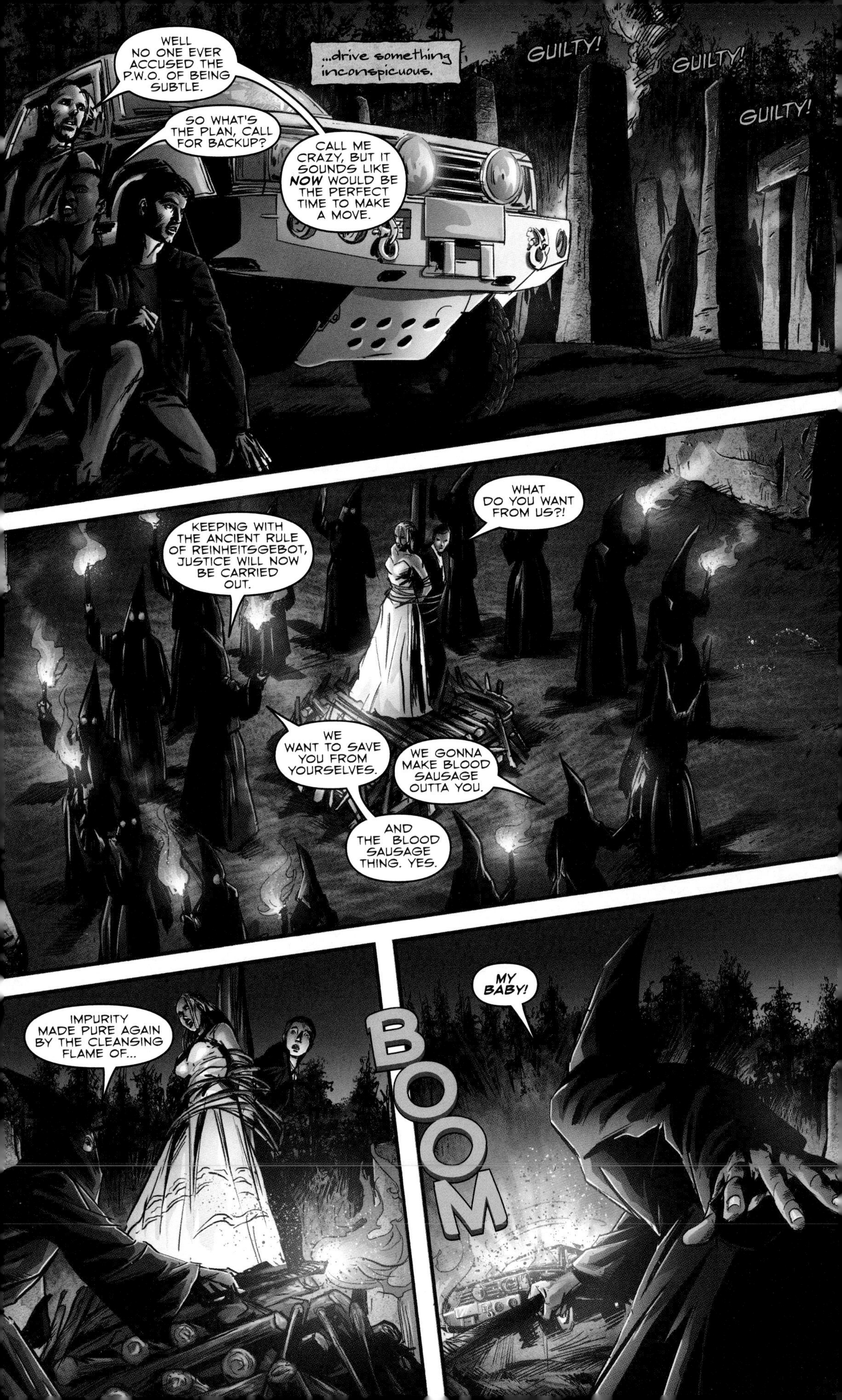
...drive something inconspicuous.
WELL NO ONE EVER ACCUSED THE P.W.O. OF BEING SUBTLE.
SO WHAT'S THE PLAN, CALL FOR BACKUP?
CALL ME CRAZY, BUT IT SOUNDS LIKE NOW WOULD BE THE PERFECT TIME TO MAKE A MOVE.
GUILTY!
GUILTY!
GUILTY!
KEEPING WITH THE ANCIENT RULE OF REINHEITSGEBOT, JUSTICE WILL NOW BE CARRIED OUT.
WHAT DO YOU WANT FROM US?!
WE WANT TO SAVE YOU FROM YOURSELVES.
WE GONNA MAKE BLOOD SAUSAGE OUTTA YOU.
AND THE BLOOD SAUSAGE THING. YES.
IMPURITY MADE PURE AGAIN BY THE CLEANSING FLAME OF...
BOOM
MY BABY!

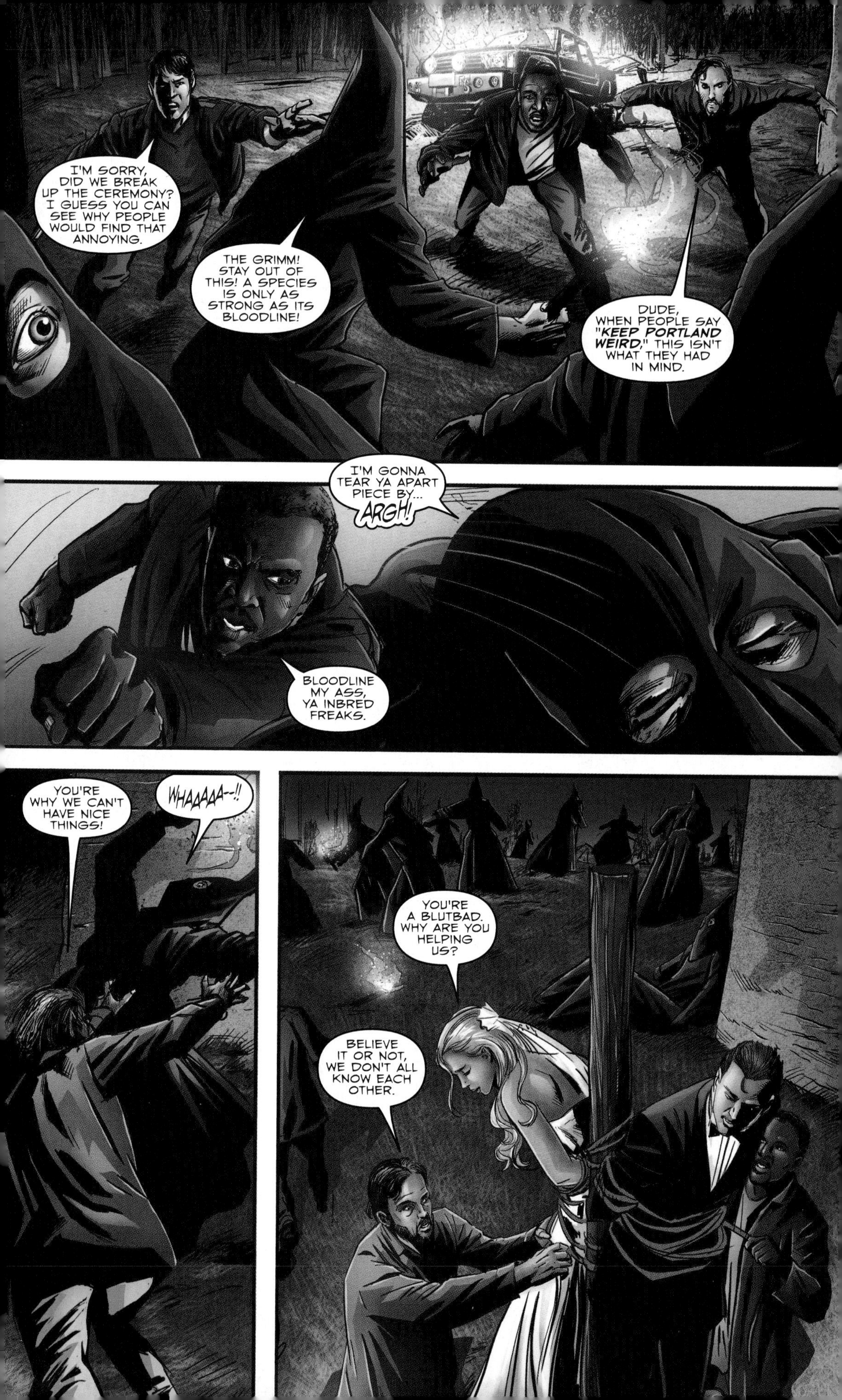
I'M SORRY, DID WE BREAK UP THE CEREMONY? I GUESS YOU CAN SEE WHY PEOPLE WOULD FIND THAT ANNOYING.
THE GRIMM! STAY OUT OF THIS! A SPECIES IS ONLY AS STRONG AS ITS BLOODLINE!
DUDE, WHEN PEOPLE SAY "KEEP PORTLAND WEIRD," THIS ISN'T WHAT THEY HAD IN MIND.
I'M GONNA TEAR YA APART PIECE BY... ARGH!
BLOODLINE MY ASS, YA INBRED FREAKS.
YOU'RE WHY WE CAN'T HAVE NICE THINGS!
WHAAAAA--!!
YOU'RE A BLUTBAD. WHY ARE YOU HELPING US?
BELIEVE IT OR NOT, WE DON'T ALL KNOW EACH OTHER.

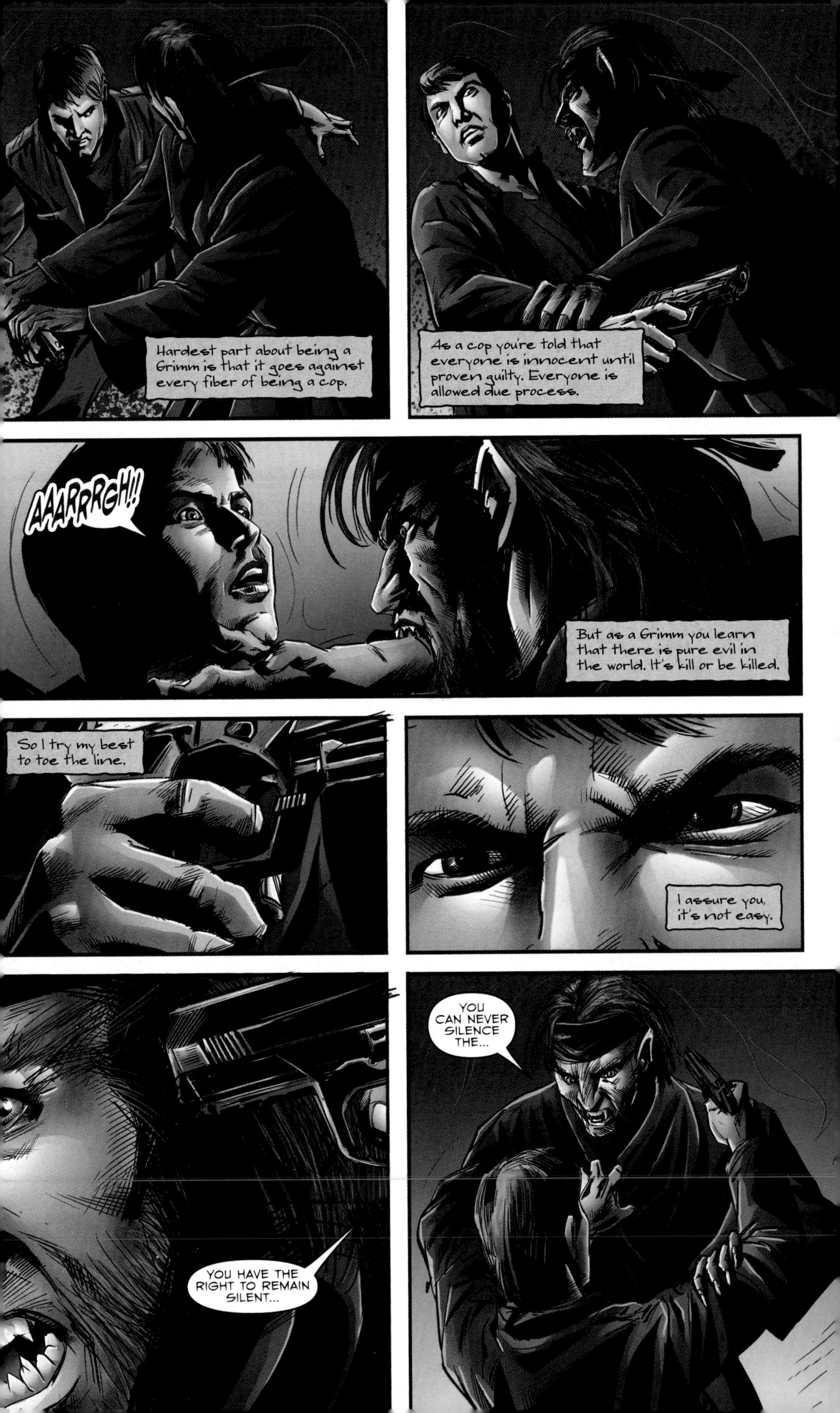
Hardest part about being a Grimm is that it goes against every fiber of being a cop.
As a cop you're told that everyone is innocent until proven guilty. Everyone is allowed due process.
AAARRRGH!!
But as a Grimm you learn that there is pure evil in the world. It's kill or be killed.
So I try my best to toe the line.
I assure you, it's not easy.
YOU HAVE THE RIGHT TO REMAIN SILENT...
YOU CAN NEVER SILENCE THE...

OOPS, GUESS YOU'RE WRONG ABOUT THAT TOO.

WAP

It can be rough. But sometimes all you need is something as simple as a proper nap to set you straight.

Which seems to rarely happen nowadays.

BZZT BZZT

BURKHARDT.

NICKY?

MOM?! WHERE ARE YOU?

VIENNA. THE VERRAT KNOW I'M IN EUROPE WITH THE COINS. *I'VE HIDDEN THEM.* I COULDN'T CHANCE THEM FALLING INTO THEIR HANDS AGAIN.

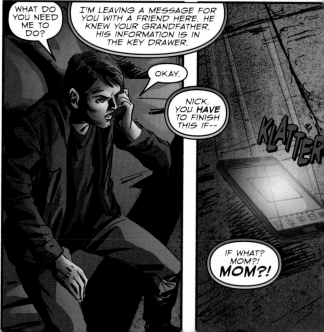

WHAT DO YOU NEED ME TO DO?

I'M LEAVING A MESSAGE FOR YOU WITH A FRIEND HERE. HE KNEW YOUR GRANDFATHER. HIS INFORMATION IS IN THE KEY DRAWER.

OKAY.

NICK, YOU *HAVE* TO FINISH THIS IF--

KLATTER

IF WHAT? MOM?! MOM?!

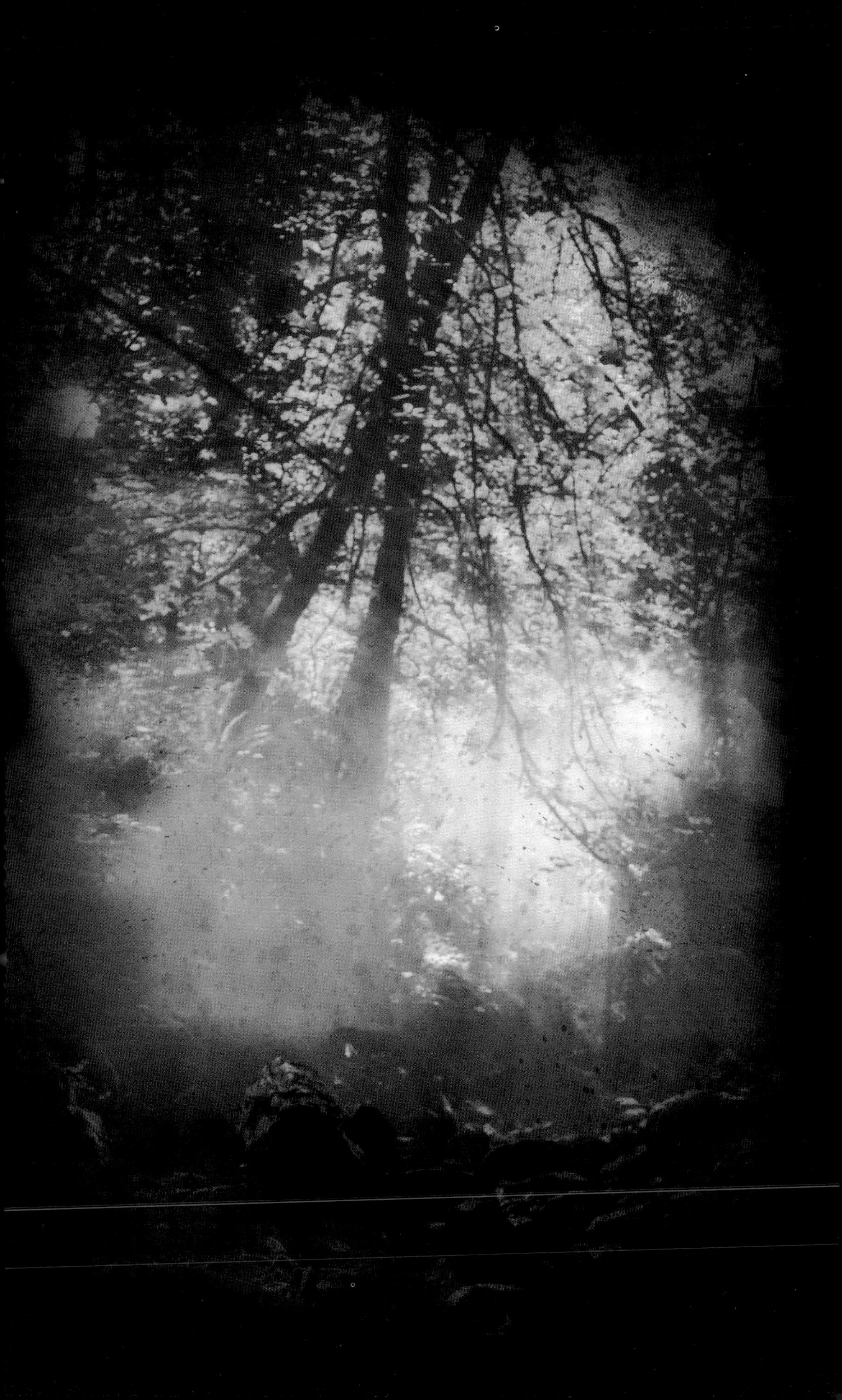

Murciélago

Llegué a América del Sur ya hace varios miles siguiendo la pista de un Murciélago que se embarcó a un buque de vapor en Málaga despues de haber cometido una serie de asesinatos. Lo seguí hasta la selva de las Amazonas, donde parece que toda criatura tiene los

Aprendí despues de habe las víctimas del Mur criaturas producen un agudo que puede ma hombre, mujer o bestia

La selva un refug

Aprendí des víctimas del producen un matar a en pocos

El sonido p arañazos de la explotar a los reventar a los nasales, estalla tripas, y causa muchísimo d interno

En mis batalla descubierto q muchas veces tiene que pagar la misma mone como sospechab sonidos fuertes debilitar a los

El sonido puede explota a los Murcielago

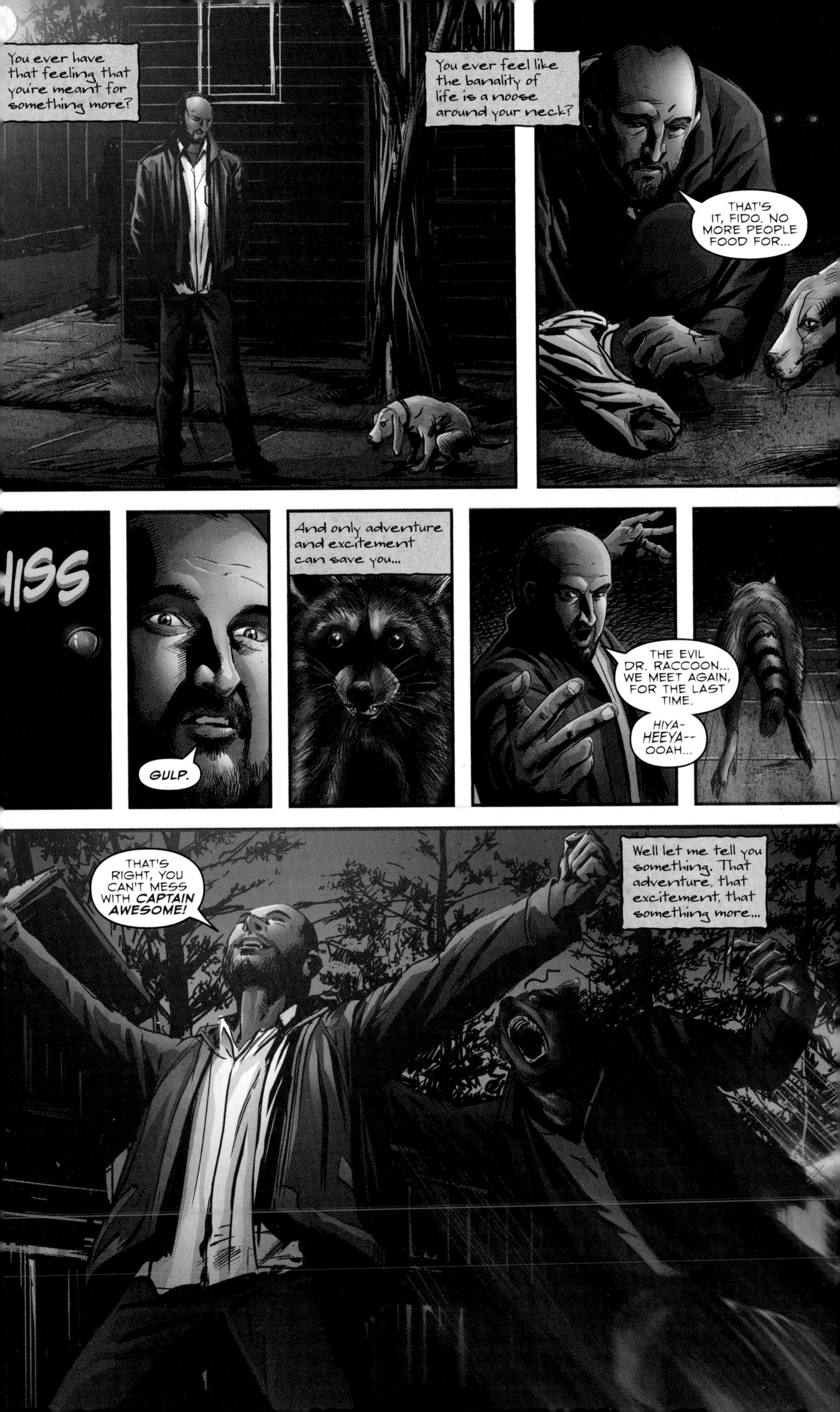
You ever have that feeling that you're meant for something more?
You ever feel like the banality of life is a noose around your neck?
THAT'S IT, FIDO. NO MORE PEOPLE FOOD FOR...
HISS
GULP.
And only adventure and excitement can save you...
THE EVIL DR. RACCOON... WE MEET AGAIN, FOR THE LAST TIME.
HIYA-HEEYA--OOAH...
THAT'S RIGHT, YOU CAN'T MESS WITH CAPTAIN AWESOME!
Well let me tell you something. That adventure, that excitement, that something more...

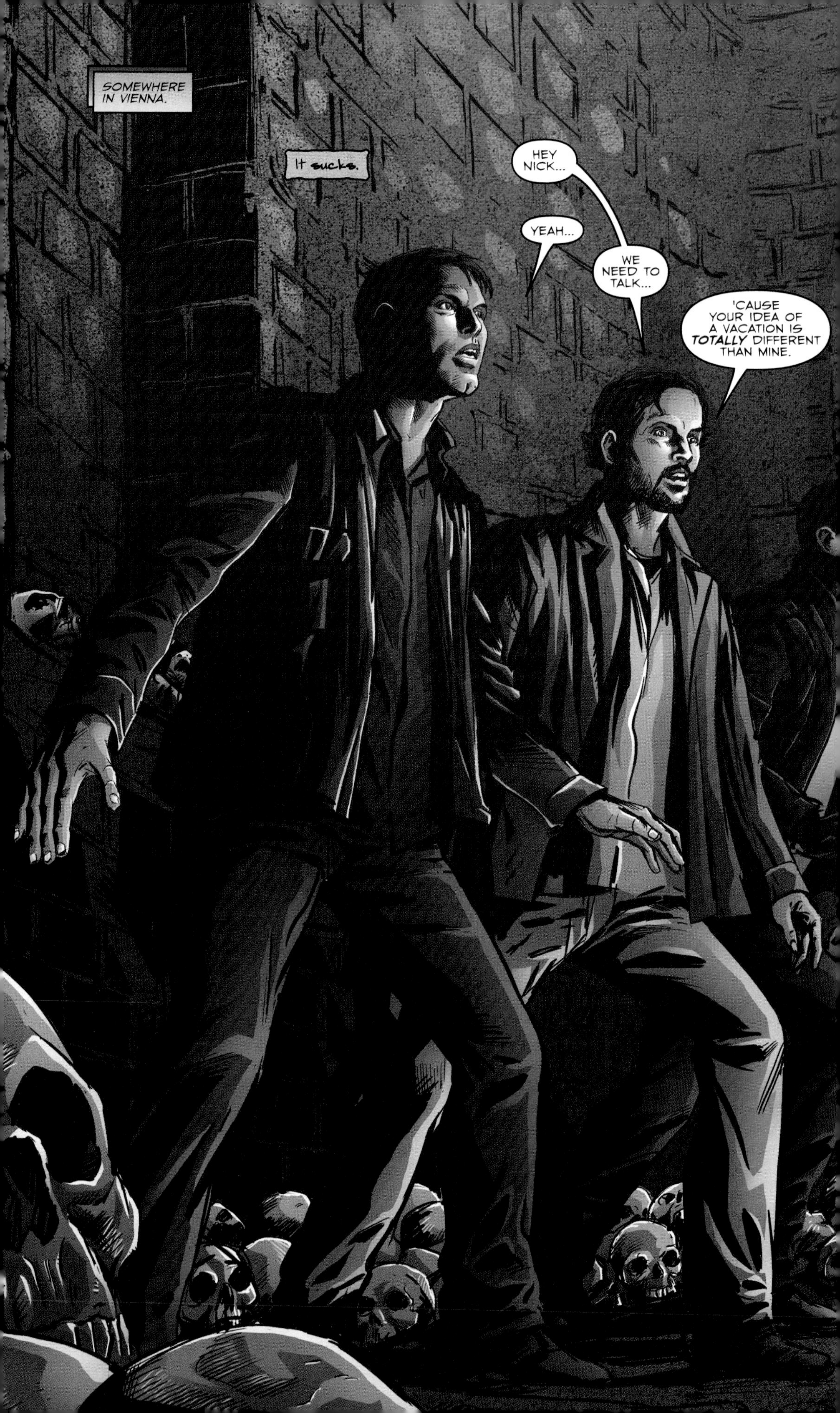
SOMEWHERE IN VIENNA.
It sucks.
HEY NICK...
YEAH...
WE NEED TO TALK...
'CAUSE YOUR IDEA OF A VACATION IS TOTALLY DIFFERENT THAN MINE.

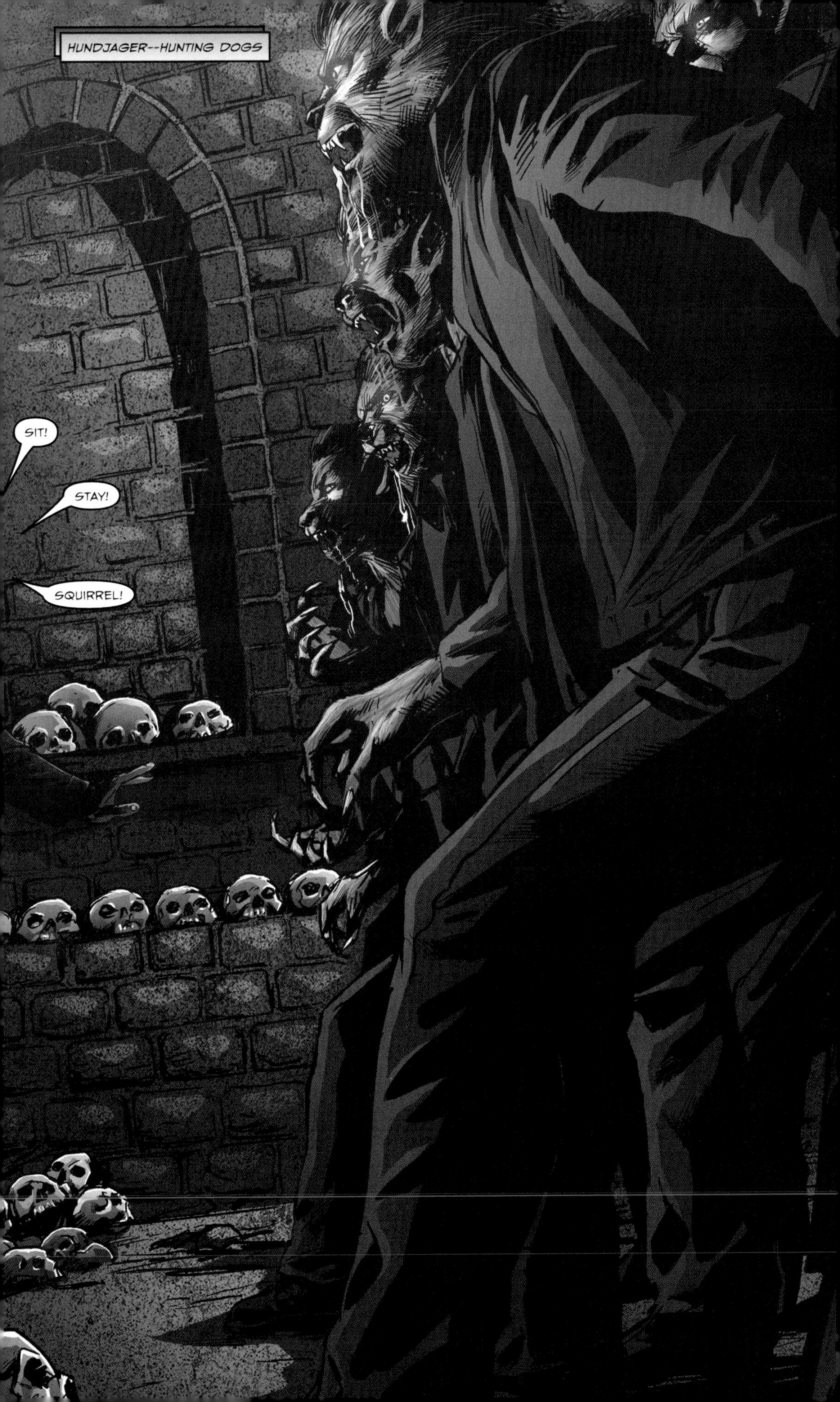
HUNDJAGER--HUNTING DOGS
SIT!
STAY!
SQUIRREL!

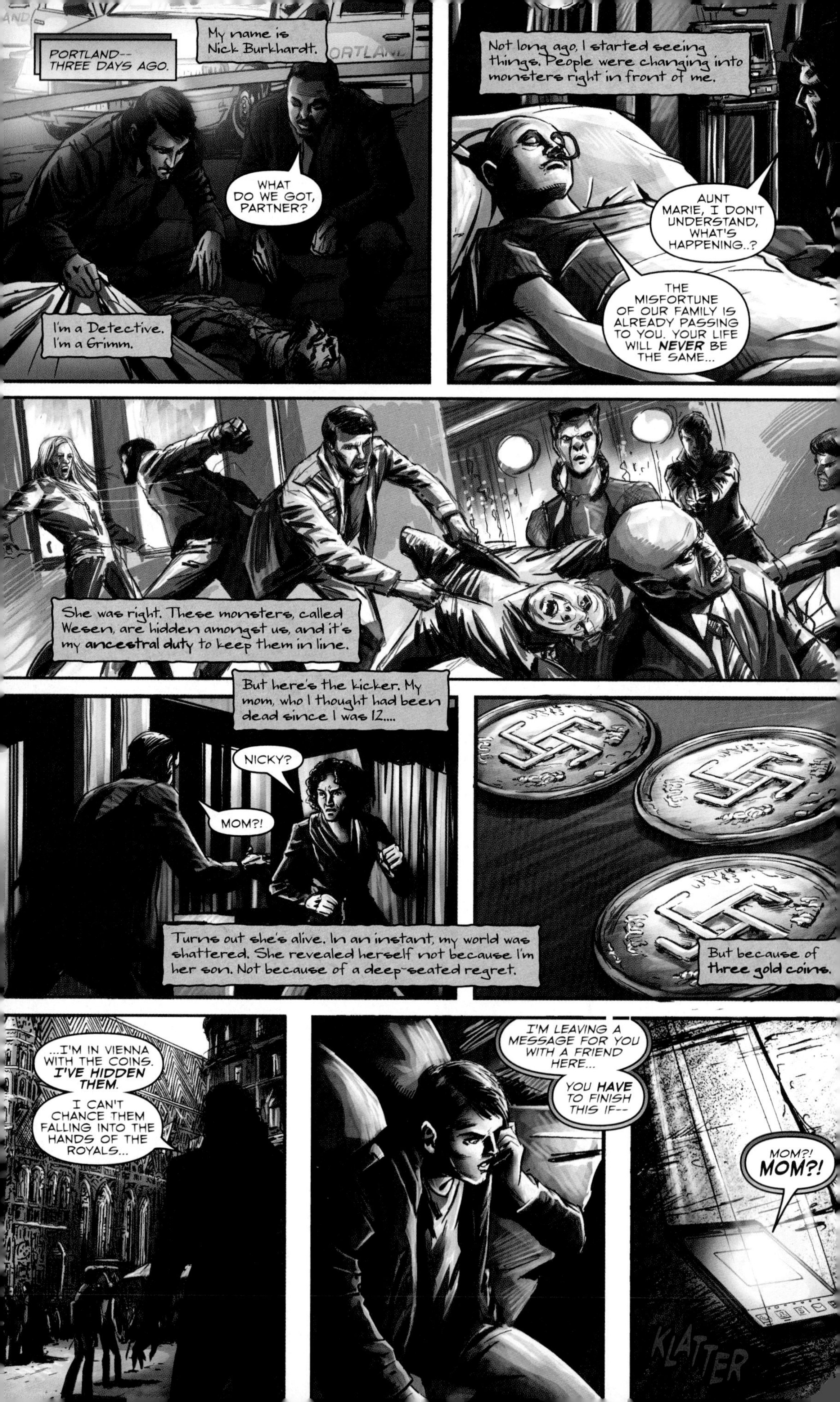
PORTLAND-- THREE DAYS AGO.
My name is Nick Burkhardt.
WHAT DO WE GOT, PARTNER?
I'm a Detective. I'm a Grimm.
Not long ago, I started seeing things. People were changing into monsters right in front of me.
AUNT MARIE, I DON'T UNDERSTAND, WHAT'S HAPPENING..?
THE MISFORTUNE OF OUR FAMILY IS ALREADY PASSING TO YOU. YOUR LIFE WILL NEVER BE THE SAME...
She was right. These monsters, called Wesen, are hidden amongst us, and it's my ancestral duty to keep them in line.
But here's the kicker. My mom, who I thought had been dead since I was 12....
NICKY?
MOM?!
Turns out she's alive. In an instant, my world was shattered. She revealed herself not because I'm her son. Not because of a deep-seated regret.
But because of three gold coins.
...I'M IN VIENNA WITH THE COINS. I'VE HIDDEN THEM.
I CAN'T CHANCE THEM FALLING INTO THE HANDS OF THE ROYALS...
I'M LEAVING A MESSAGE FOR YOU WITH A FRIEND HERE...
YOU HAVE TO FINISH THIS IF--
MOM?! MOM?!
KLATTER

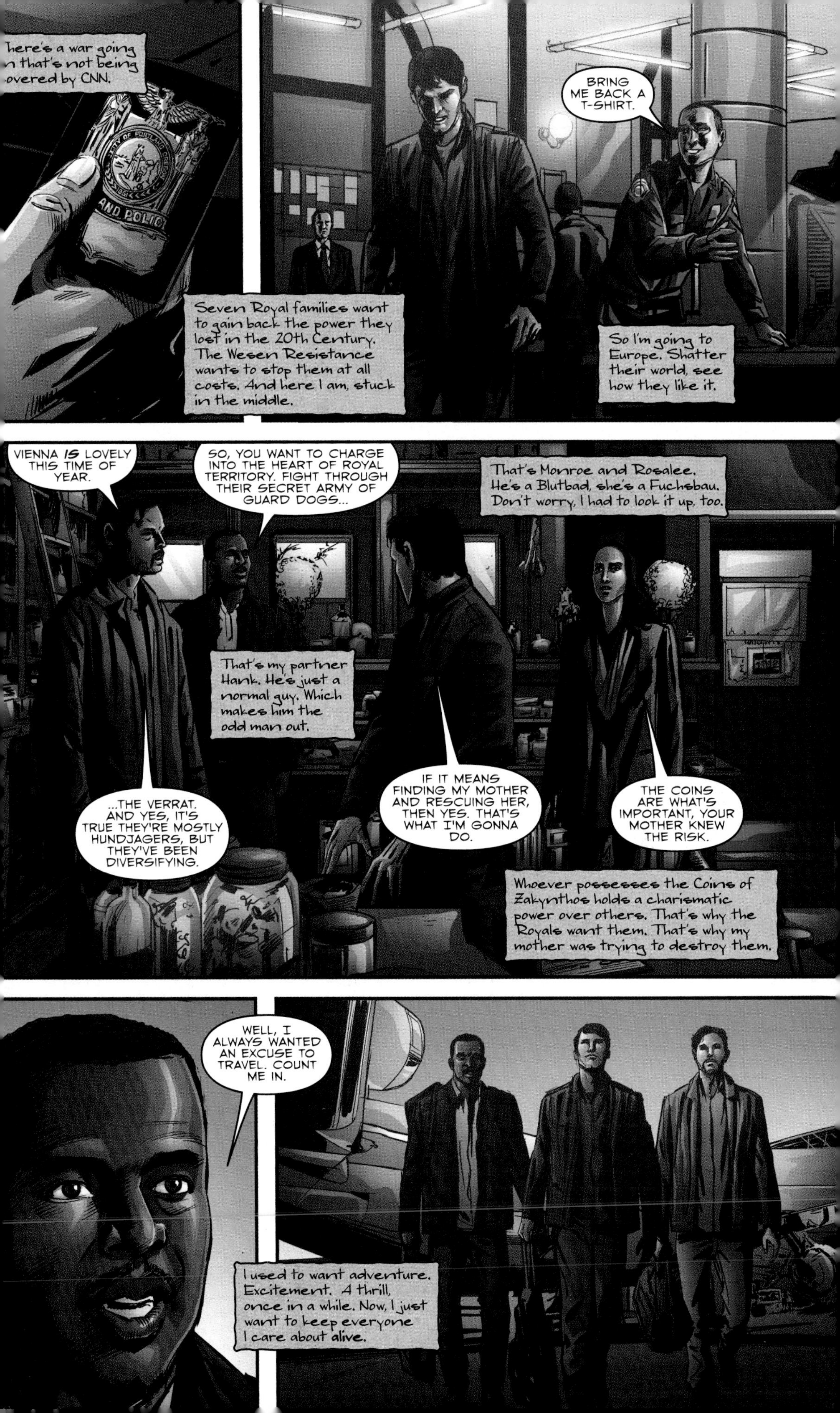

here's a war going
n that's not being
overed by CNN.
AND POLICE
BRING ME BACK A T-SHIRT.
Seven Royal families want to gain back the power they lost in the 20th Century. The Wesen Resistance wants to stop them at all costs. And here I am, stuck in the middle.
So I'm going to Europe. Shatter their world, see how they like it.
VIENNA IS LOVELY THIS TIME OF YEAR.
SO, YOU WANT TO CHARGE INTO THE HEART OF ROYAL TERRITORY. FIGHT THROUGH THEIR SECRET ARMY OF GUARD DOGS...
That's Monroe and Rosalee. He's a Blutbad, she's a Fuchsbau. Don't worry, I had to look it up, too.
That's my partner Hank. He's just a normal guy. Which makes him the odd man out.
...THE VERRAT. AND YES, IT'S TRUE THEY'RE MOSTLY HUNDJAGERS, BUT THEY'VE BEEN DIVERSIFYING.
IF IT MEANS FINDING MY MOTHER AND RESCUING HER, THEN YES. THAT'S WHAT I'M GONNA DO.
THE COINS ARE WHAT'S IMPORTANT, YOUR MOTHER KNEW THE RISK.
Whoever possesses the Coins of Zakynthos holds a charismatic power over others. That's why the Royals want them. That's why my mother was trying to destroy them.
WELL, I ALWAYS WANTED AN EXCUSE TO TRAVEL. COUNT ME IN.
I used to want adventure. Excitement. A thrill, once in a while. Now, I just want to keep everyone I care about alive.

VIENNA, AUSTRIA.

YOU'RE GOING THE WRONG WAY!

TAXI

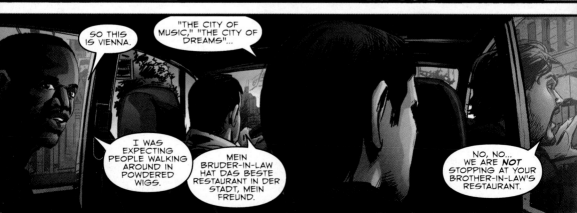

SO THIS IS VIENNA.

"THE CITY OF MUSIC," "THE CITY OF DREAMS"...

I WAS EXPECTING PEOPLE WALKING AROUND IN POWDERED WIGS.

MEIN BRUDER-IN-LAW HAT DAS BESTE RESTAURANT IN DER STADT, MEIN FREUND.

NO, NO... WE ARE *NOT* STOPPING AT YOUR BROTHER-IN-LAW'S RESTAURANT.

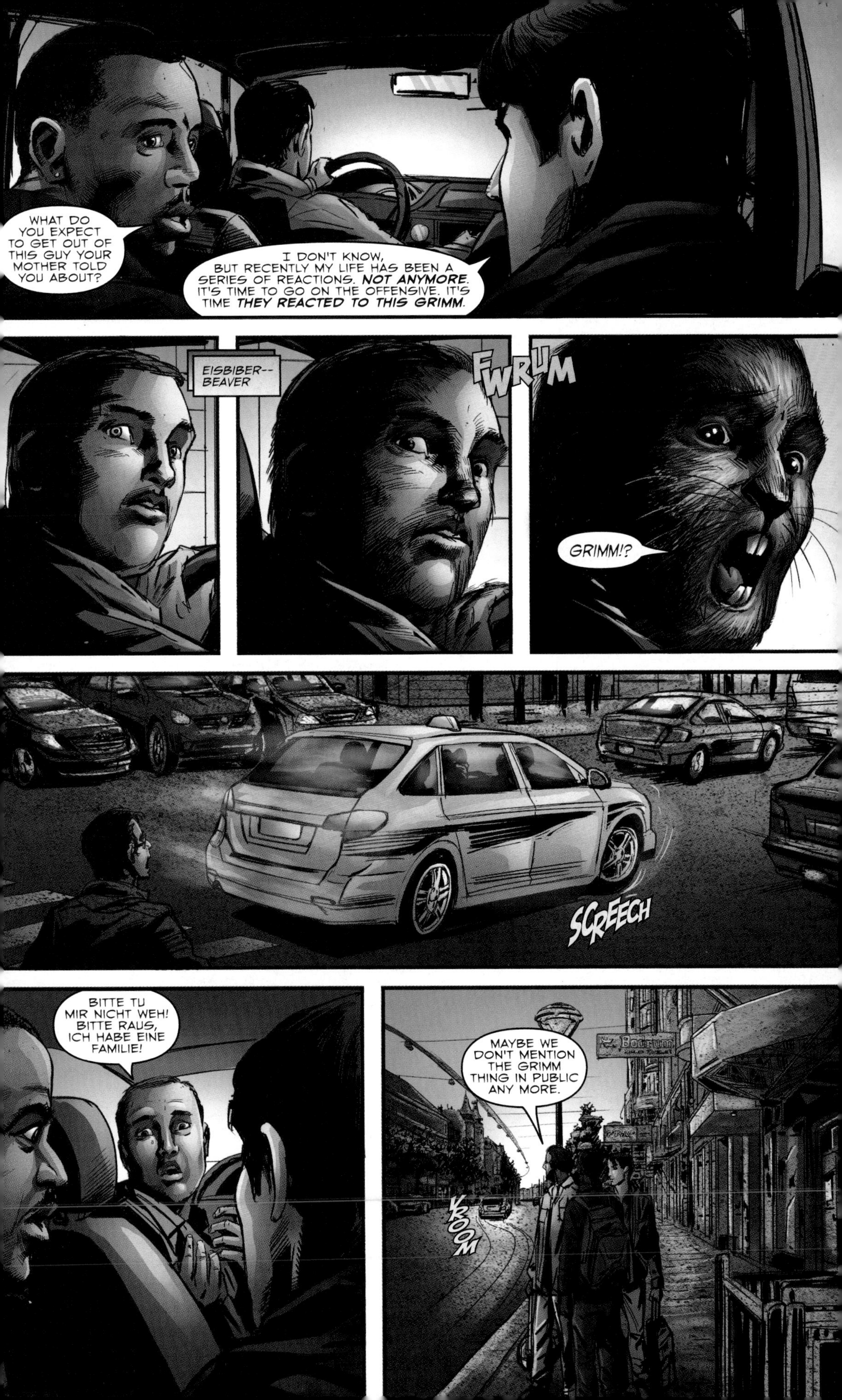
WHAT DO YOU EXPECT TO GET OUT OF THIS GUY YOUR MOTHER TOLD YOU ABOUT?
I DON'T KNOW, BUT RECENTLY MY LIFE HAS BEEN A SERIES OF REACTIONS. NOT ANYMORE. IT'S TIME TO GO ON THE OFFENSIVE. IT'S TIME THEY REACTED TO THIS GRIMM.
EISBIBER-- BEAVER
FWRUM
GRIMM!?
SCREECH
BITTE TU MIR NICHT WEH! BITTE RAUS, ICH HABE EINE FAMILIE!
MAYBE WE DON'T MENTION THE GRIMM THING IN PUBLIC ANY MORE.
KROOM

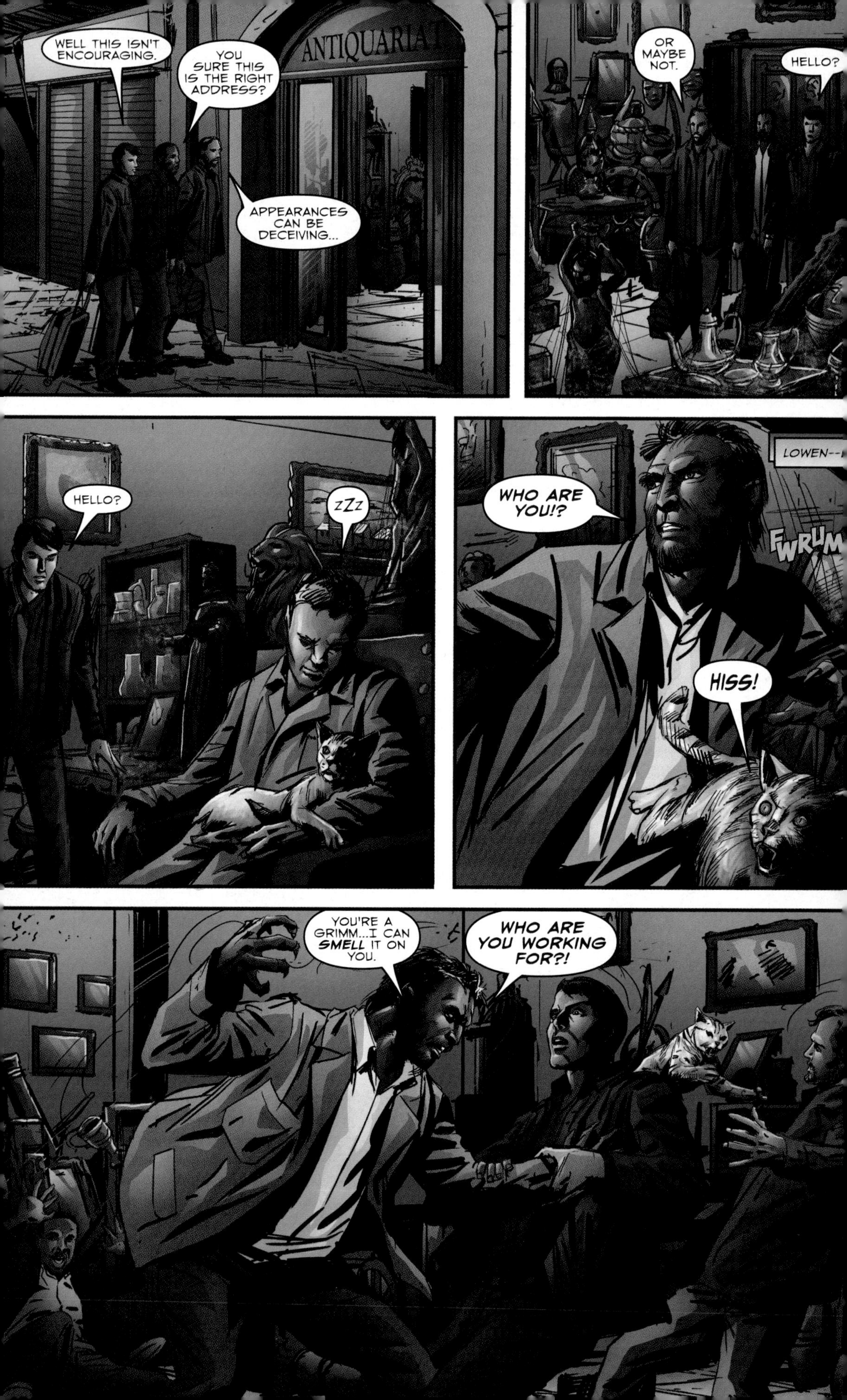
ANTIQUARIAT
WELL THIS ISN'T ENCOURAGING.
YOU SURE THIS IS THE RIGHT ADDRESS?
APPEARANCES CAN BE DECEIVING...
OR MAYBE NOT.
HELLO?
HELLO?
ZZZ
WHO ARE YOU!?
LOWEN--!
FWRUM
HISS!
YOU'RE A GRIMM...I CAN SMELL IT ON YOU.
WHO ARE YOU WORKING FOR?!

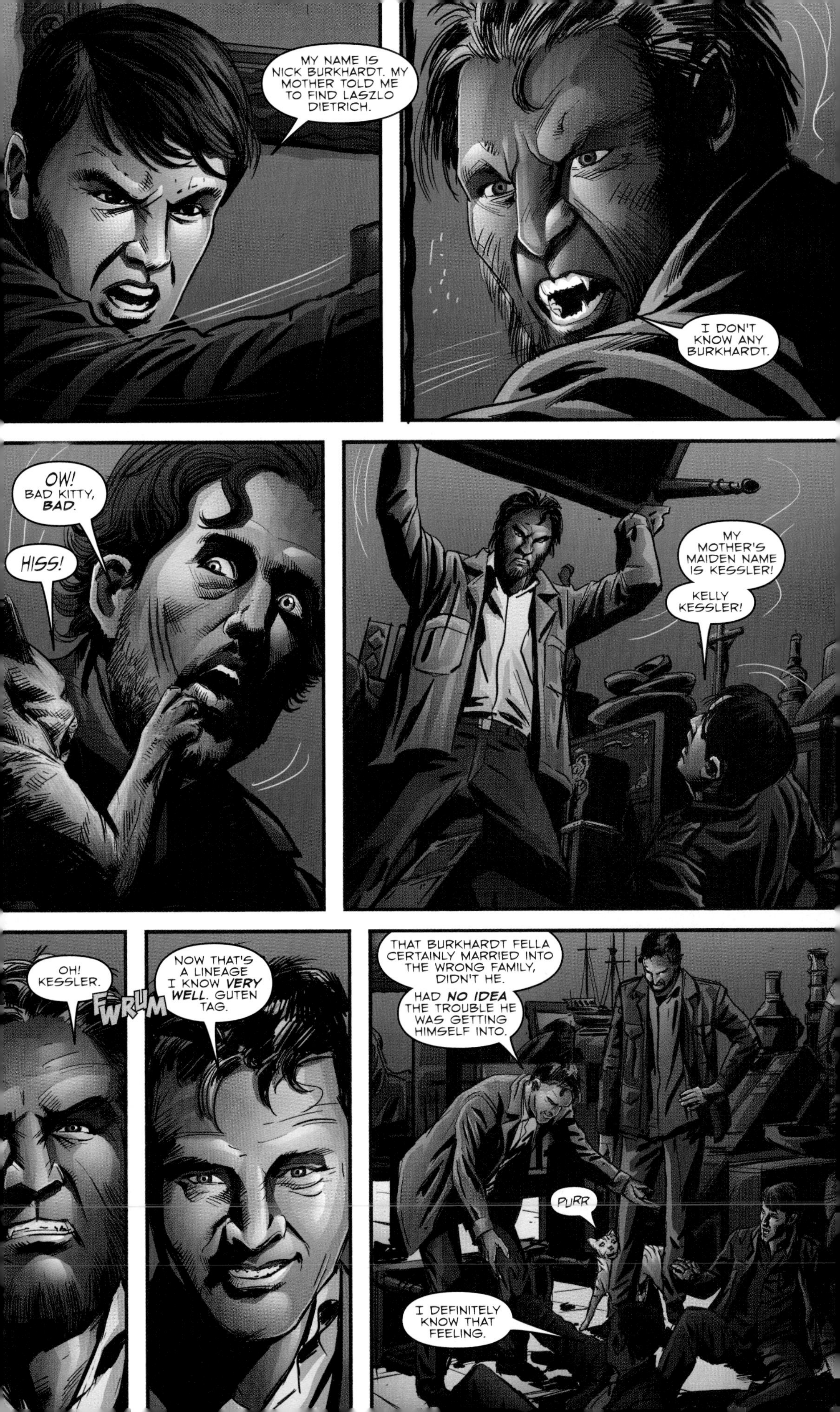
MY NAME IS NICK BURKHARDT. MY MOTHER TOLD ME TO FIND LASZLO DIETRICH.
I DON'T KNOW ANY BURKHARDT.
OW! BAD KITTY, BAD.
HISS!
MY MOTHER'S MAIDEN NAME IS KESSLER!
KELLY KESSLER!
OH! KESSLER.
FWRUM
NOW THAT'S A LINEAGE I KNOW VERY WELL. GUTEN TAG.
THAT BURKHARDT FELLA CERTAINLY MARRIED INTO THE WRONG FAMILY, DIDN'T HE.
HAD NO IDEA THE TROUBLE HE WAS GETTING HIMSELF INTO.
PURR
I DEFINITELY KNOW THAT FEELING.

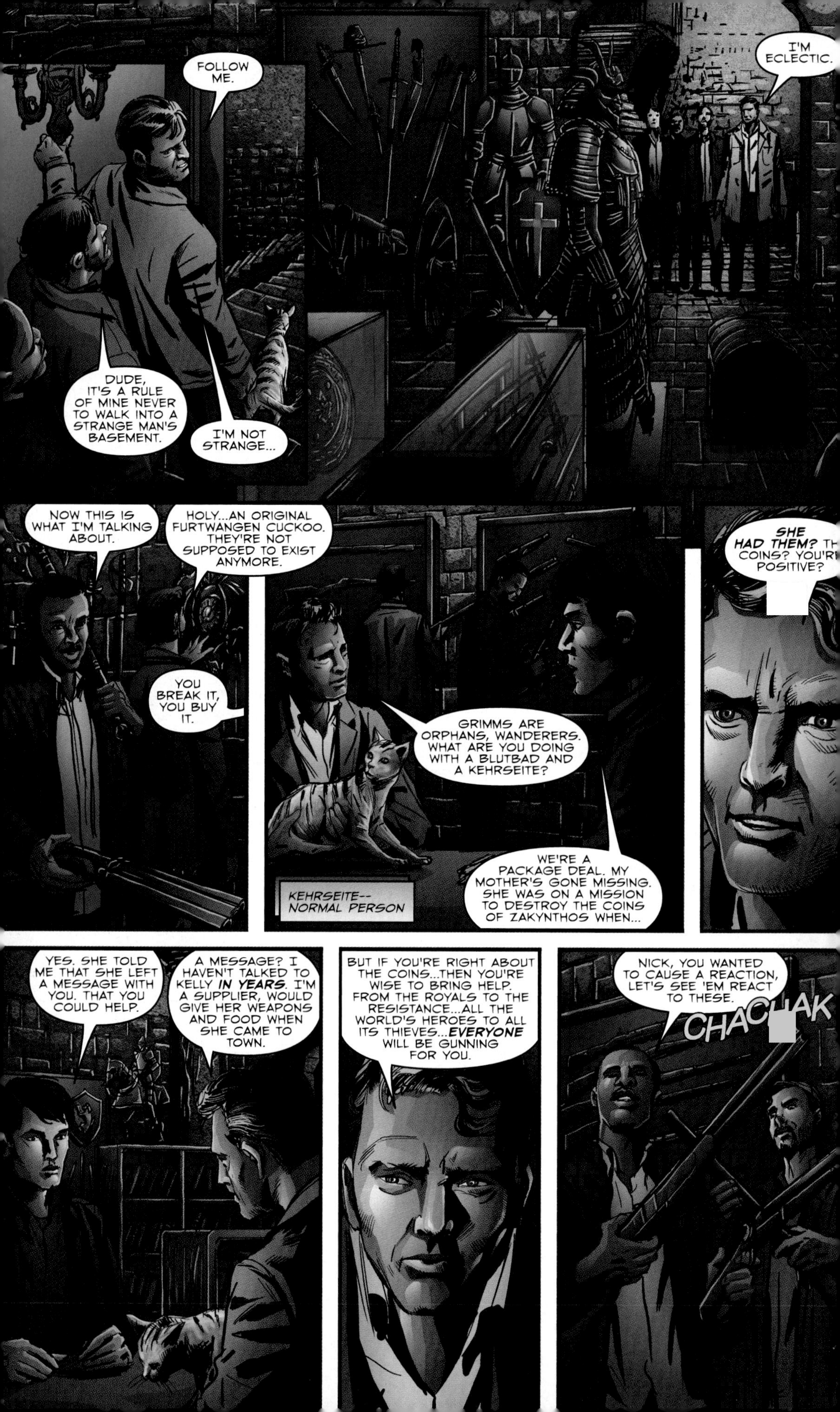
FOLLOW ME.
DUDE, IT'S A RULE OF MINE NEVER TO WALK INTO A STRANGE MAN'S BASEMENT.
I'M NOT STRANGE...
I'M ECLECTIC.
NOW THIS IS WHAT I'M TALKING ABOUT.
HOLY...AN ORIGINAL FURTWANGEN CUCKOO. THEY'RE NOT SUPPOSED TO EXIST ANYMORE.
YOU BREAK IT, YOU BUY IT.
GRIMMS ARE ORPHANS, WANDERERS. WHAT ARE YOU DOING WITH A BLUTBAD AND A KEHRSEITE?
KEHRSEITE-- NORMAL PERSON
WE'RE A PACKAGE DEAL. MY MOTHER'S GONE MISSING. SHE WAS ON A MISSION TO DESTROY THE COINS OF ZAKYNTHOS WHEN...
SHE HAD THEM? TH COINS? YOU'R POSITIVE?
YES. SHE TOLD ME THAT SHE LEFT A MESSAGE WITH YOU. THAT YOU COULD HELP.
A MESSAGE? I HAVEN'T TALKED TO KELLY ***IN YEARS***. I'M A SUPPLIER, WOULD GIVE HER WEAPONS AND FOOD WHEN SHE CAME TO TOWN.
BUT IF YOU'RE RIGHT ABOUT THE COINS...THEN YOU'RE WISE TO BRING HELP. FROM THE ROYALS TO THE RESISTANCE...ALL THE WORLD'S HEROES TO ALL ITS THIEVES...***EVERYONE*** WILL BE GUNNING FOR YOU.
NICK, YOU WANTED TO CAUSE A REACTION, LET'S SEE 'EM REACT TO THESE.
CHACHAK

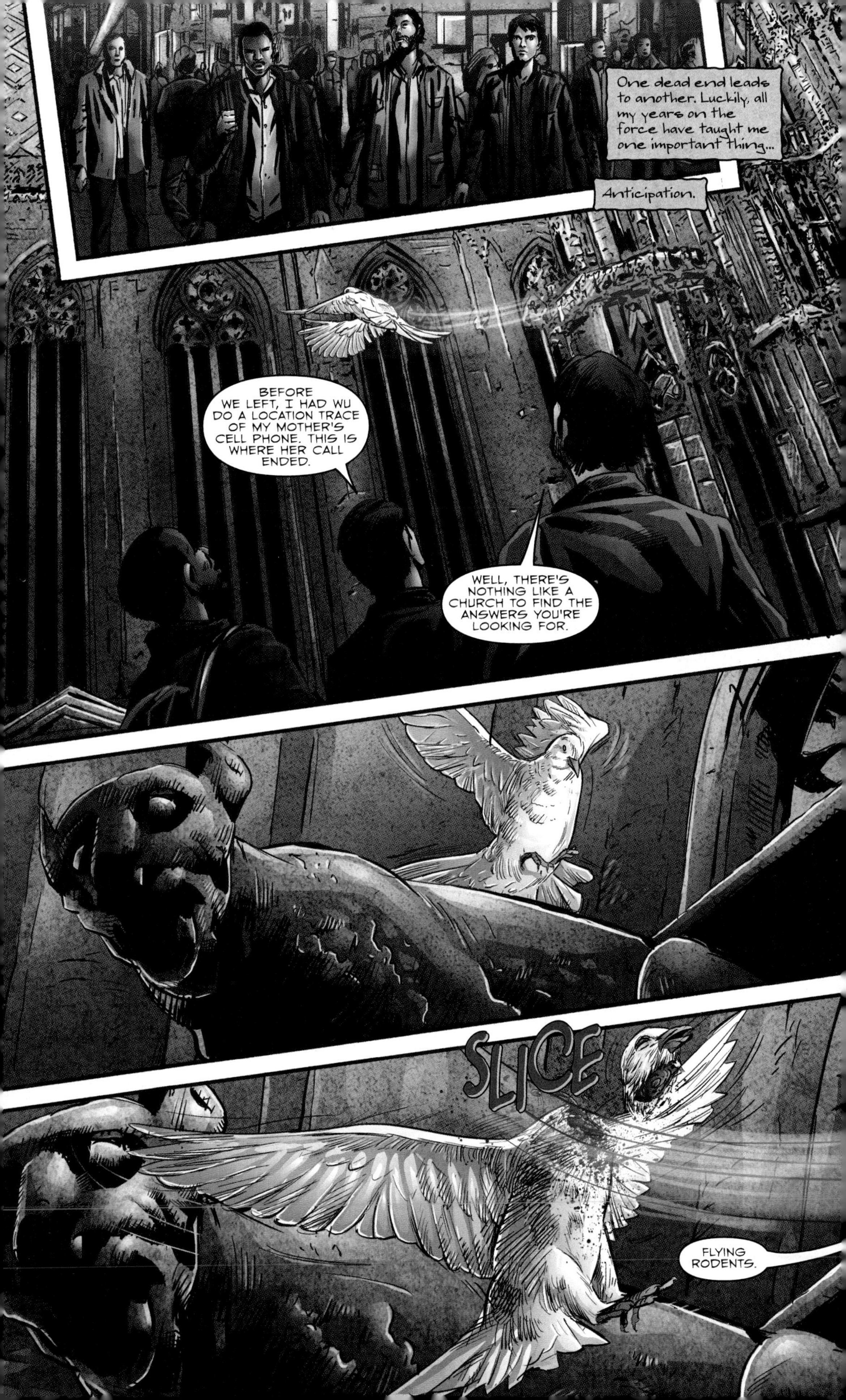
One dead end leads to another. Luckily, all my years on the force have taught me one important thing...
Anticipation.
BEFORE WE LEFT, I HAD WU DO A LOCATION TRACE OF MY MOTHER'S CELL PHONE. THIS IS WHERE HER CALL ENDED.
WELL, THERE'S NOTHING LIKE A CHURCH TO FIND THE ANSWERS YOU'RE LOOKING FOR.
SLICE
FLYING RODENTS.

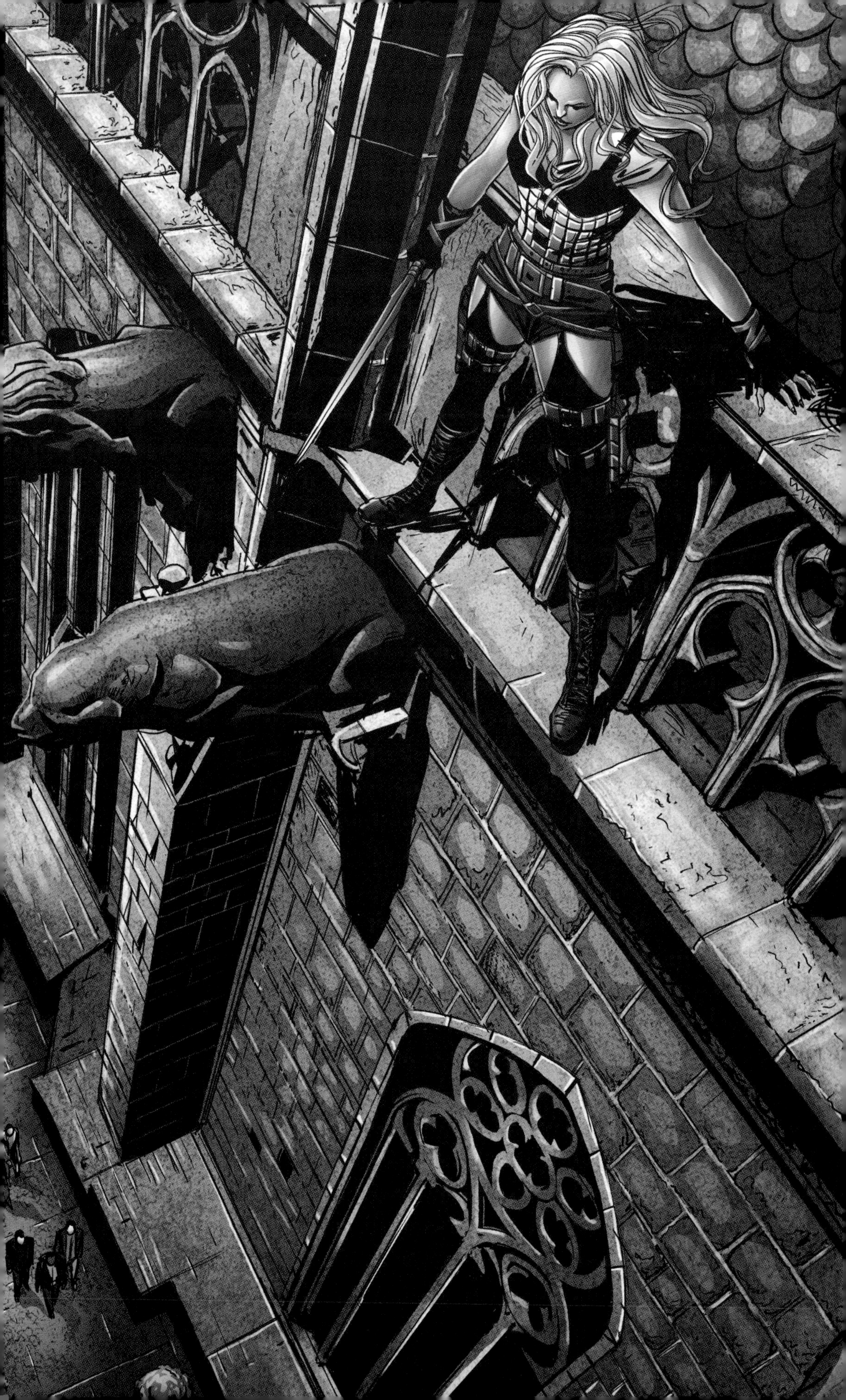

UNKNOWN LOCATION.
I don't want to be here.
I could be at home, knitting a sweater by the fire, watching a sitcom on television.
But that's just not me. My name is Kelly Burkhardt. I'm a Grimm. And who am I kidding? Truth be told...
I LOVE IT.
SORRY, WHAT DID YOU SAY?

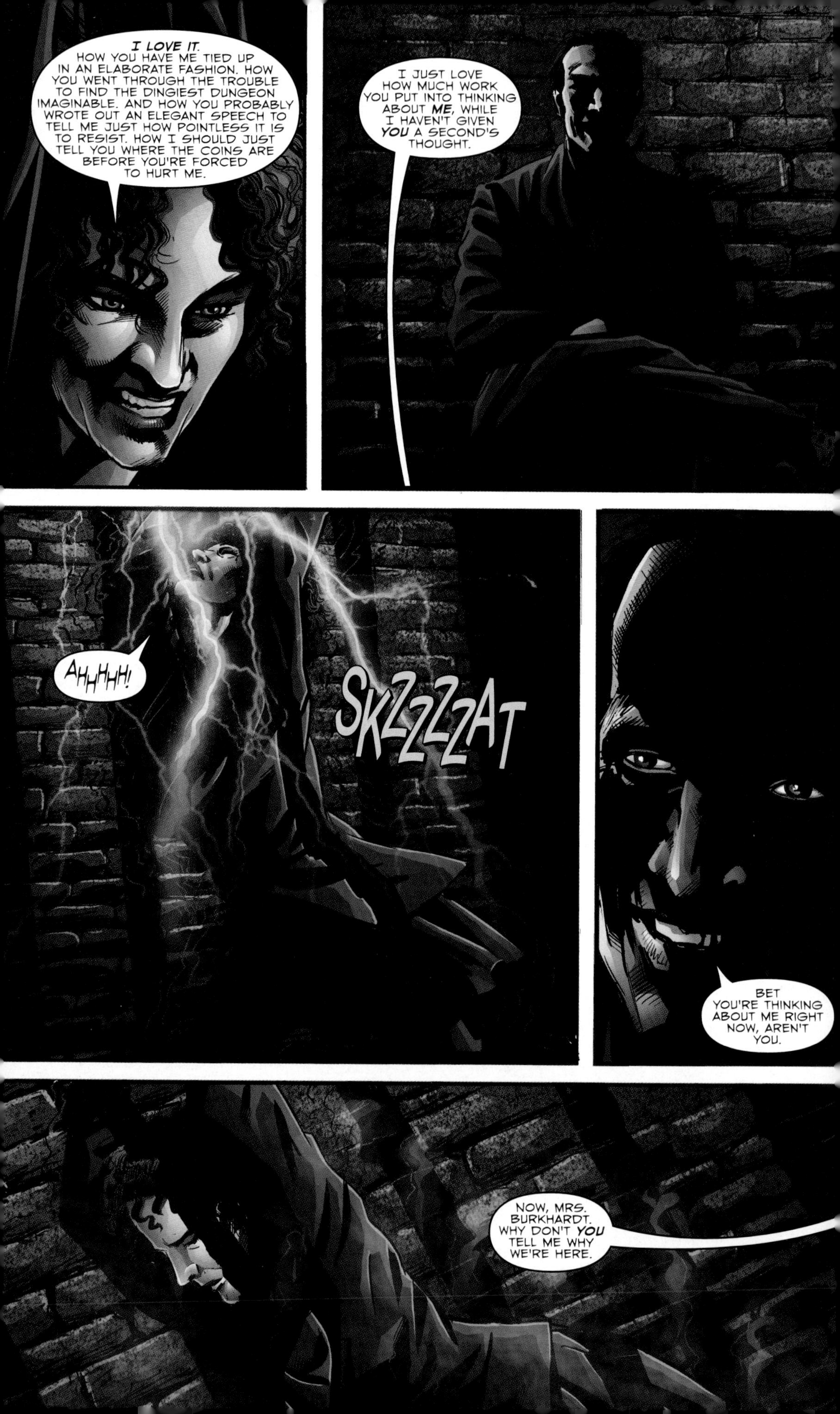
I LOVE IT. HOW YOU HAVE ME TIED UP IN AN ELABORATE FASHION. HOW YOU WENT THROUGH THE TROUBLE TO FIND THE DINGIEST DUNGEON IMAGINABLE. AND HOW YOU PROBABLY WROTE OUT AN ELEGANT SPEECH TO TELL ME JUST HOW POINTLESS IT IS TO RESIST. HOW I SHOULD JUST TELL YOU WHERE THE COINS ARE BEFORE YOU'RE FORCED TO HURT ME.
I JUST LOVE HOW MUCH WORK YOU PUT INTO THINKING ABOUT ME, WHILE I HAVEN'T GIVEN YOU A SECOND'S THOUGHT.
AHHHHH!
SKZZZZZAT
BET YOU'RE THINKING ABOUT ME RIGHT NOW, AREN'T YOU.
NOW, MRS. BURKHARDT. WHY DON'T YOU TELL ME WHY WE'RE HERE.

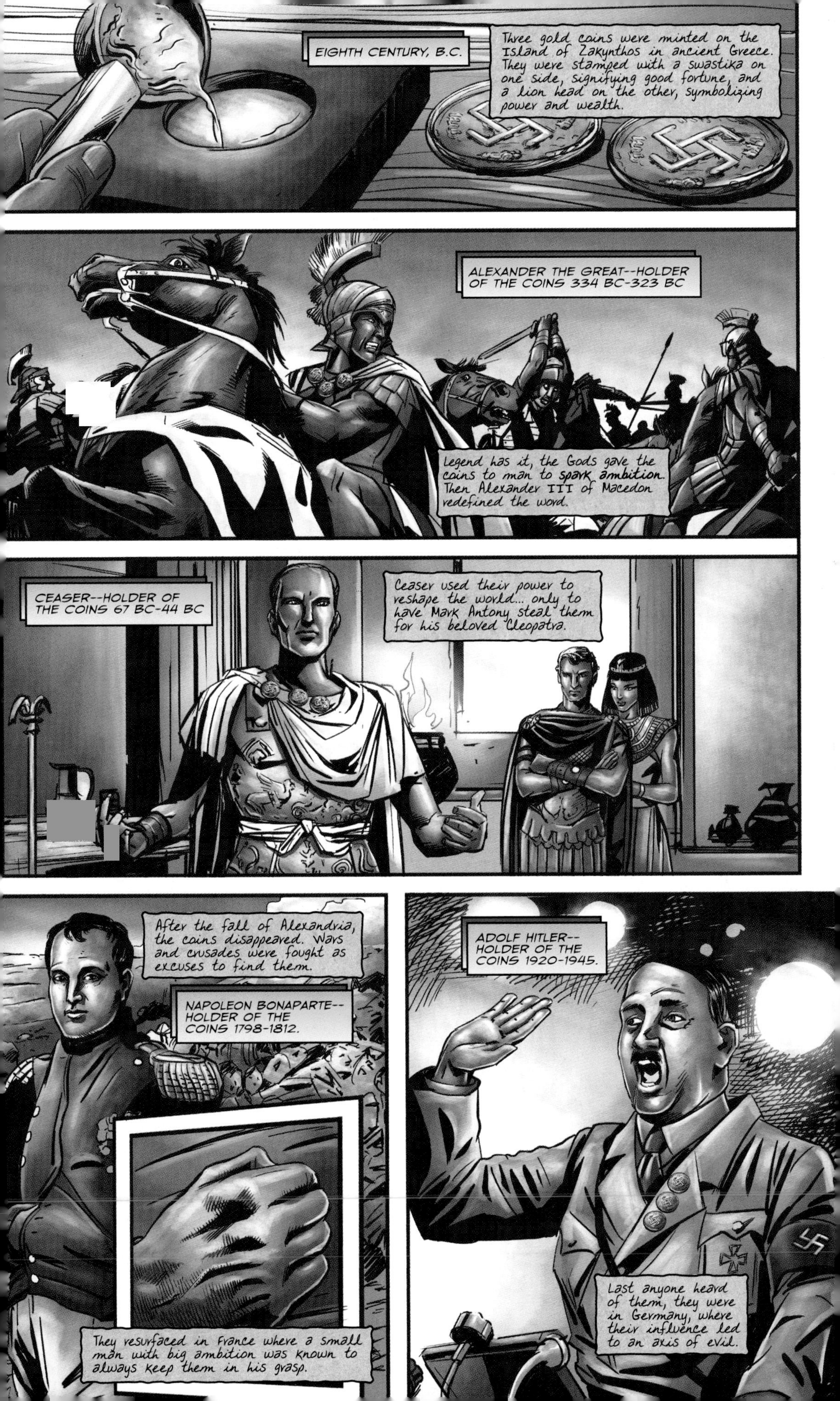
EIGHTH CENTURY, B.C.
Three gold coins were minted on the Island of Zakynthos in ancient Greece. They were stamped with a swastika on one side, signifying good fortune, and a lion head on the other, symbolizing power and wealth.
ALEXANDER THE GREAT--HOLDER OF THE COINS 334 BC-323 BC
Legend has it, the Gods gave the coins to man to spark ambition. Then Alexander III of Macedon redefined the word.
CEASER--HOLDER OF THE COINS 67 BC-44 BC
Ceaser used their power to reshape the world... only to have Mark Antony steal them for his beloved Cleopatra.
After the fall of Alexandria, the coins disappeared. Wars and crusades were fought as excuses to find them.
NAPOLEON BONAPARTE--HOLDER OF THE COINS 1798-1812.
They resurfaced in France where a small man with big ambition was known to always keep them in his grasp.
ADOLF HITLER--HOLDER OF THE COINS 1920-1945.
Last anyone heard of them, they were in Germany, where their influence led to an axis of evil.

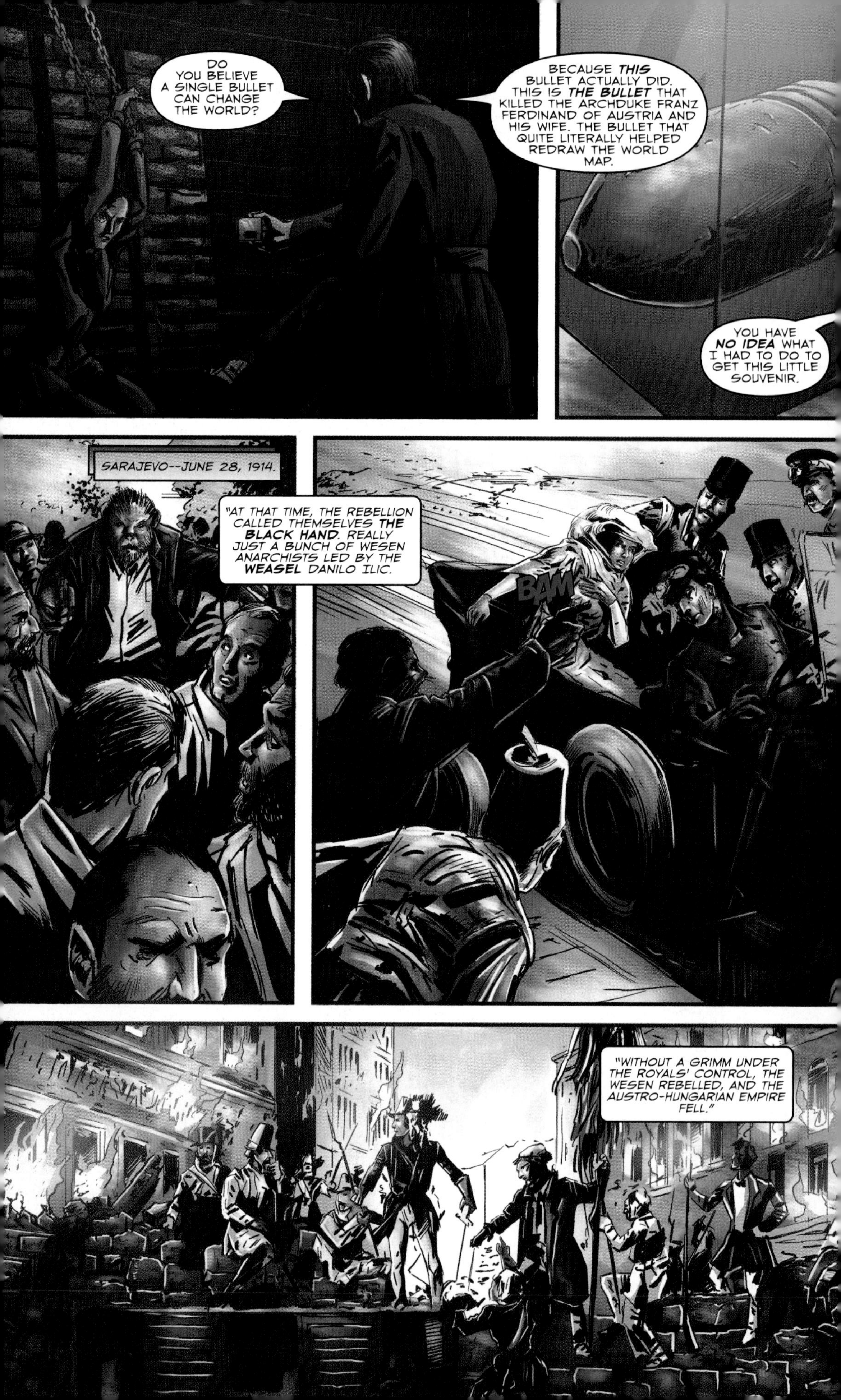
DO YOU BELIEVE A SINGLE BULLET CAN CHANGE THE WORLD?
BECAUSE THIS BULLET ACTUALLY DID. THIS IS THE BULLET THAT KILLED THE ARCHDUKE FRANZ FERDINAND OF AUSTRIA AND HIS WIFE. THE BULLET THAT QUITE LITERALLY HELPED REDRAW THE WORLD MAP.
YOU HAVE NO IDEA WHAT I HAD TO DO TO GET THIS LITTLE SOUVENIR.
SARAJEVO--JUNE 28, 1914.
"AT THAT TIME, THE REBELLION CALLED THEMSELVES THE BLACK HAND. REALLY JUST A BUNCH OF WESEN ANARCHISTS LED BY THE WEASEL DANILO ILIC.
BAM
"WITHOUT A GRIMM UNDER THE ROYALS' CONTROL, THE WESEN REBELLED, AND THE AUSTRO-HUNGARIAN EMPIRE FELL."

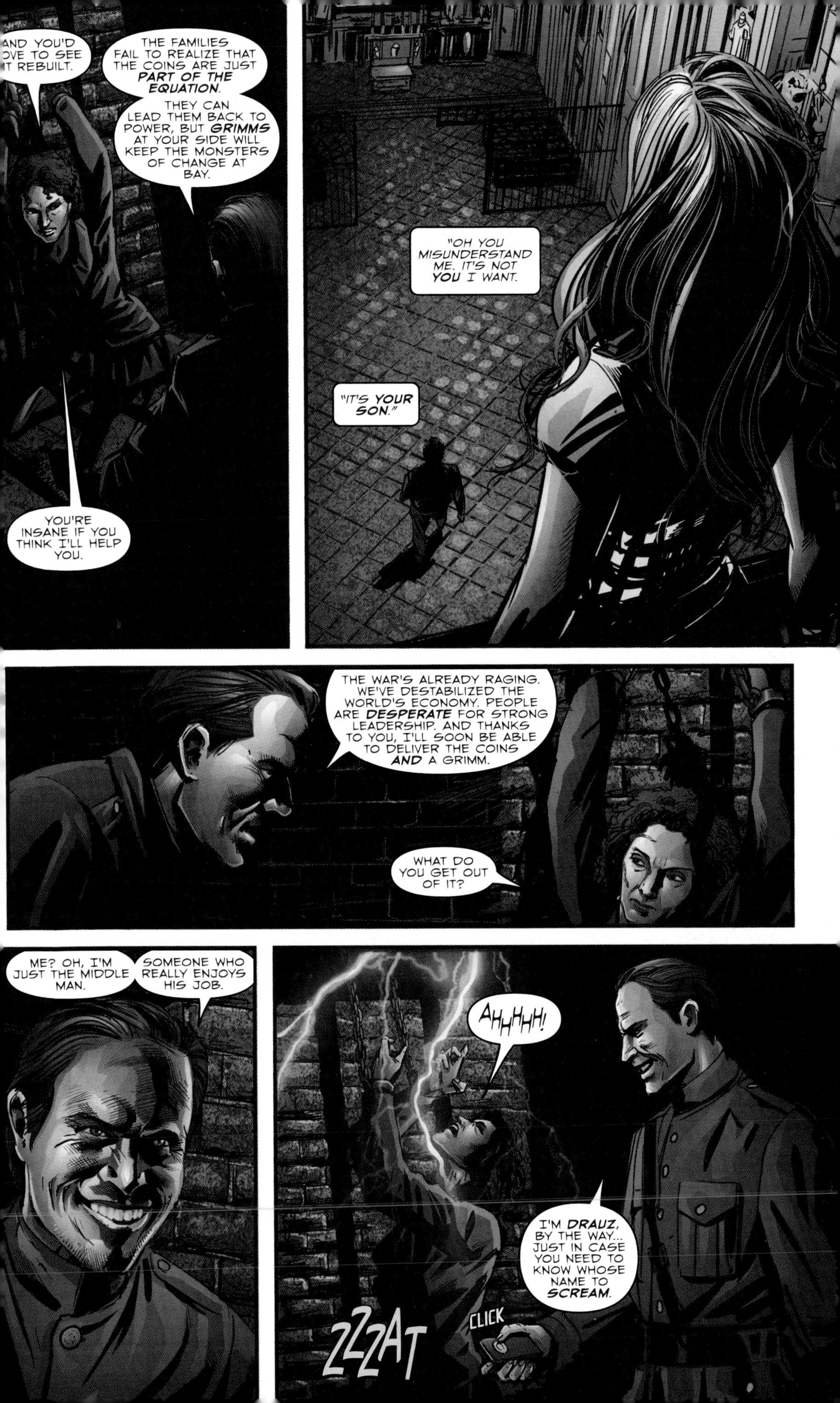
AND YOU'D LOVE TO SEE IT REBUILT.
THE FAMILIES FAIL TO REALIZE THAT THE COINS ARE JUST **PART OF THE EQUATION**.
THEY CAN LEAD THEM BACK TO POWER, BUT **GRIMMS** AT YOUR SIDE WILL KEEP THE MONSTERS OF CHANGE AT BAY.
YOU'RE INSANE IF YOU THINK I'LL HELP YOU.
"OH YOU MISUNDERSTAND ME. IT'S NOT **YOU** I WANT.
"IT'S **YOUR SON**."
THE WAR'S ALREADY RAGING. WE'VE DESTABILIZED THE WORLD'S ECONOMY. PEOPLE ARE **DESPERATE** FOR STRONG LEADERSHIP. AND THANKS TO YOU, I'LL SOON BE ABLE TO DELIVER THE COINS **AND** A GRIMM.
WHAT DO YOU GET OUT OF IT?
ME? OH, I'M JUST THE MIDDLE MAN.
SOMEONE WHO REALLY ENJOYS HIS JOB.
AHHHHH!
I'M **DRAUZ**, BY THE WAY... JUST IN CASE YOU NEED TO KNOW WHOSE NAME TO **SCREAM**.
ZZZAT
CLICK

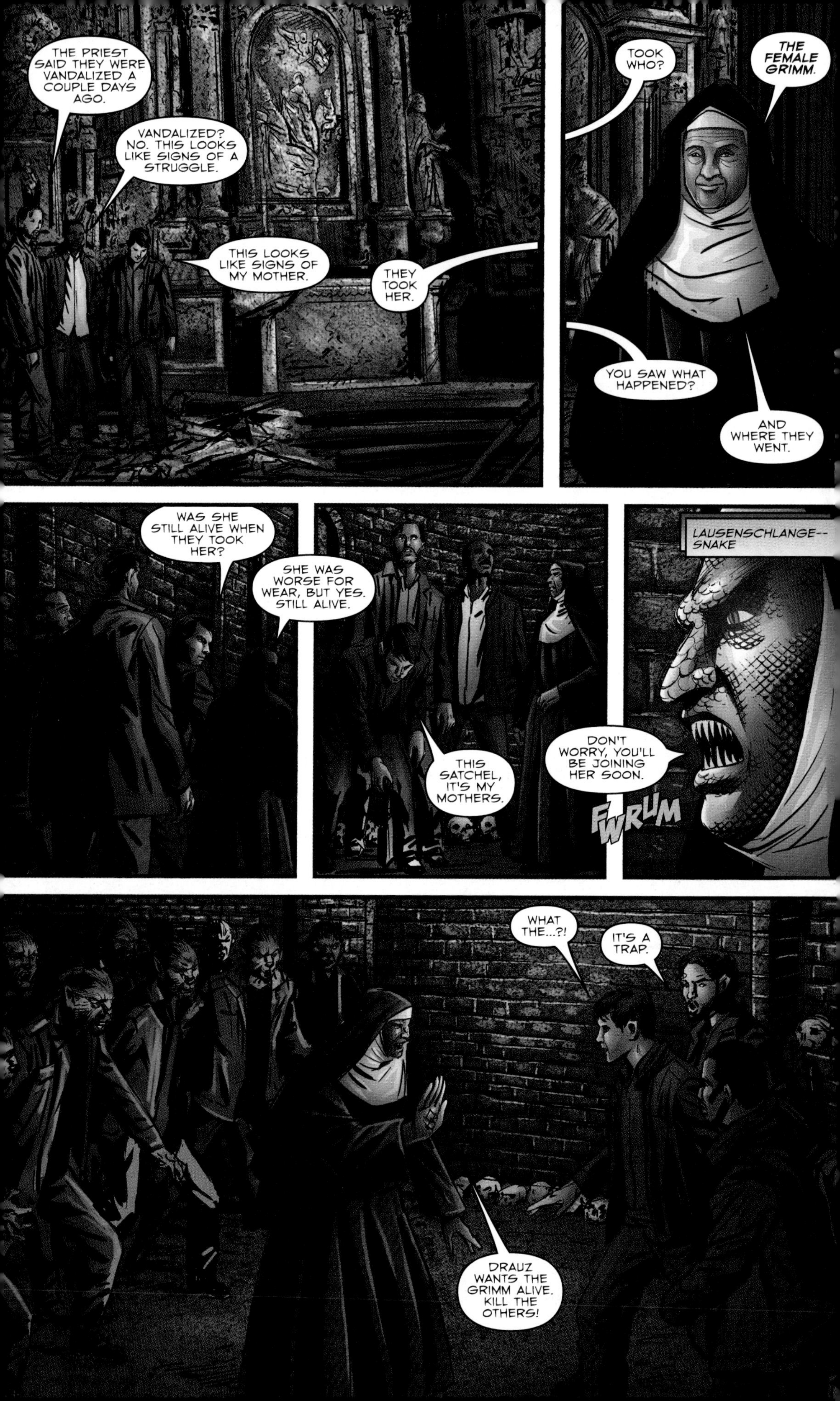
THE PRIEST SAID THEY WERE VANDALIZED A COUPLE DAYS AGO.
VANDALIZED? NO. THIS LOOKS LIKE SIGNS OF A STRUGGLE.
THIS LOOKS LIKE SIGNS OF MY MOTHER.
THEY TOOK HER.
TOOK WHO?
THE FEMALE GRIMM.
YOU SAW WHAT HAPPENED?
AND WHERE THEY WENT.
WAS SHE STILL ALIVE WHEN THEY TOOK HER?
SHE WAS WORSE FOR WEAR, BUT YES. STILL ALIVE.
THIS SATCHEL, IT'S MY MOTHERS.
LAUSENSCHLANGE--SNAKE
DON'T WORRY, YOU'LL BE JOINING HER SOON.
FWRUM
WHAT THE...?!
IT'S A TRAP.
DRAUZ WANTS THE GRIMM ALIVE. KILL THE OTHERS!

WHAK

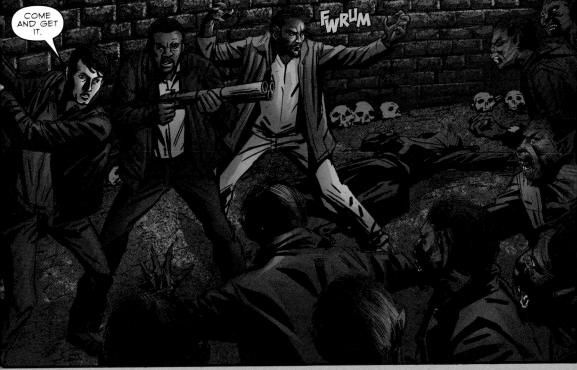

COME AND GET IT.

FWRUM

BOOM

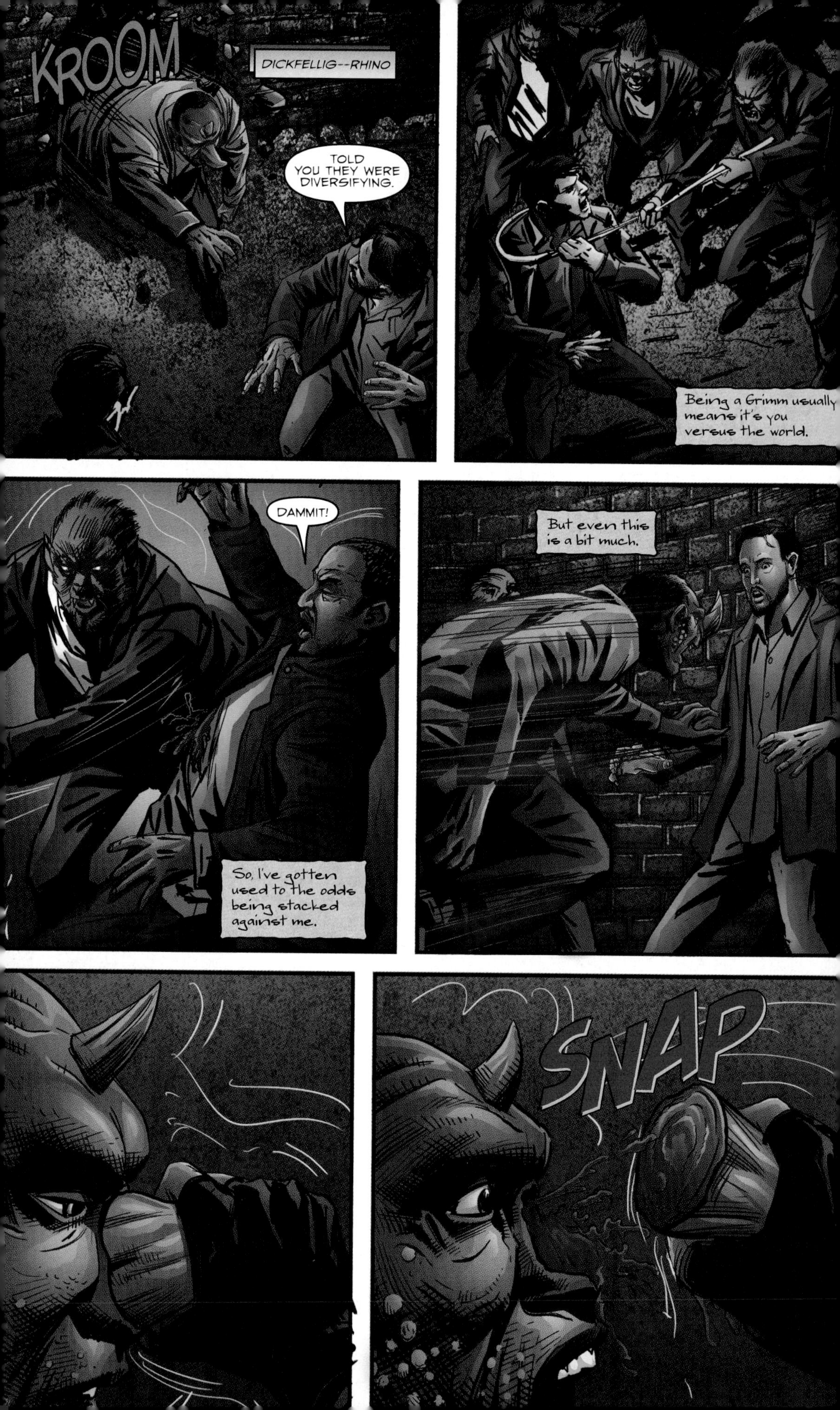
KROOM
DICKFELLIG--RHINO
TOLD YOU THEY WERE DIVERSIFYING.
Being a Grimm usually means it's you versus the world.
DAMMIT!
So, I've gotten used to the odds being stacked against me.
But even this is a bit much.
SNAP

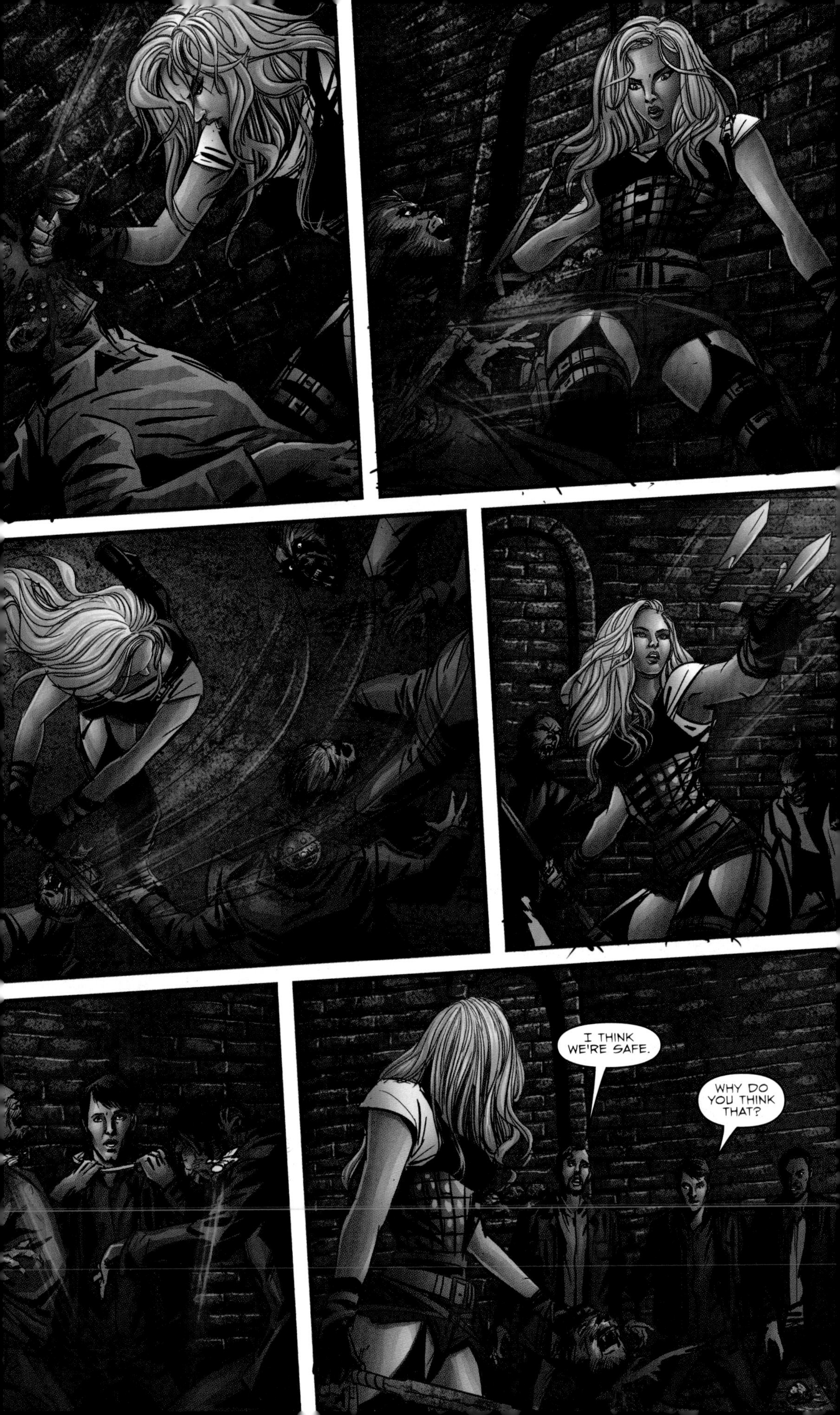
I THINK WE'RE SAFE.
WHY DO YOU THINK THAT?

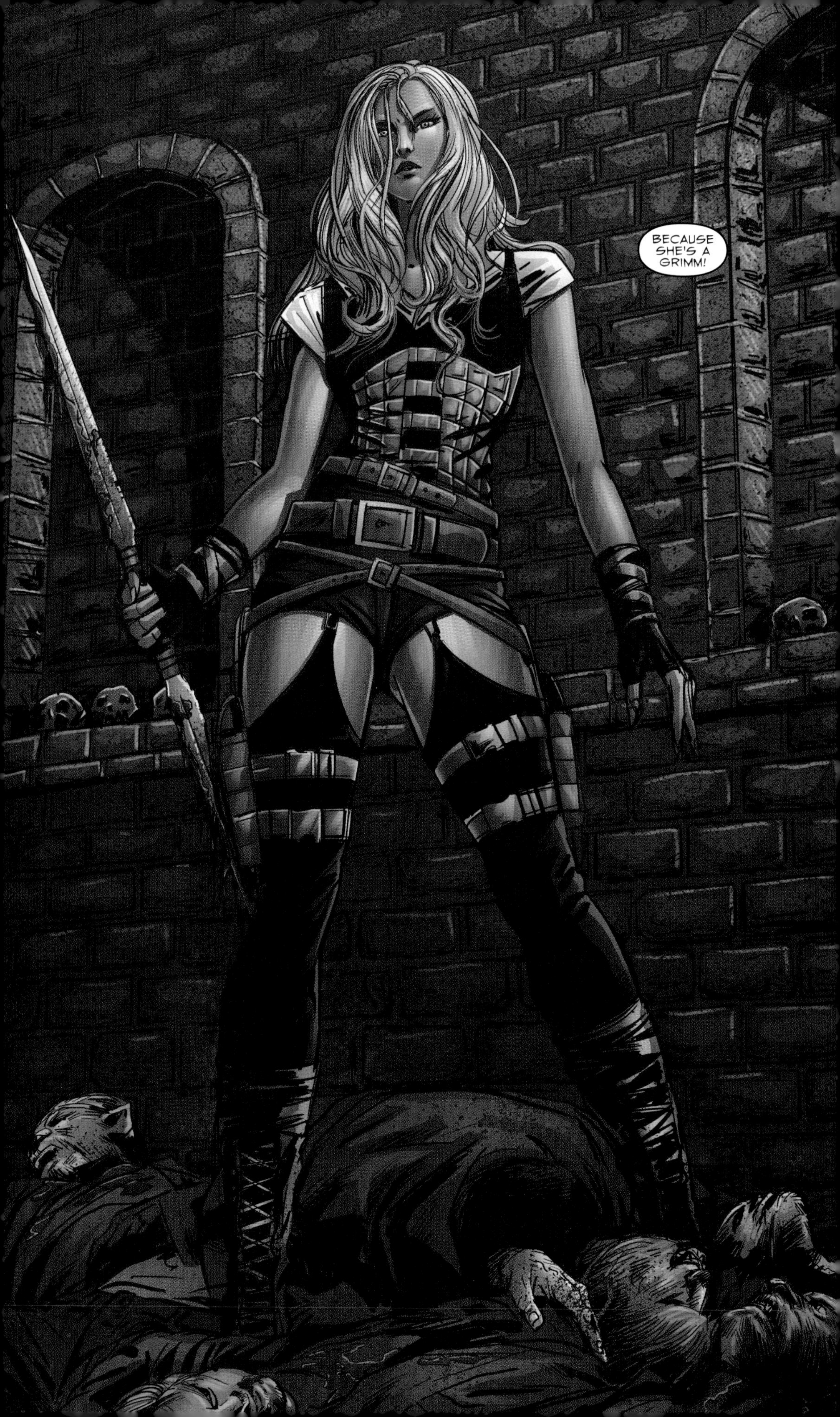
BECAUSE SHE'S A GRIMM!

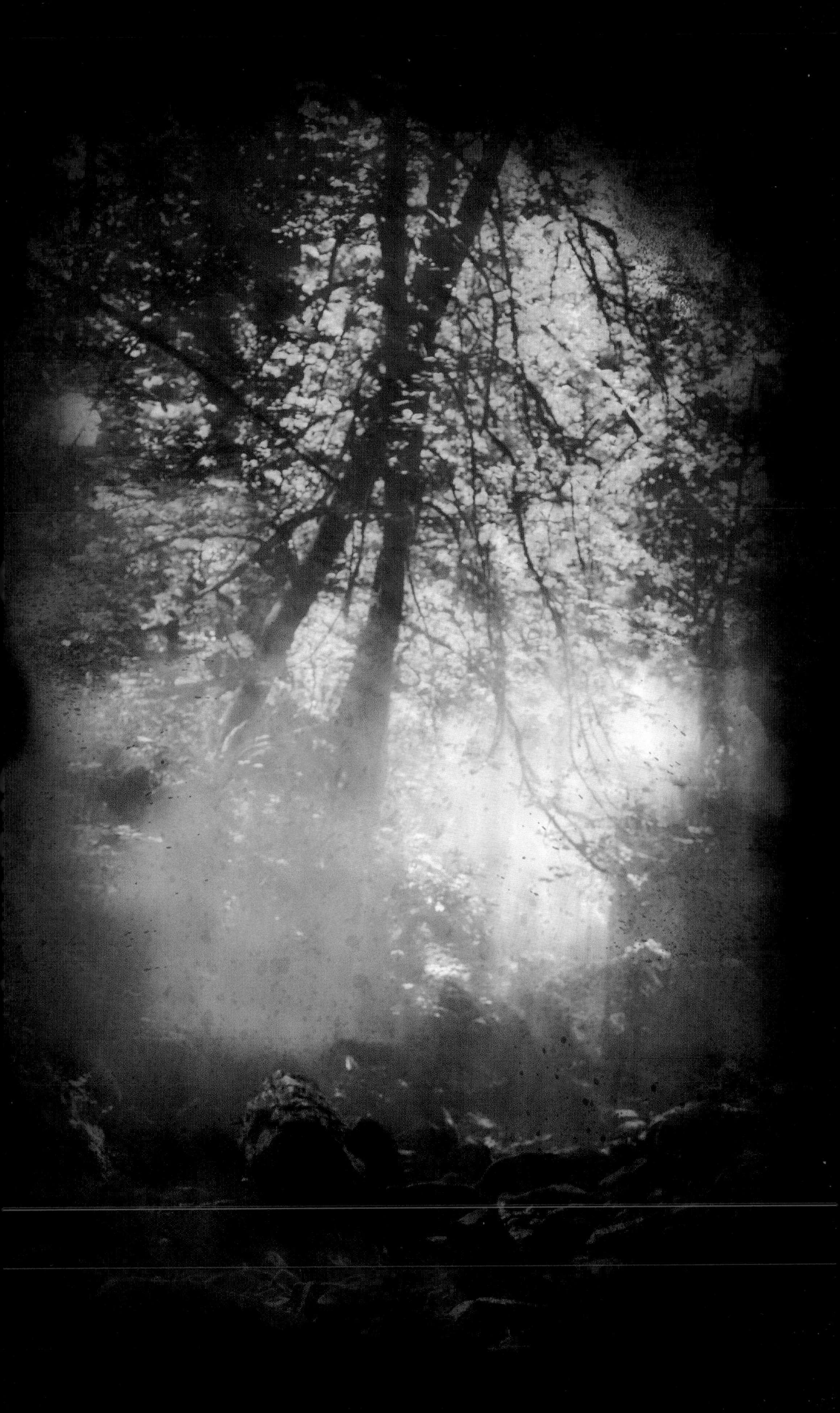

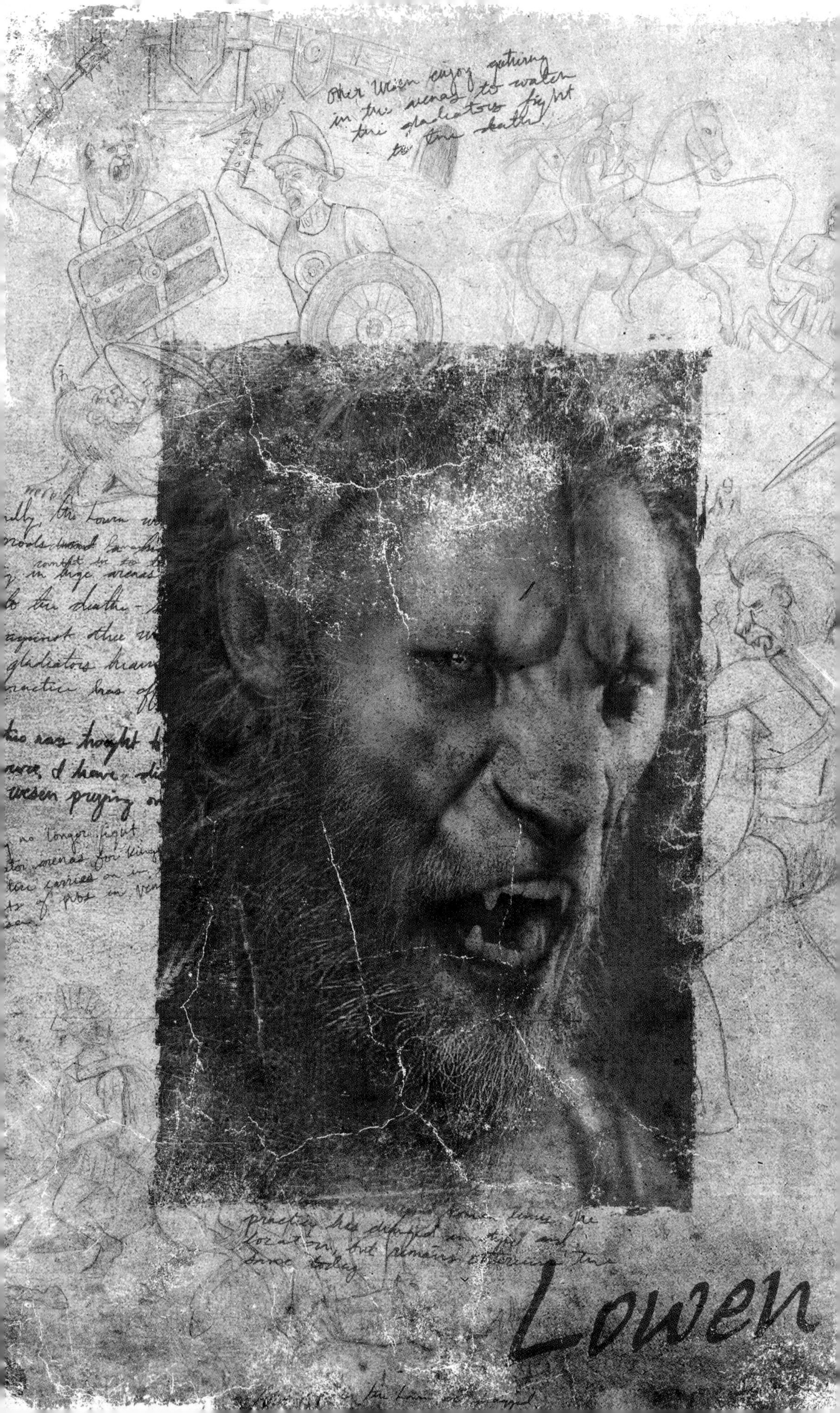
Other Wesen enjoy gathering
in the arenas to watch
the gladiators fight
to the death
Lowen

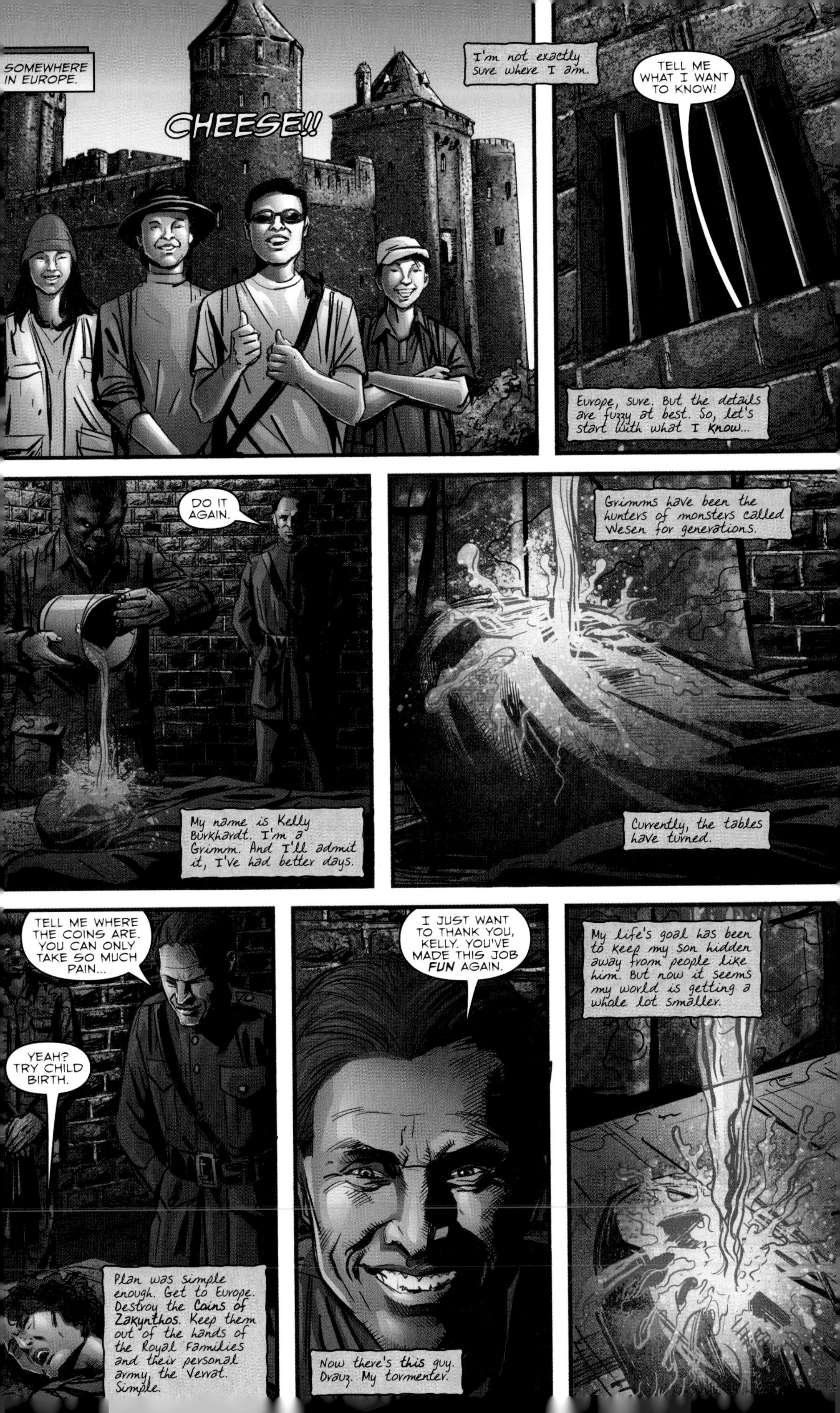
SOMEWHERE IN EUROPE.
CHEESE!!
I'm not exactly sure where I am.
TELL ME WHAT I WANT TO KNOW!
Europe, sure. But the details are fuzzy at best. So, let's start with what I know...
DO IT AGAIN.
My name is Kelly Burkhardt. I'm a Grimm. And I'll admit it, I've had better days.
Grimms have been the hunters of monsters called Wesen for generations.
Currently, the tables have turned.
TELL ME WHERE THE COINS ARE. YOU CAN ONLY TAKE SO MUCH PAIN...
YEAH? TRY CHILD BIRTH.
Plan was simple enough. Get to Europe. Destroy the Coins of Zakynthos. Keep them out of the hands of the Royal Families and their personal army, the Verrat. Simple.
I JUST WANT TO THANK YOU, KELLY. YOU'VE MADE THIS JOB FUN AGAIN.
Now there's this guy. Drauz. My tormenter.
My life's goal has been to keep my son hidden away from people like him. But now it seems my world is getting a whole lot smaller.

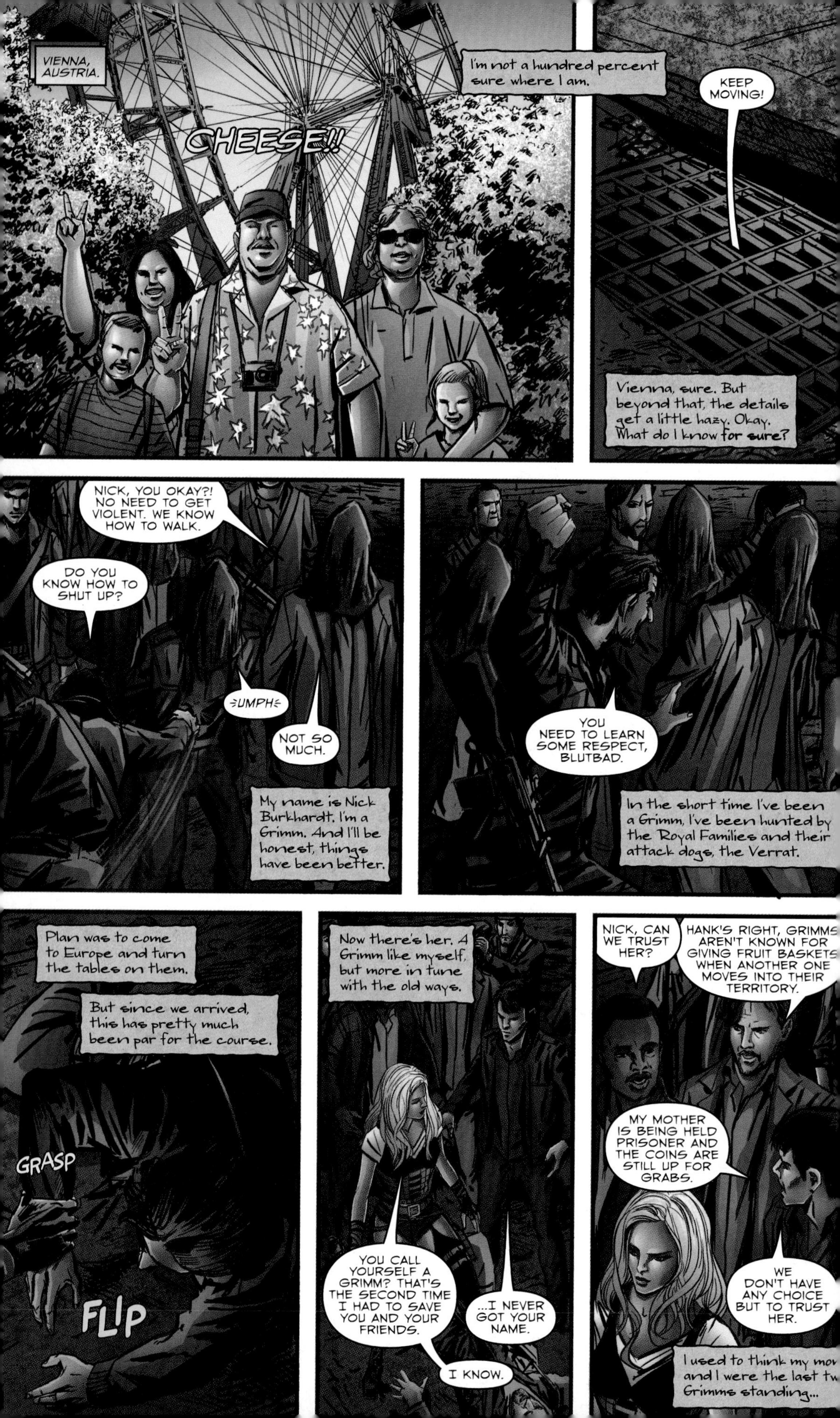
VIENNA, AUSTRIA.
I'm not a hundred percent sure where I am.
CHEESE!!
KEEP MOVING!
Vienna, sure. But beyond that, the details get a little hazy. Okay. What do I know for sure?
NICK, YOU OKAY?! NO NEED TO GET VIOLENT. WE KNOW HOW TO WALK.
DO YOU KNOW HOW TO SHUT UP?
UMPH
NOT SO MUCH.
My name is Nick Burkhardt. I'm a Grimm. And I'll be honest, things have been better.
YOU NEED TO LEARN SOME RESPECT, BLUTBAD.
In the short time I've been a Grimm, I've been hunted by the Royal Families and their attack dogs, the Verrat.
Plan was to come to Europe and turn the tables on them.
But since we arrived, this has pretty much been par for the course.
GRASP
FLIP
Now there's her. A Grimm like myself, but more in tune with the old ways.
YOU CALL YOURSELF A GRIMM? THAT'S THE SECOND TIME I HAD TO SAVE YOU AND YOUR FRIENDS.
...I NEVER GOT YOUR NAME.
I KNOW.
NICK, CAN WE TRUST HER?
HANK'S RIGHT, GRIMMS AREN'T KNOWN FOR GIVING FRUIT BASKETS WHEN ANOTHER ONE MOVES INTO THEIR TERRITORY.
MY MOTHER IS BEING HELD PRISONER AND THE COINS ARE STILL UP FOR GRABS.
WE DON'T HAVE ANY CHOICE BUT TO TRUST HER.
I used to think my mo and I were the last tw Grimms standing...

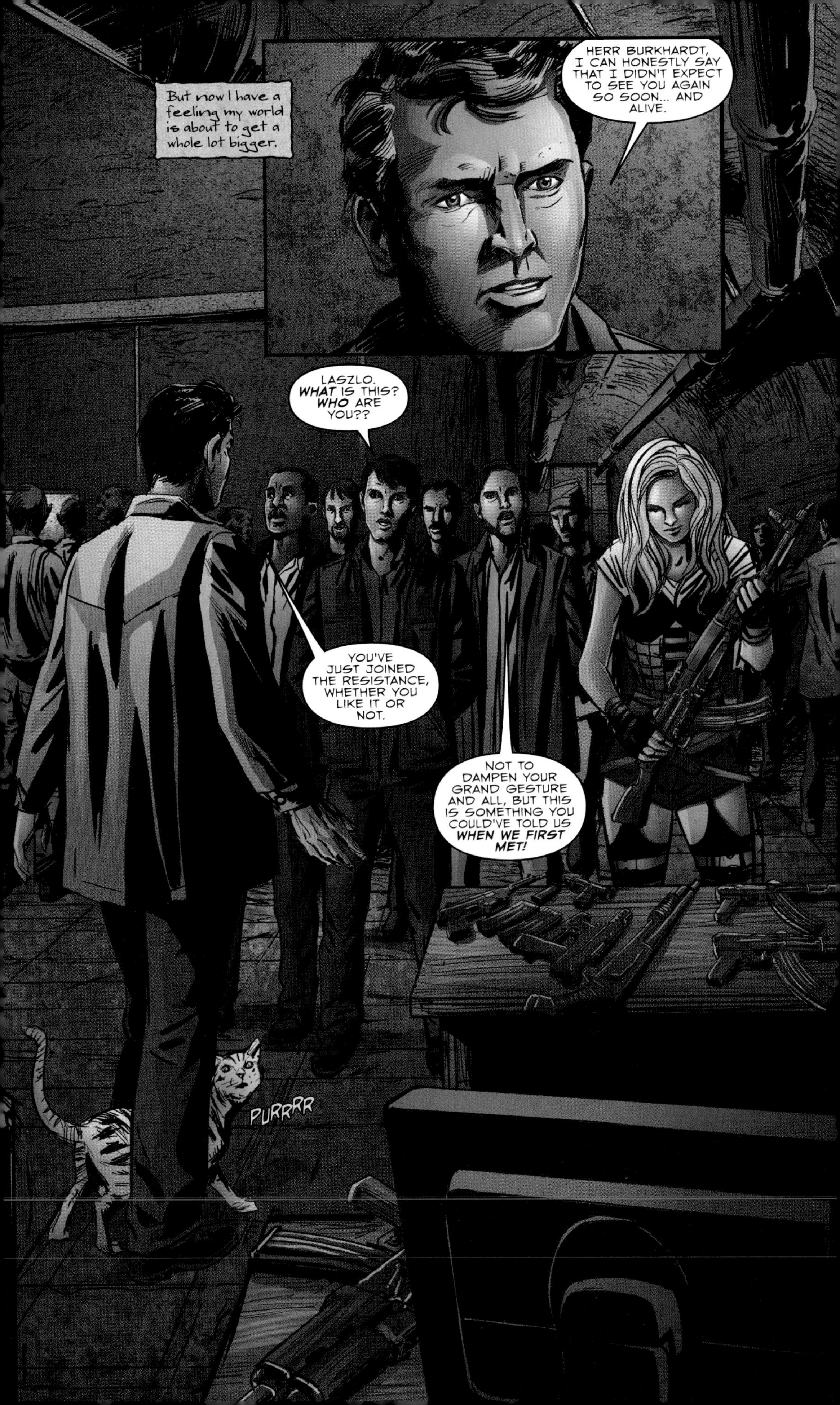

But now I have a feeling my world is about to get a whole lot bigger.
HERR BURKHARDT, I CAN HONESTLY SAY THAT I DIDN'T EXPECT TO SEE YOU AGAIN SO SOON... AND ALIVE.
LASZLO. WHAT IS THIS? WHO ARE YOU??
YOU'VE JUST JOINED THE RESISTANCE, WHETHER YOU LIKE IT OR NOT.
NOT TO DAMPEN YOUR GRAND GESTURE AND ALL, BUT THIS IS SOMETHING YOU COULD'VE TOLD US WHEN WE FIRST MET!
PURRRR

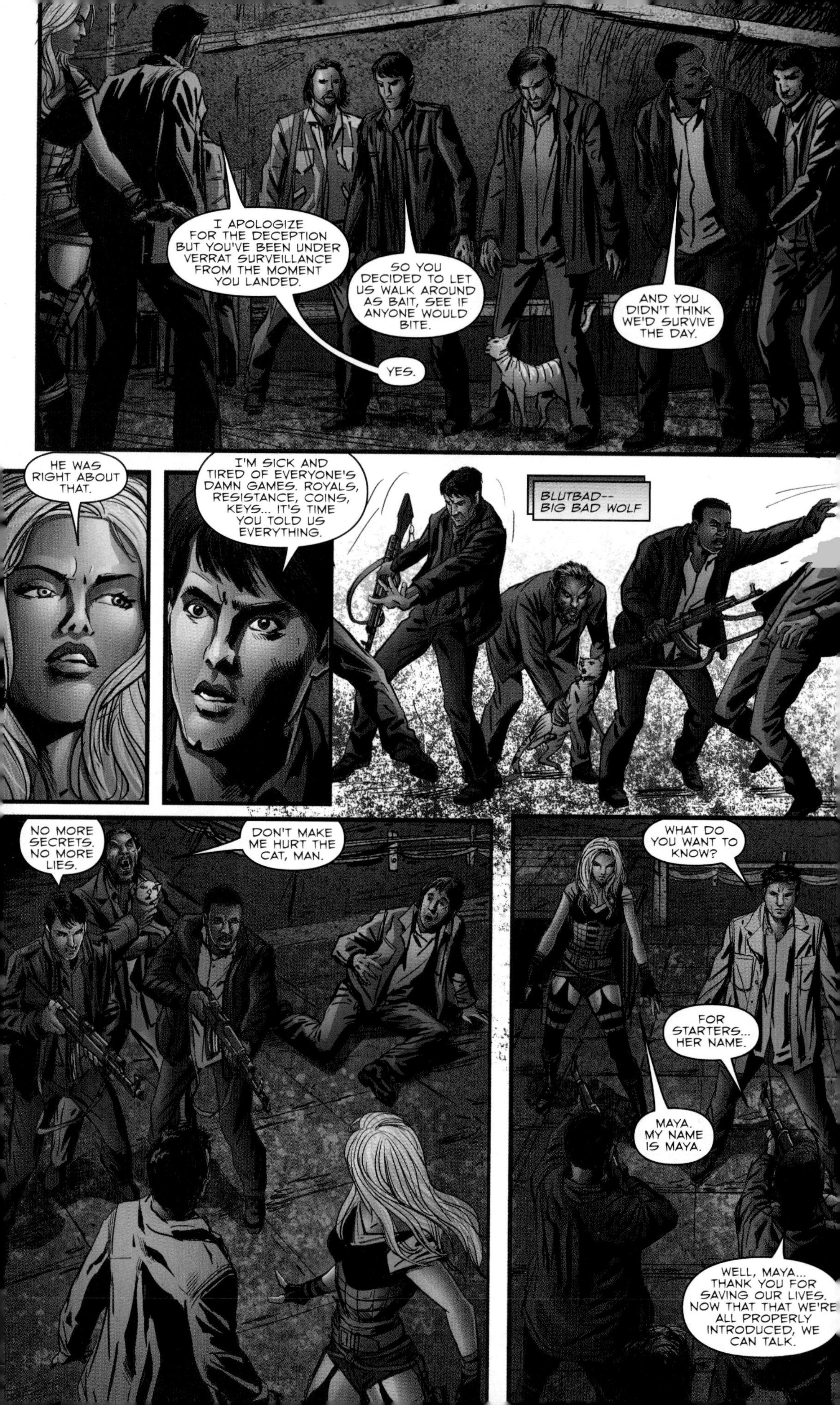
I APOLOGIZE FOR THE DECEPTION BUT YOU'VE BEEN UNDER VERRAT SURVEILLANCE FROM THE MOMENT YOU LANDED.
SO YOU DECIDED TO LET US WALK AROUND AS BAIT, SEE IF ANYONE WOULD BITE.
YES.
AND YOU DIDN'T THINK WE'D SURVIVE THE DAY.
HE WAS RIGHT ABOUT THAT.
I'M SICK AND TIRED OF EVERYONE'S DAMN GAMES. ROYALS, RESISTANCE, COINS, KEYS... IT'S TIME YOU TOLD US EVERYTHING.
BLUTBAD-- BIG BAD WOLF
NO MORE SECRETS. NO MORE LIES.
DON'T MAKE ME HURT THE CAT, MAN.
WHAT DO YOU WANT TO KNOW?
FOR STARTERS... HER NAME.
MAYA. MY NAME IS MAYA.
WELL, MAYA... THANK YOU FOR SAVING OUR LIVES. NOW THAT THAT WE'RE ALL PROPERLY INTRODUCED, WE CAN TALK.

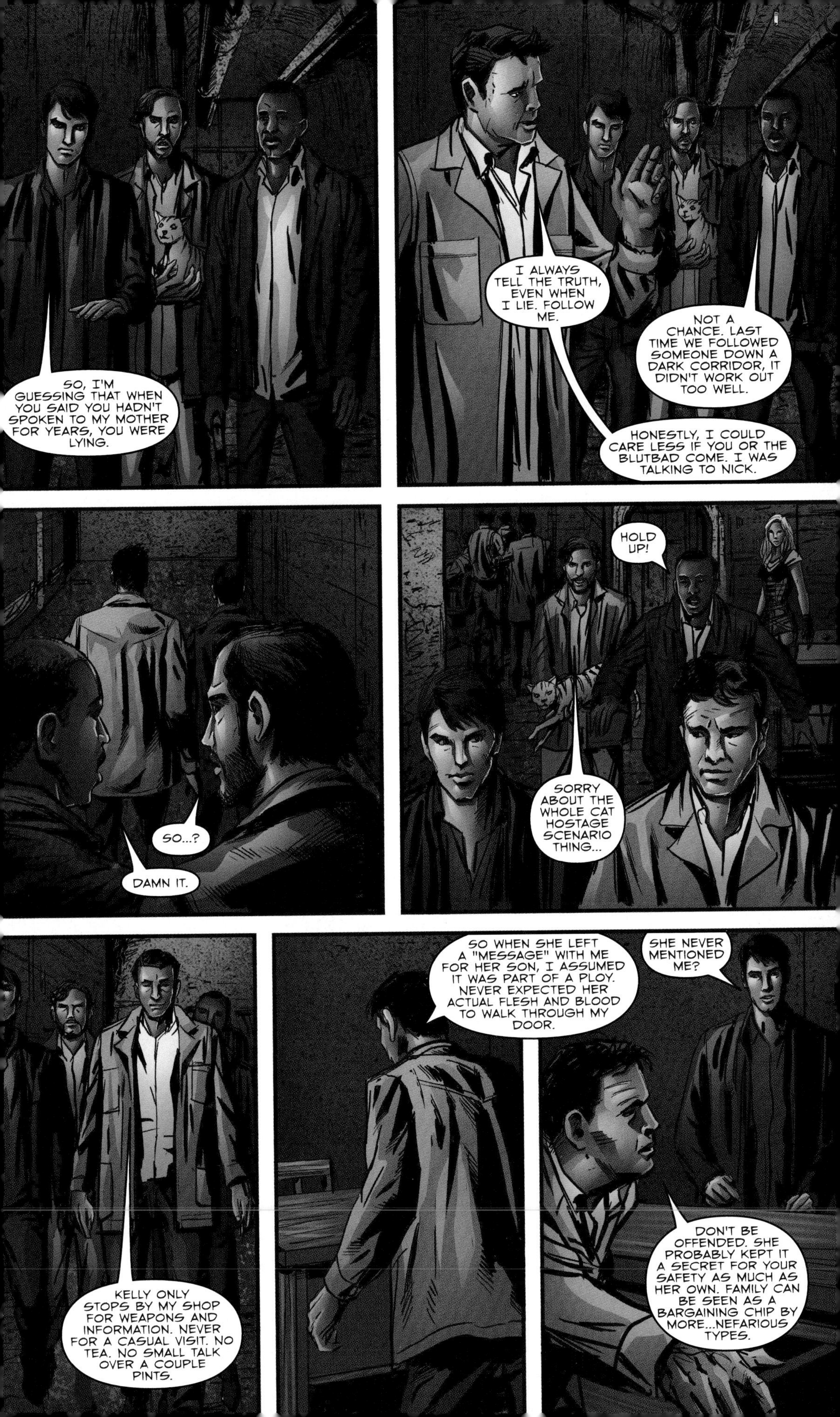
SO, I'M GUESSING THAT WHEN YOU SAID YOU HADN'T SPOKEN TO MY MOTHER FOR YEARS, YOU WERE LYING.
I ALWAYS TELL THE TRUTH, EVEN WHEN I LIE. FOLLOW ME.
NOT A CHANCE. LAST TIME WE FOLLOWED SOMEONE DOWN A DARK CORRIDOR, IT DIDN'T WORK OUT TOO WELL.
HONESTLY, I COULD CARE LESS IF YOU OR THE BLUTBAD COME. I WAS TALKING TO NICK.
SO...?
DAMN IT.
HOLD UP!
SORRY ABOUT THE WHOLE CAT HOSTAGE SCENARIO THING...
KELLY ONLY STOPS BY MY SHOP FOR WEAPONS AND INFORMATION. NEVER FOR A CASUAL VISIT. NO TEA. NO SMALL TALK OVER A COUPLE PINTS.
SO WHEN SHE LEFT A "MESSAGE" WITH ME FOR HER SON, I ASSUMED IT WAS PART OF A PLOY. NEVER EXPECTED HER ACTUAL FLESH AND BLOOD TO WALK THROUGH MY DOOR.
SHE NEVER MENTIONED ME?
DON'T BE OFFENDED. SHE PROBABLY KEPT IT A SECRET FOR YOUR SAFETY AS MUCH AS HER OWN. FAMILY CAN BE SEEN AS A BARGAINING CHIP BY MORE...NEFARIOUS TYPES.

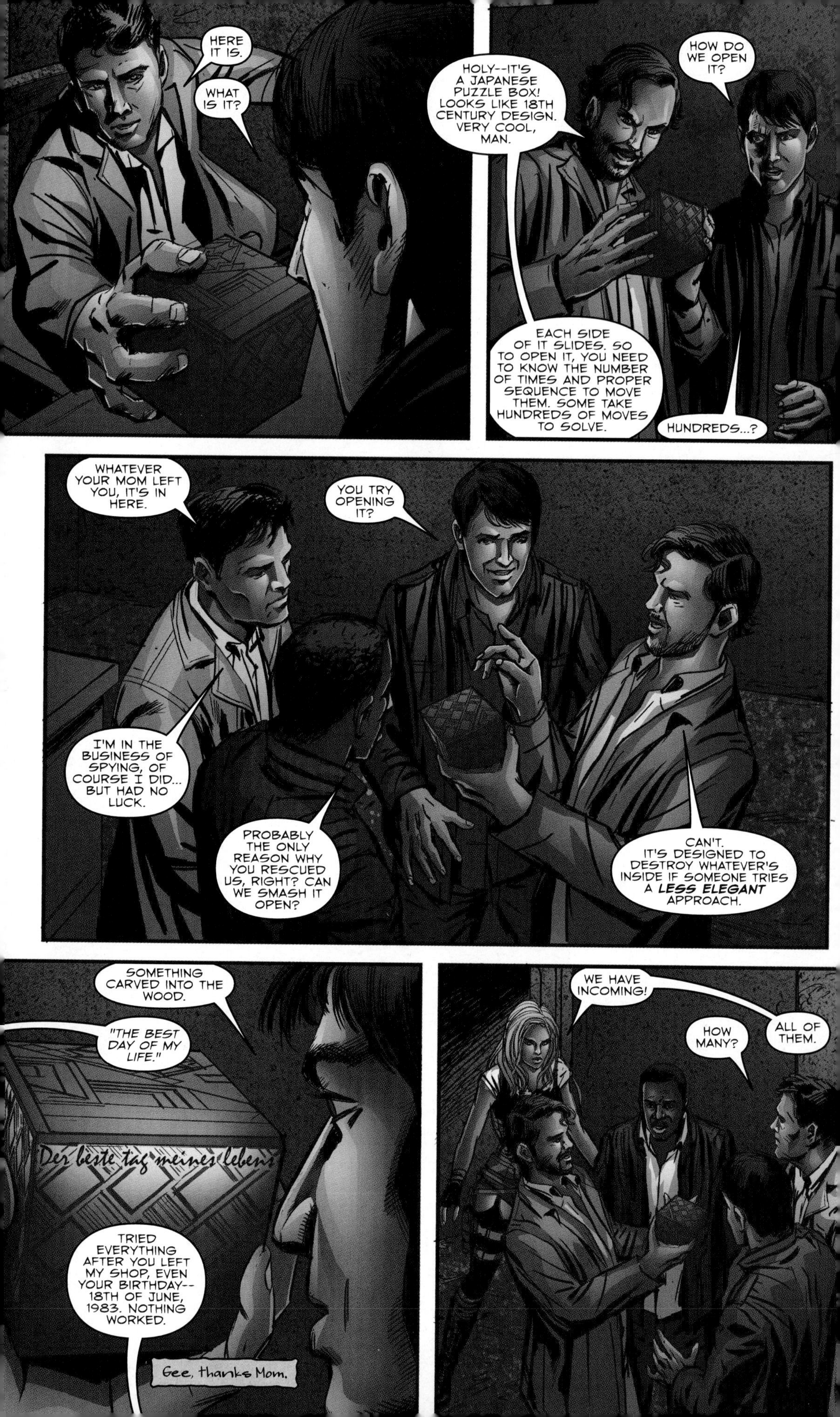
HERE IT IS.
WHAT IS IT?
HOLY--IT'S A JAPANESE PUZZLE BOX! LOOKS LIKE 18TH CENTURY DESIGN. VERY COOL, MAN.
HOW DO WE OPEN IT?
EACH SIDE OF IT SLIDES. SO TO OPEN IT, YOU NEED TO KNOW THE NUMBER OF TIMES AND PROPER SEQUENCE TO MOVE THEM. SOME TAKE HUNDREDS OF MOVES TO SOLVE.
HUNDREDS...?
WHATEVER YOUR MOM LEFT YOU, IT'S IN HERE.
YOU TRY OPENING IT?
I'M IN THE BUSINESS OF SPYING, OF COURSE I DID... BUT HAD NO LUCK.
PROBABLY THE ONLY REASON WHY YOU RESCUED US, RIGHT? CAN WE SMASH IT OPEN?
CAN'T. IT'S DESIGNED TO DESTROY WHATEVER'S INSIDE IF SOMEONE TRIES A ***LESS ELEGANT*** APPROACH.
SOMETHING CARVED INTO THE WOOD.
"THE BEST DAY OF MY LIFE."
Der beste tag meines lebens
TRIED EVERYTHING AFTER YOU LEFT MY SHOP, EVEN YOUR BIRTHDAY-- 18TH OF JUNE, 1983. NOTHING WORKED.
Gee, thanks Mom.
WE HAVE INCOMING!
HOW MANY?
ALL OF THEM.

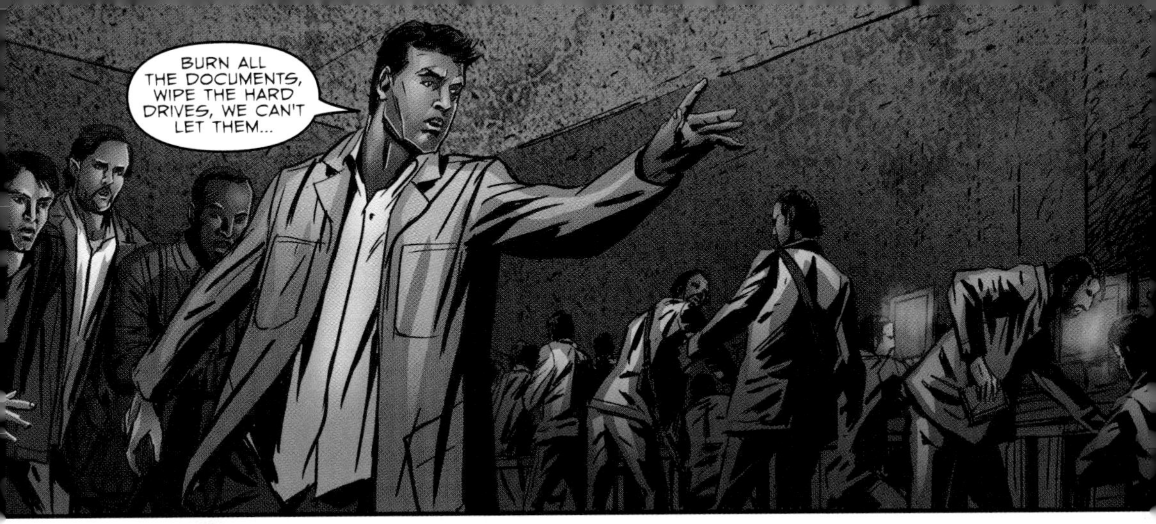
BURN ALL THE DOCUMENTS, WIPE THE HARD DRIVES, WE CAN'T LET THEM...

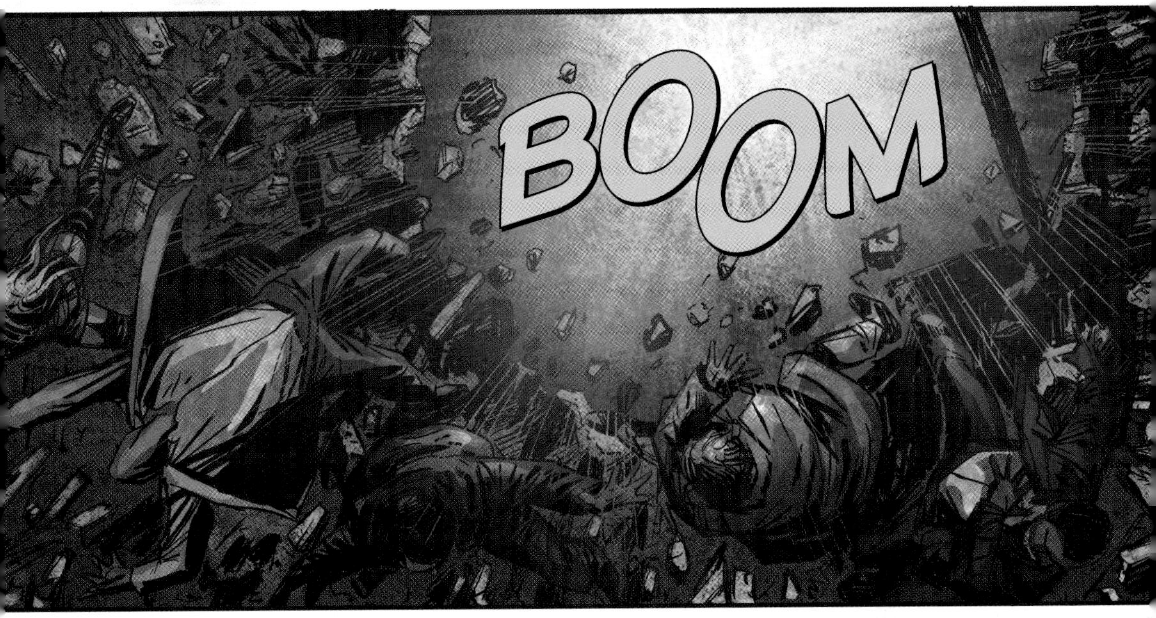
BOOM

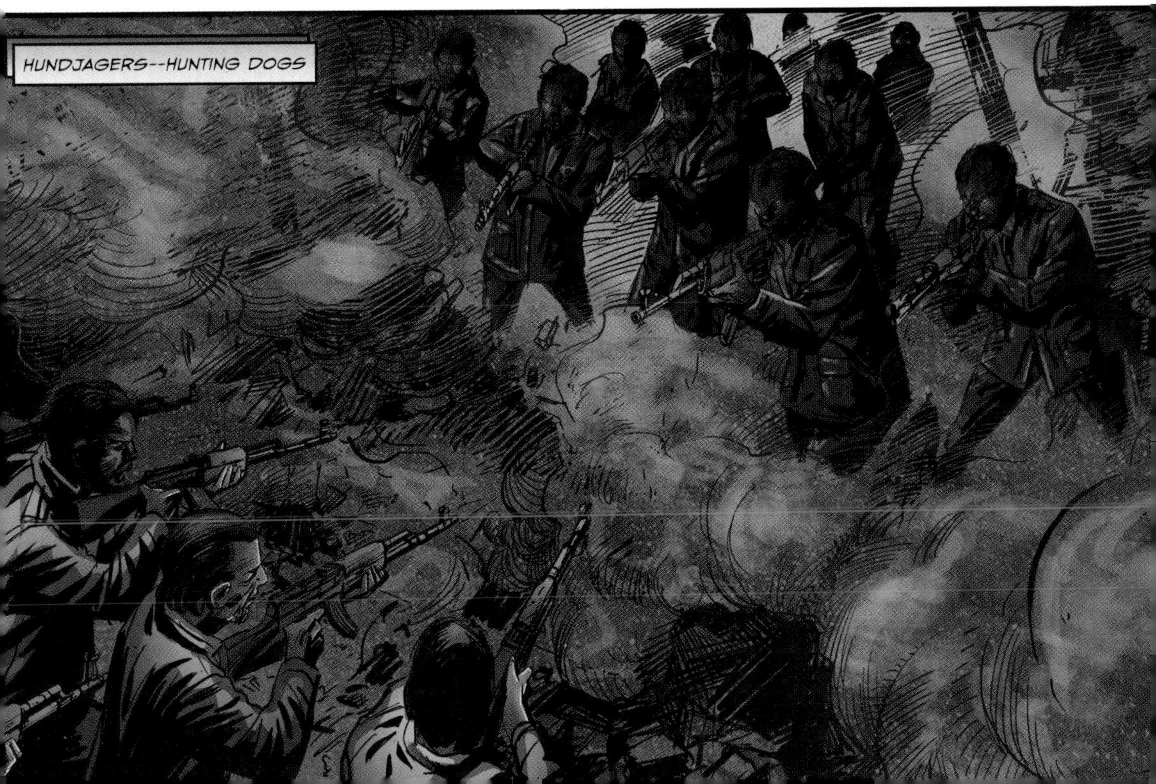
HUNDJAGERS--HUNTING DOGS

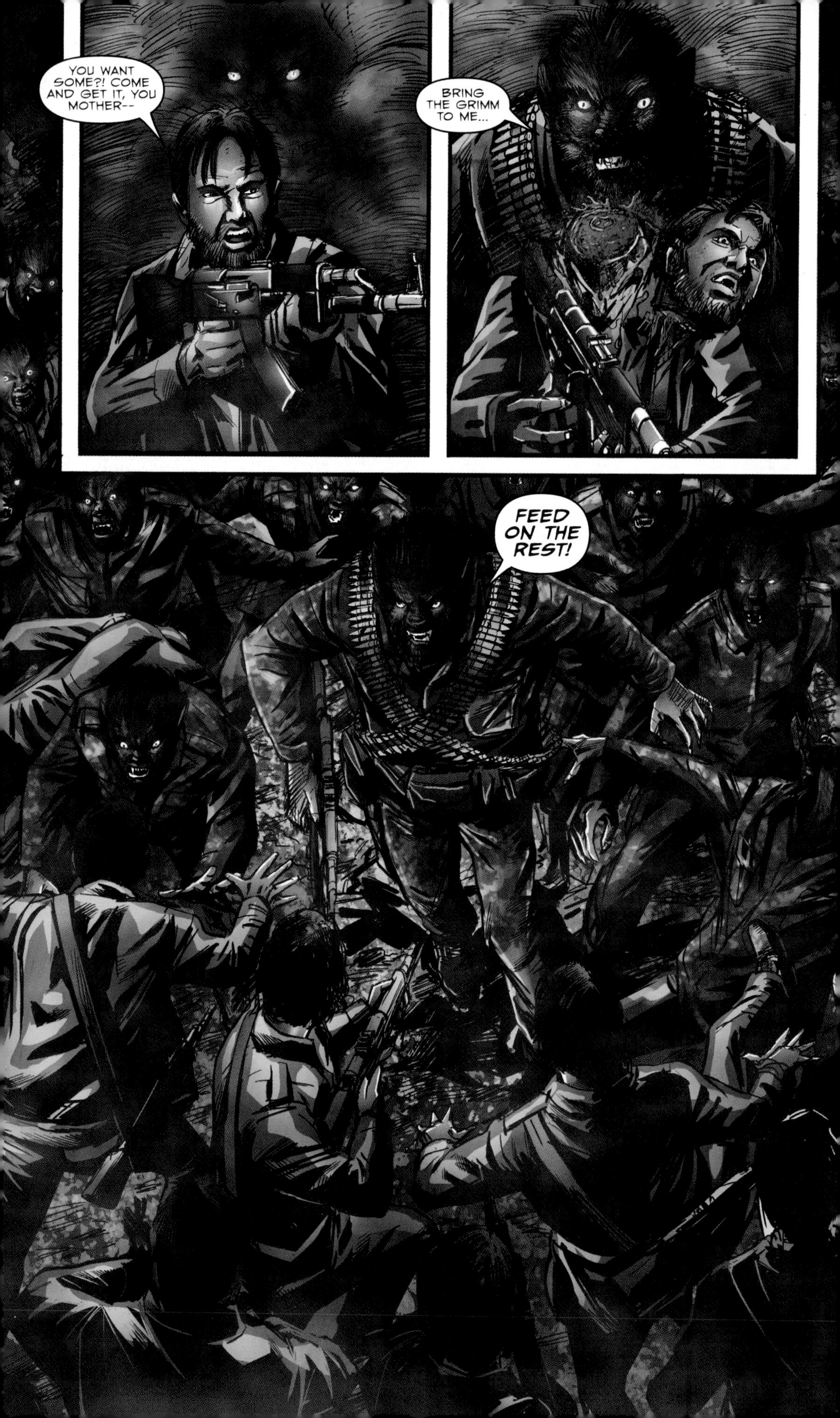
YOU WANT SOME?! COME AND GET IT, YOU MOTHER--
BRING THE GRIMM TO ME...
FEED ON THE REST!

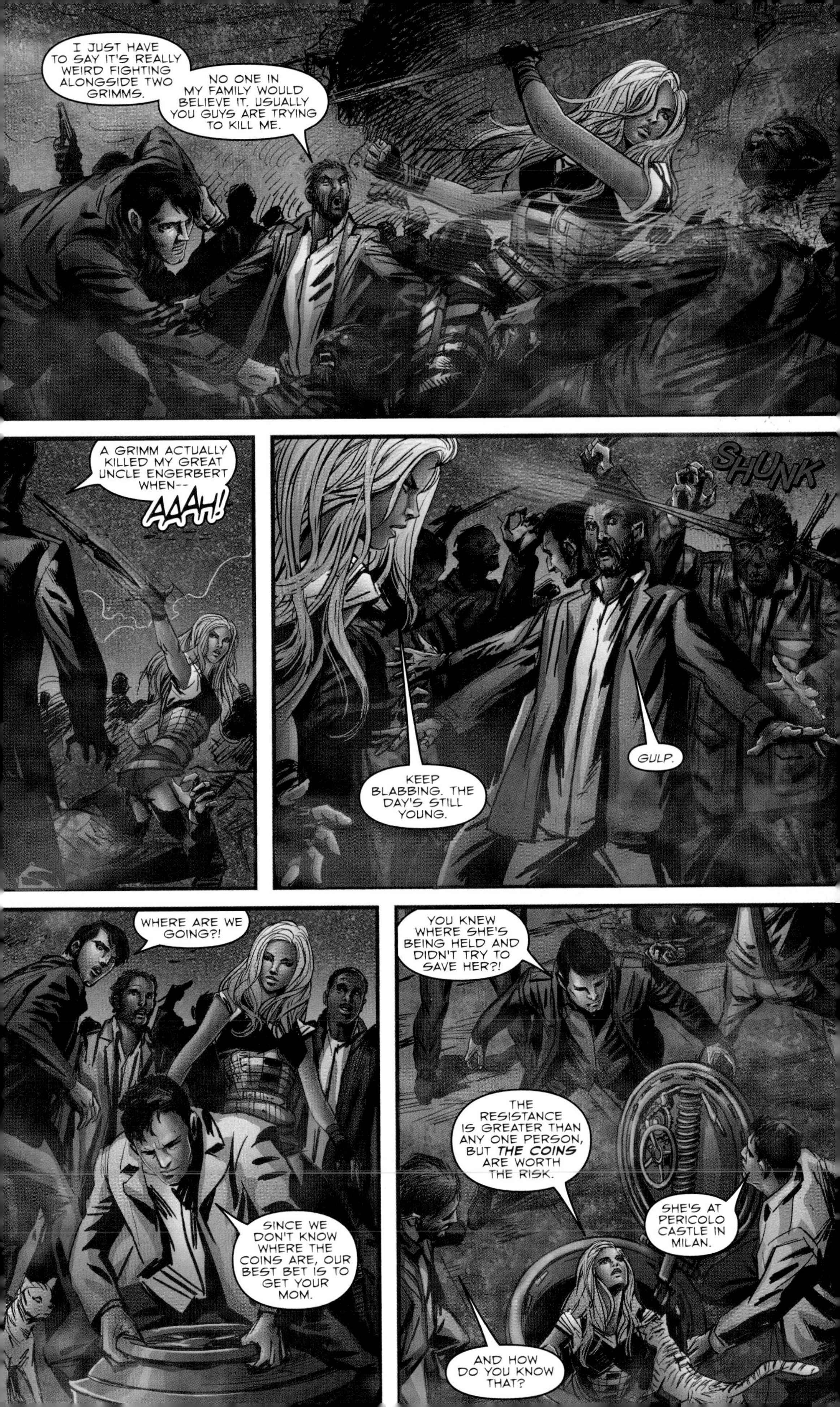
I JUST HAVE TO SAY IT'S REALLY WEIRD FIGHTING ALONGSIDE TWO GRIMMS.
NO ONE IN MY FAMILY WOULD BELIEVE IT. USUALLY YOU GUYS ARE TRYING TO KILL ME.
A GRIMM ACTUALLY KILLED MY GREAT UNCLE ENGERBERT WHEN--
AAAH!
SHUNK
KEEP BLABBING. THE DAY'S STILL YOUNG.
GULP.
WHERE ARE WE GOING?!
SINCE WE DON'T KNOW WHERE THE COINS ARE, OUR BEST BET IS TO GET YOUR MOM.
YOU KNEW WHERE SHE'S BEING HELD AND DIDN'T TRY TO SAVE HER?!
THE RESISTANCE IS GREATER THAN ANY ONE PERSON, BUT THE COINS ARE WORTH THE RISK.
SHE'S AT PERICOLO CASTLE IN MILAN.
AND HOW DO YOU KNOW THAT?

"I HAVE AN INSIDE MAN."

In situations like this, patience is the key. Sooner or later your enemy makes a mistake.

You just have to make the most of those opportunities.

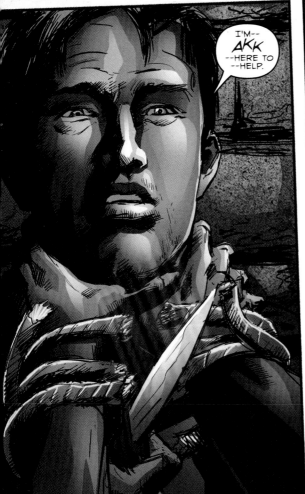

I'M--

AKK

--HERE TO --HELP.

LASZLO SENT ME.

WELL THEN...LET'S GO.

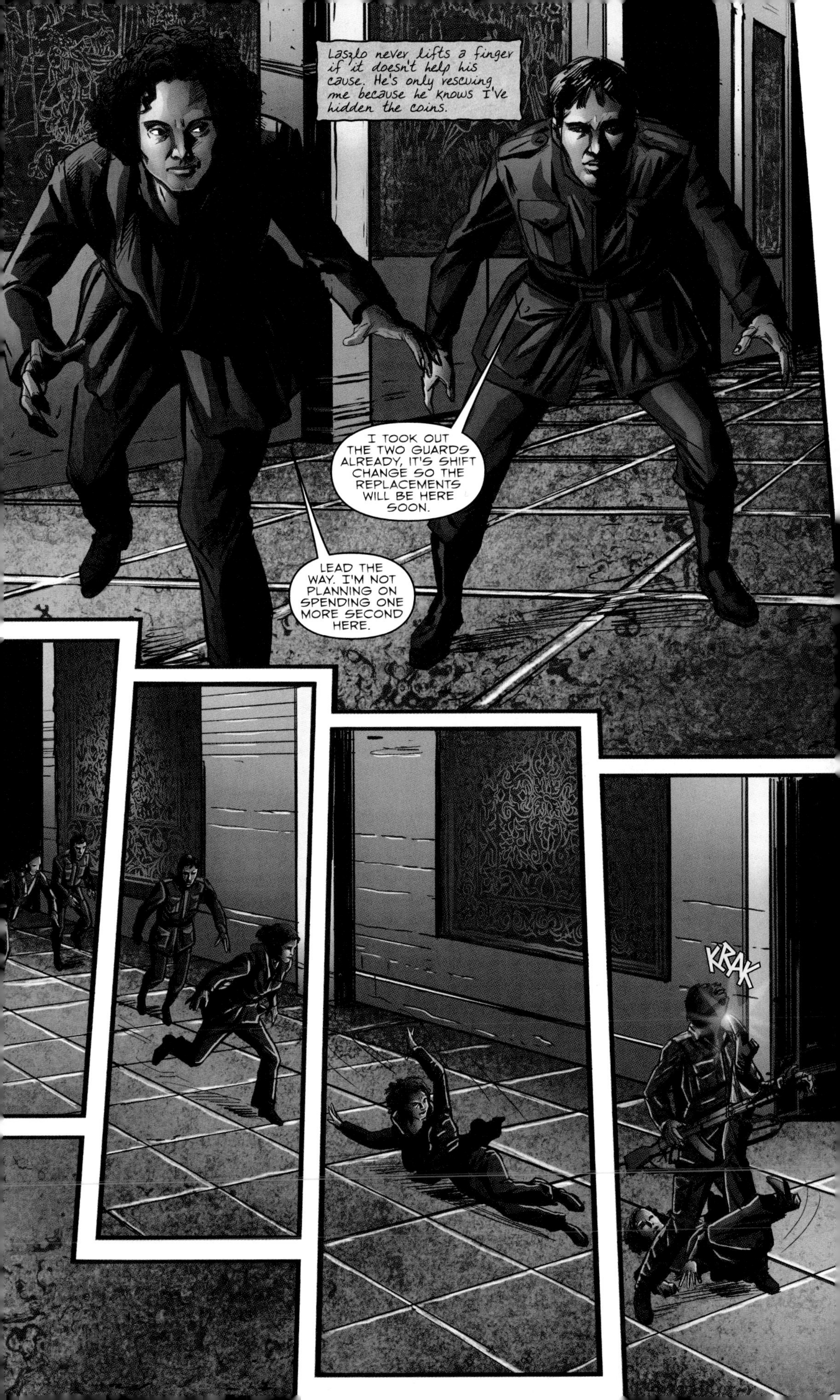

Laszlo never lifts a finger if it doesn't help his cause. He's only rescuing me because he knows I've hidden the coins.
I TOOK OUT THE TWO GUARDS ALREADY, IT'S SHIFT CHANGE SO THE REPLACEMENTS WILL BE HERE SOON.
LEAD THE WAY. I'M NOT PLANNING ON SPENDING ONE MORE SECOND HERE.
KRAK

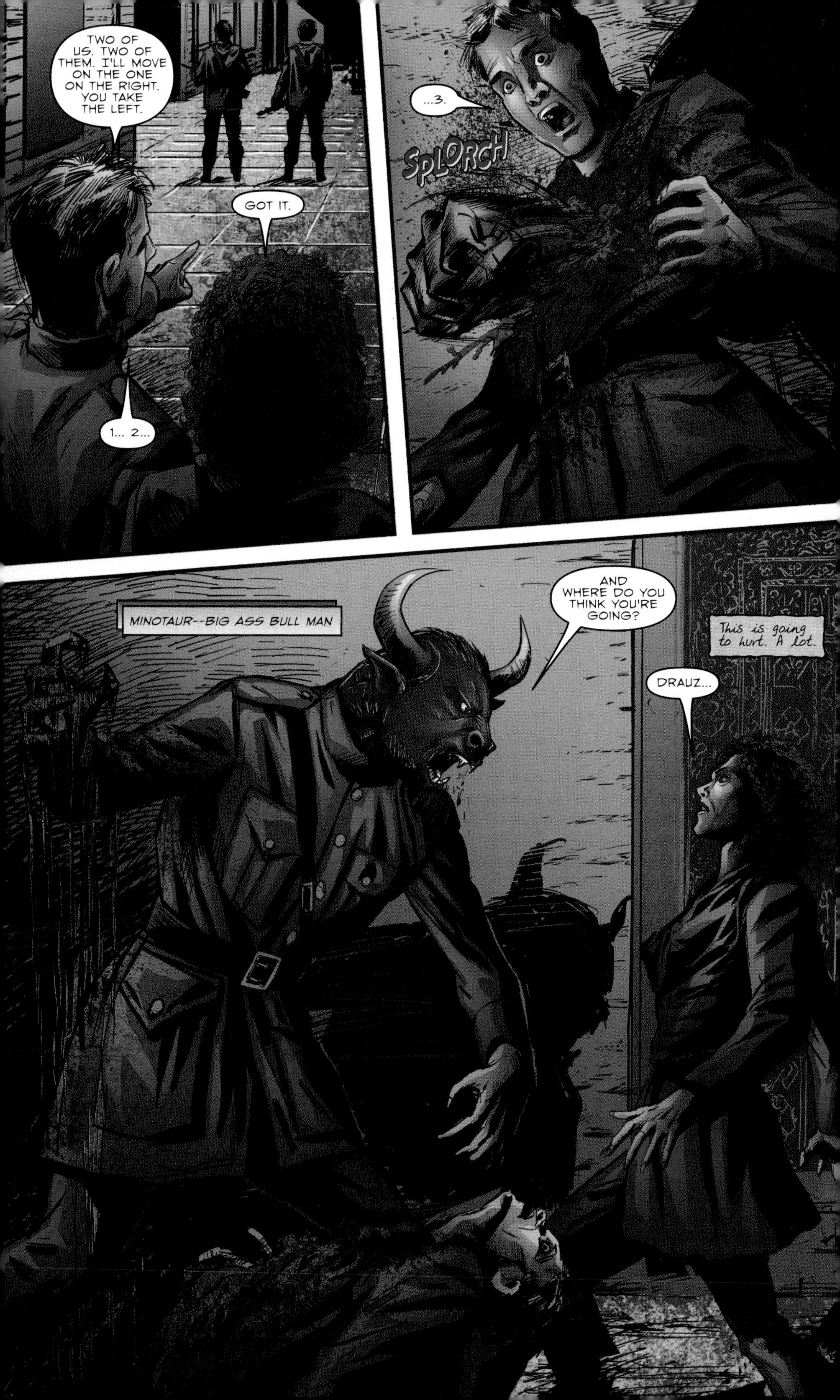
TWO OF US. TWO OF THEM. I'LL MOVE ON THE ONE ON THE RIGHT. YOU TAKE THE LEFT.
GOT IT.
1... 2...
...3.
SPLORCH
MINOTAUR--BIG ASS BULL MAN
AND WHERE DO YOU THINK YOU'RE GOING?
This is going to hurt. A lot.
DRAUZ...

ITALY.

"BEST DAY OF MY LIFE..." IT'S OBVIOUSLY A CLUE."

HANK IS KEEPING LASZLO AND THE OTHERS BUSY, LETS FIGURE THIS OUT.

OKAY. WE NEED A SEQUENCE OF NUMBERS.

SIX SIDES, SIX NUMBERS. WHICH MEANS WE'RE LOOKING FOR A SPECIFIC DATE, RIGHT?

THE BEST DAY OF HER LIFE COULD BE THE DAY SHE KILLED HER FIRST WESEN...OR HELL, A DAY SHE WENT GO-CARTING.

WHAT ABOUT THE DAY YOUR PARENTS GOT MARRIED?

NINETEEN SEVENTY... SOMETHING?

DUDE...

WHAT... LIKE YOU REMEMBER ALL YOUR PARENTS ANNIVERSARIES?

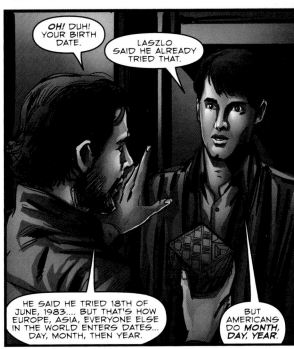

OH! DUH! YOUR BIRTH DATE.

LASZLO SAID HE ALREADY TRIED THAT.

HE SAID HE TRIED 18TH OF JUNE, 1983.... BUT THAT'S HOW EUROPE, ASIA, EVERYONE ELSE IN THE WORLD ENTERS DATES... DAY, MONTH, THEN YEAR.

BUT AMERICANS DO MONTH, DAY, YEAR.

CLICK

WE GOT IT! WHAT'S INSIDE?

U.S.A.! SUCK IT EUROPE, WITH YOUR METRIC SYSTEM AND WEIRD DATES.

LOOKS LIKE A G.P.S. TRACKER.

WITH ONLY ONE SAVED LOCATION-- IT'S THE COINS.

WHO KNEW YOUR OLD SCHOOL MOM WOULD BE SO TECHY.

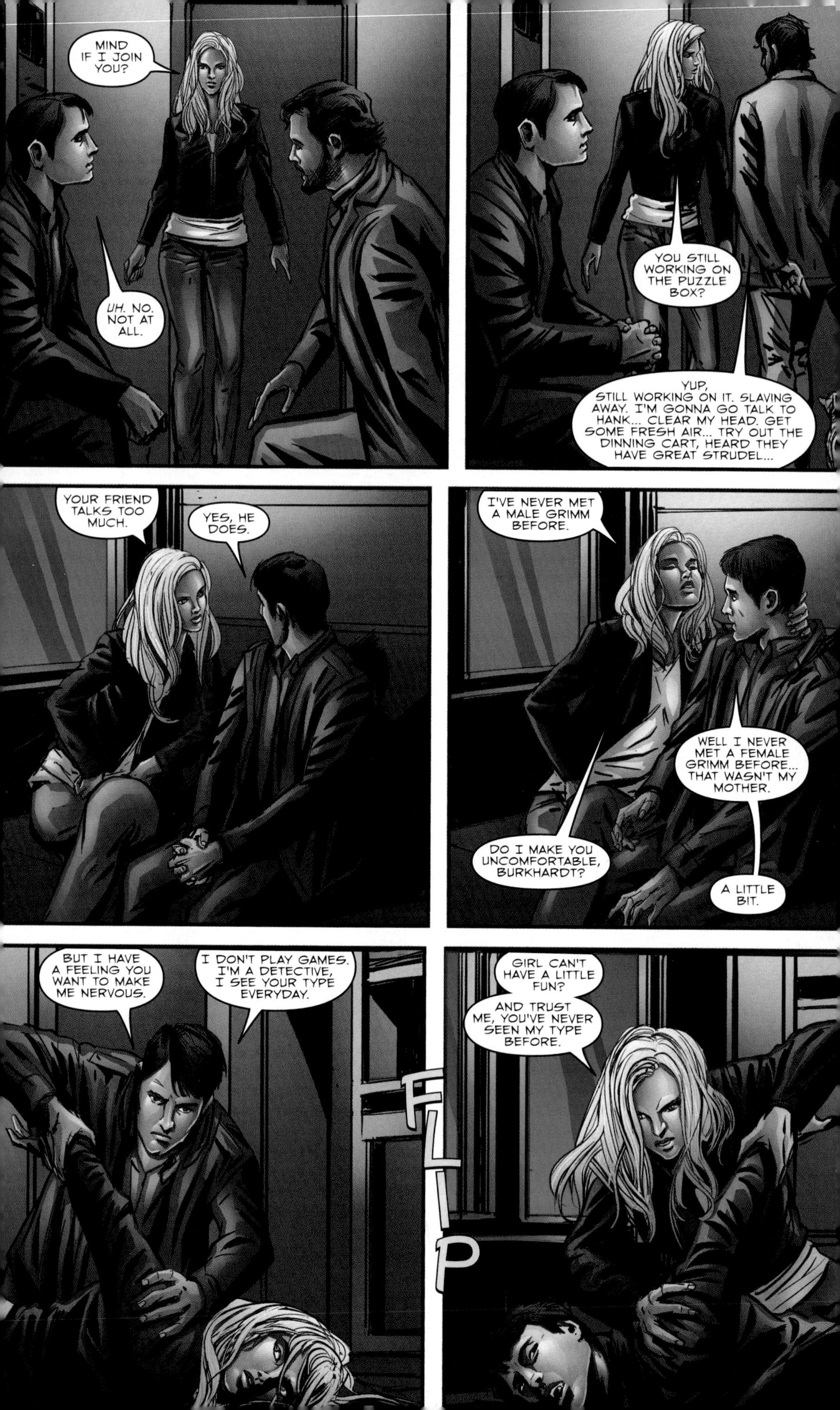
MIND IF I JOIN YOU?
UH. NO. NOT AT ALL.
YOU STILL WORKING ON THE PUZZLE BOX?
YUP, STILL WORKING ON IT. SLAVING AWAY. I'M GONNA GO TALK TO HANK... CLEAR MY HEAD. GET SOME FRESH AIR... TRY OUT THE DINNING CART, HEARD THEY HAVE GREAT STRUDEL...
YOUR FRIEND TALKS TOO MUCH.
YES, HE DOES.
I'VE NEVER MET A MALE GRIMM BEFORE.
WELL I NEVER MET A FEMALE GRIMM BEFORE... THAT WASN'T MY MOTHER.
DO I MAKE YOU UNCOMFORTABLE, BURKHARDT?
A LITTLE BIT.
BUT I HAVE A FEELING YOU WANT TO MAKE ME NERVOUS.
I DON'T PLAY GAMES. I'M A DETECTIVE, I SEE YOUR TYPE EVERYDAY.
FLIP
GIRL CAN'T HAVE A LITTLE FUN?
AND TRUST ME, YOU'VE NEVER SEEN MY TYPE BEFORE.

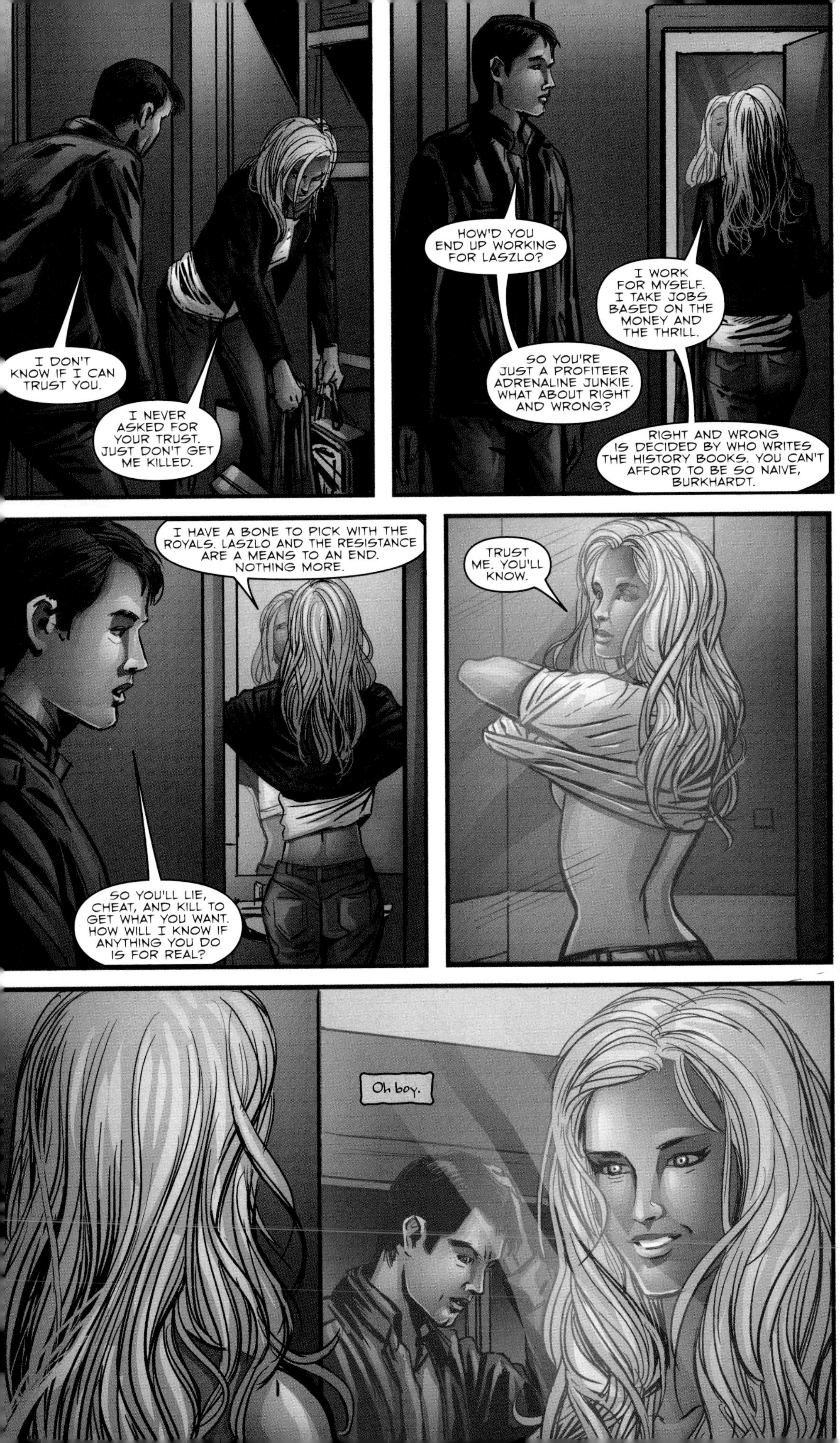
I DON'T KNOW IF I CAN TRUST YOU.
I NEVER ASKED FOR YOUR TRUST. JUST DON'T GET ME KILLED.
HOW'D YOU END UP WORKING FOR LASZLO?
I WORK FOR MYSELF. I TAKE JOBS BASED ON THE MONEY AND THE THRILL.
SO YOU'RE JUST A PROFITEER ADRENALINE JUNKIE. WHAT ABOUT RIGHT AND WRONG?
RIGHT AND WRONG IS DECIDED BY WHO WRITES THE HISTORY BOOKS. YOU CAN'T AFFORD TO BE SO NAIVE, BURKHARDT.
I HAVE A BONE TO PICK WITH THE ROYALS. LASZLO AND THE RESISTANCE ARE A MEANS TO AN END. NOTHING MORE.
SO YOU'LL LIE, CHEAT, AND KILL TO GET WHAT YOU WANT. HOW WILL I KNOW IF ANYTHING YOU DO IS FOR REAL?
TRUST ME. YOU'LL KNOW.
Oh boy.

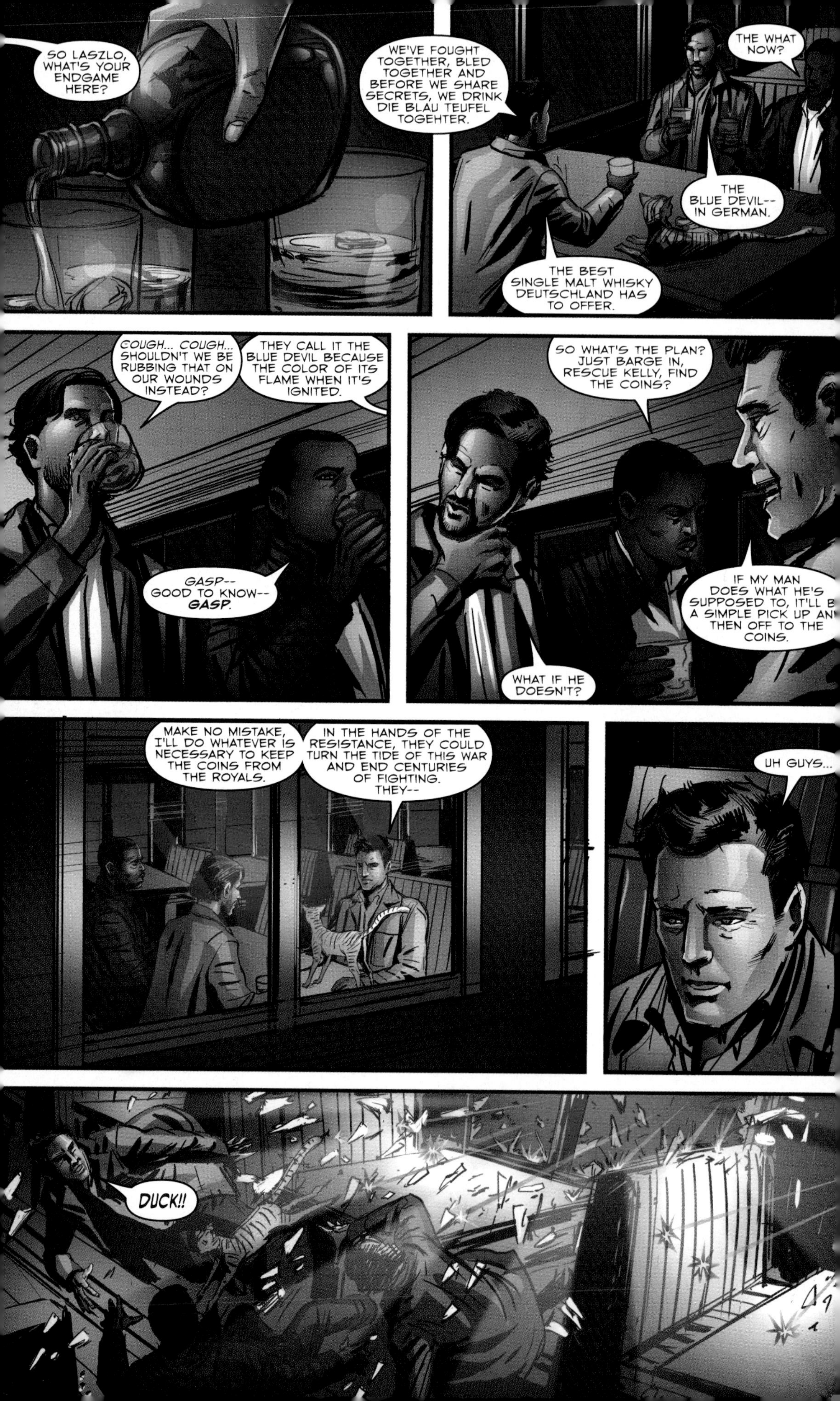
SO LASZLO, WHAT'S YOUR ENDGAME HERE?
WE'VE FOUGHT TOGETHER, BLED TOGETHER AND BEFORE WE SHARE SECRETS, WE DRINK DIE BLAU TEUFEL TOGEHTER.
THE WHAT NOW?
THE BLUE DEVIL-- IN GERMAN.
THE BEST SINGLE MALT WHISKY DEUTSCHLAND HAS TO OFFER.
COUGH... COUGH... SHOULDN'T WE BE RUBBING THAT ON OUR WOUNDS INSTEAD?
THEY CALL IT THE BLUE DEVIL BECAUSE THE COLOR OF ITS FLAME WHEN IT'S IGNITED.
GASP-- GOOD TO KNOW-- GASP.
SO WHAT'S THE PLAN? JUST BARGE IN, RESCUE KELLY, FIND THE COINS?
IF MY MAN DOES WHAT HE'S SUPPOSED TO, IT'LL B A SIMPLE PICK UP AN THEN OFF TO THE COINS.
WHAT IF HE DOESN'T?
MAKE NO MISTAKE, I'LL DO WHATEVER IS NECESSARY TO KEEP THE COINS FROM THE ROYALS.
IN THE HANDS OF THE RESISTANCE, THEY COULD TURN THE TIDE OF THIS WAR AND END CENTURIES OF FIGHTING. THEY--
UH GUYS...
DUCK!!

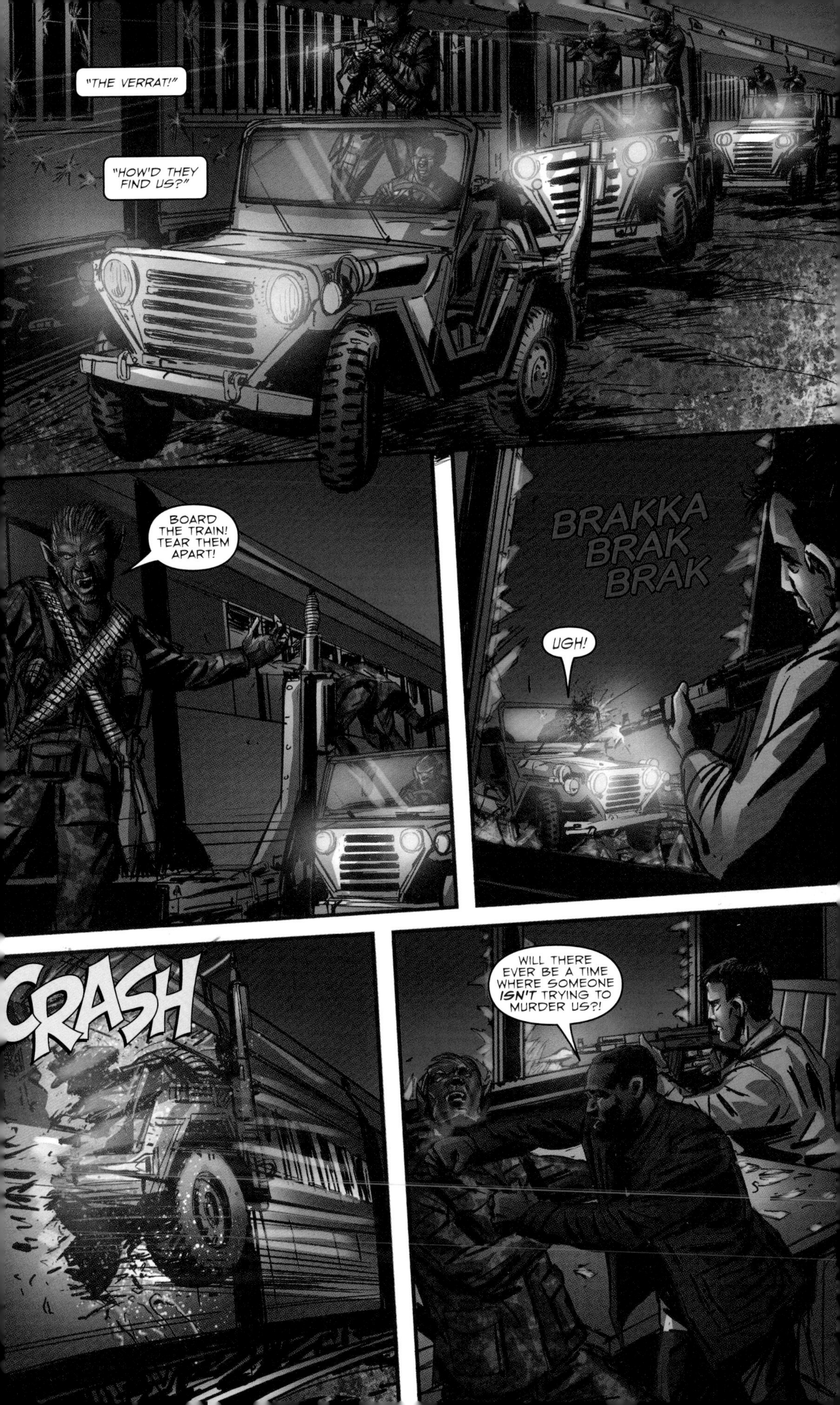

"THE VERRAT!"
"HOW'D THEY FIND US?"
BOARD THE TRAIN! TEAR THEM APART!
BRAKKA BRAK BRAK
UGH!
CRASH
WILL THERE EVER BE A TIME WHERE SOMEONE ISN'T TRYING TO MURDER US?!

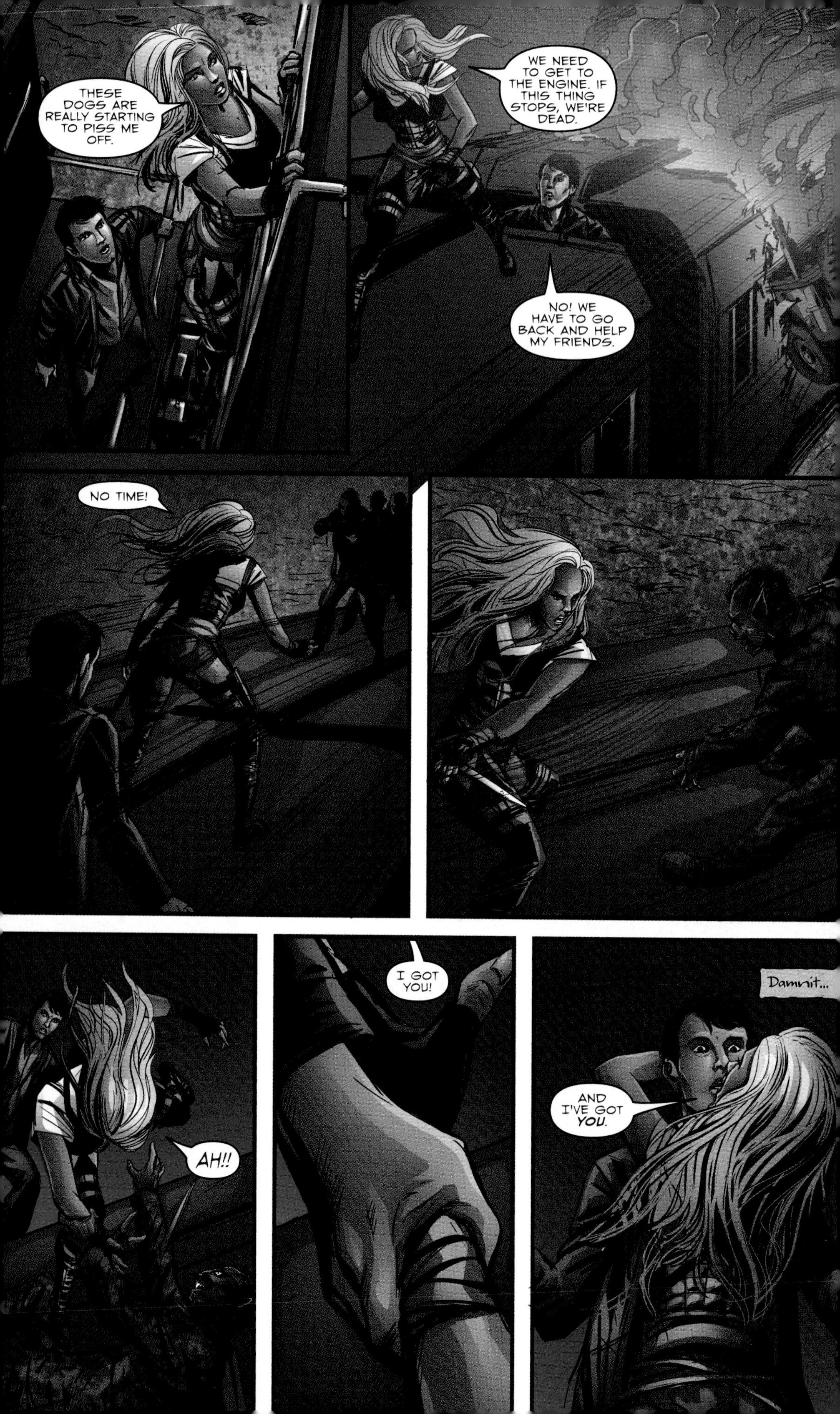
THESE DOGS ARE REALLY STARTING TO PISS ME OFF.
WE NEED TO GET TO THE ENGINE. IF THIS THING STOPS, WE'RE DEAD.
NO! WE HAVE TO GO BACK AND HELP MY FRIENDS.
NO TIME!
AH!!
I GOT YOU!
Damnit...
AND I'VE GOT *YOU*.

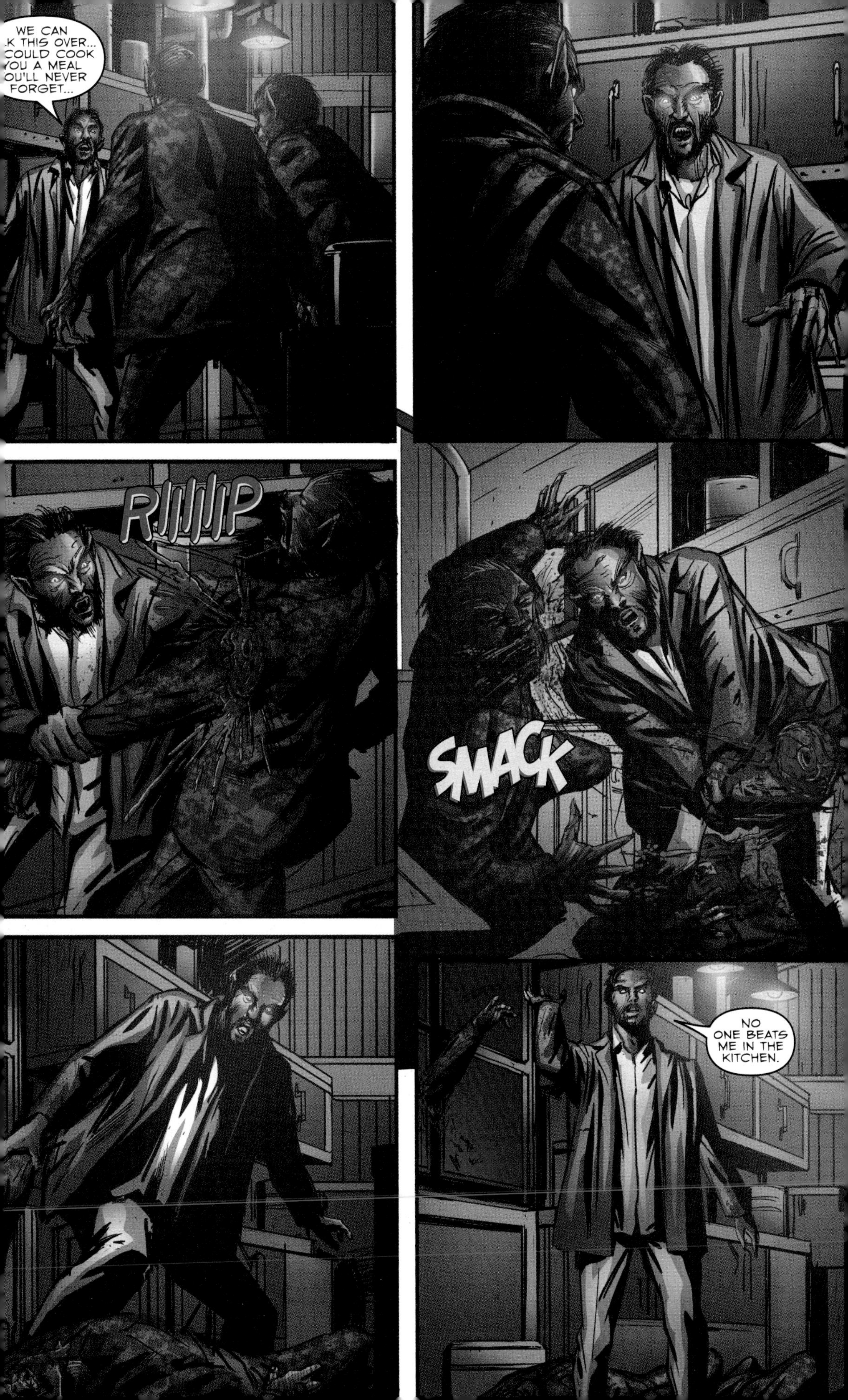
WE CAN ...K THIS OVER... ...COULD COOK ...YOU A MEAL ...OU'LL NEVER FORGET...
RIIIIIP
SMACK
NO ONE BEATS ME IN THE KITCHEN.

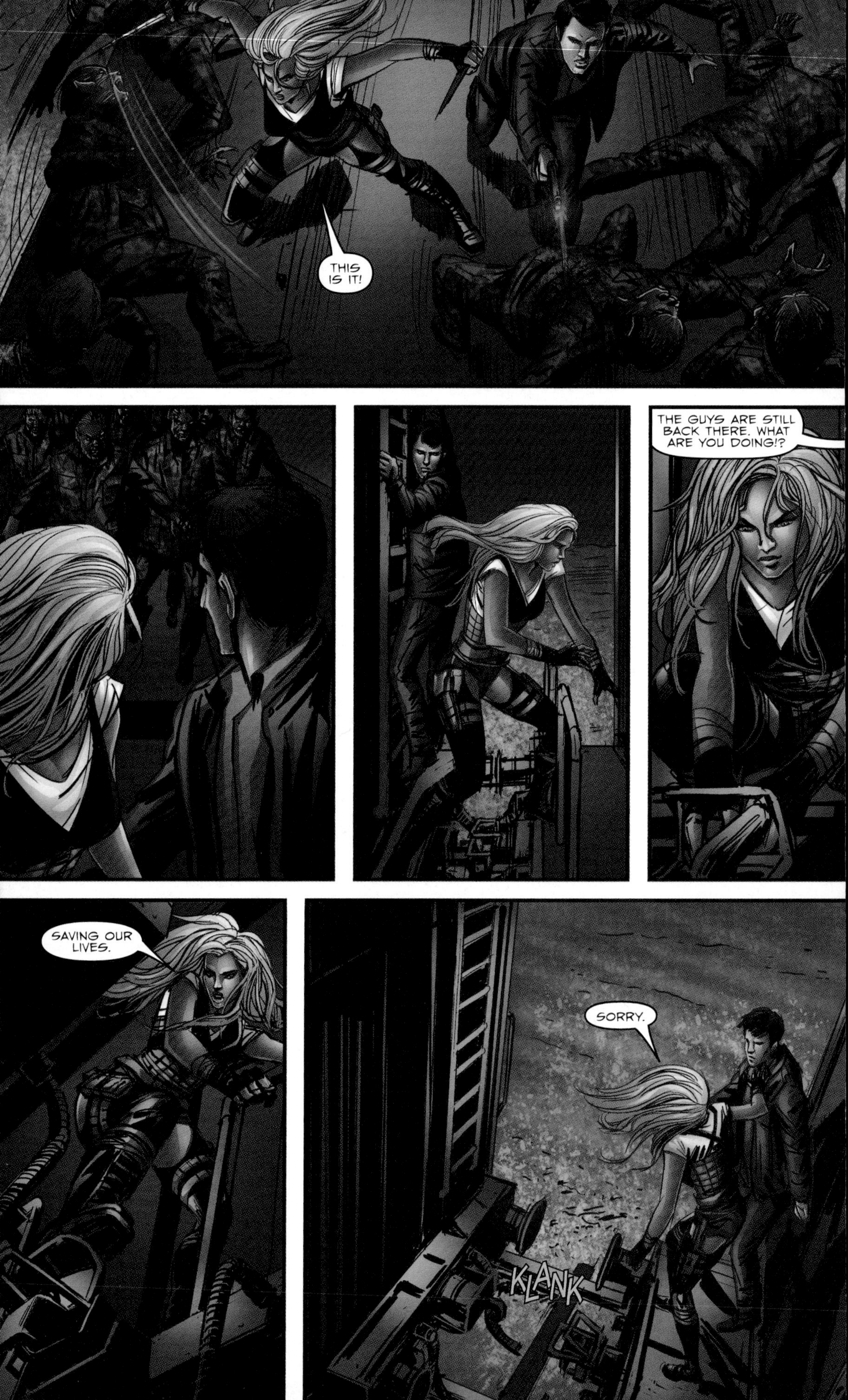
THIS IS IT!
THE GUYS ARE STILL BACK THERE. WHAT ARE YOU DOING!?
SAVING OUR LIVES.
SORRY.
KLANK

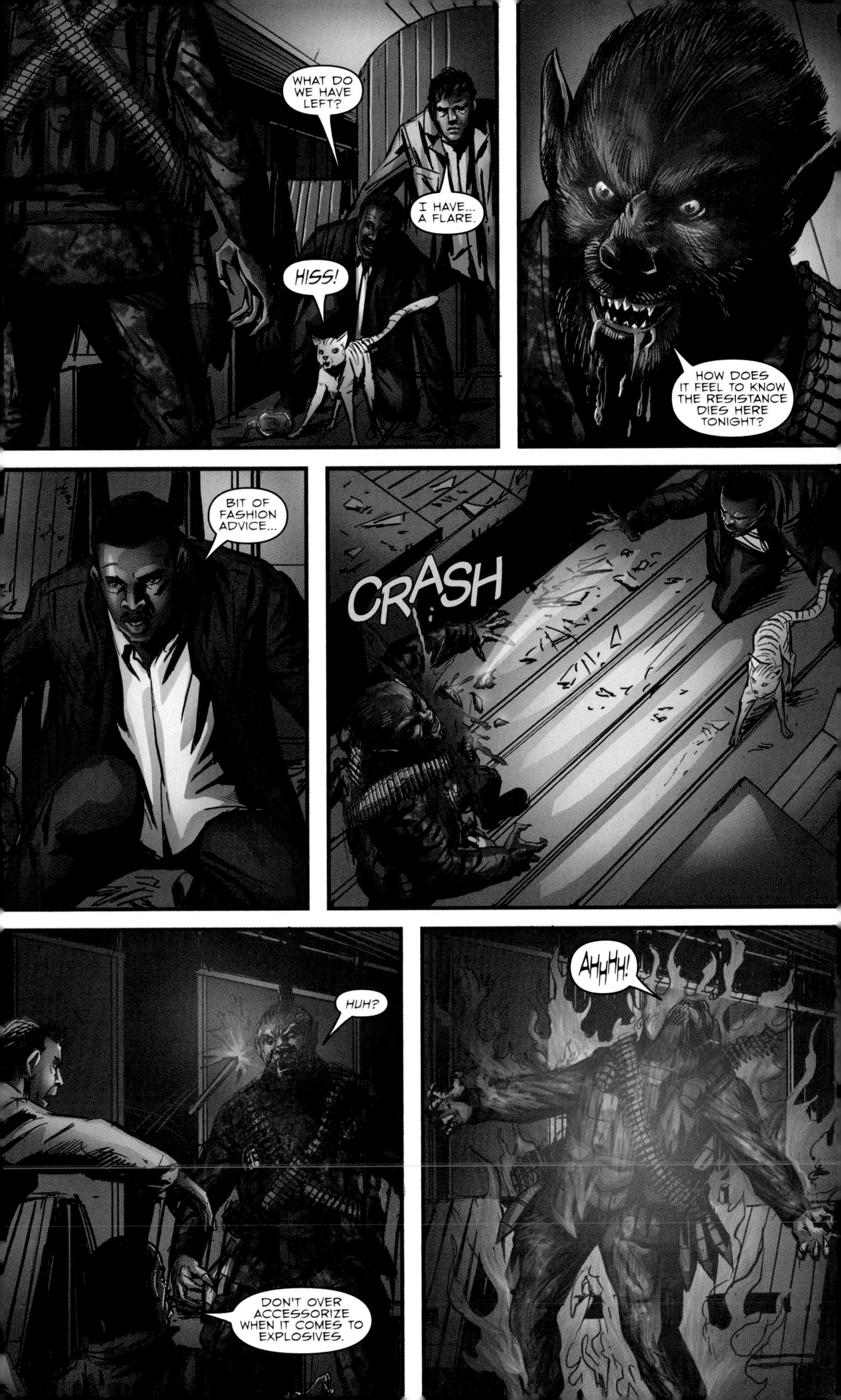
WHAT DO WE HAVE LEFT?
I HAVE... A FLARE.
HISS!
HOW DOES IT FEEL TO KNOW THE RESISTANCE DIES HERE TONIGHT?
BIT OF FASHION ADVICE...
CRASH
HUH?
DON'T OVER ACCESSORIZE WHEN IT COMES TO EXPLOSIVES.
AHHHH!

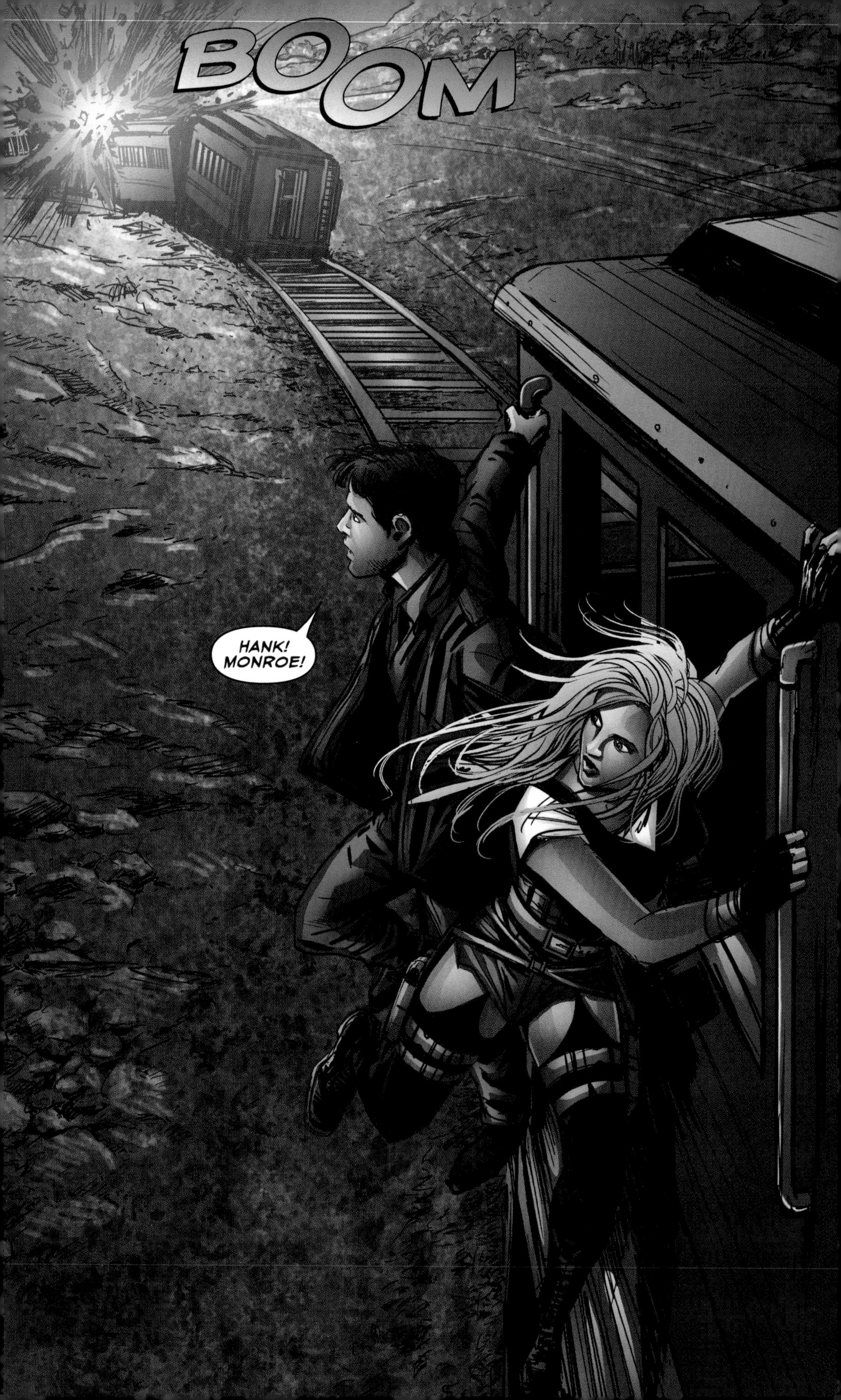
BOOM
HANK! MONROE!

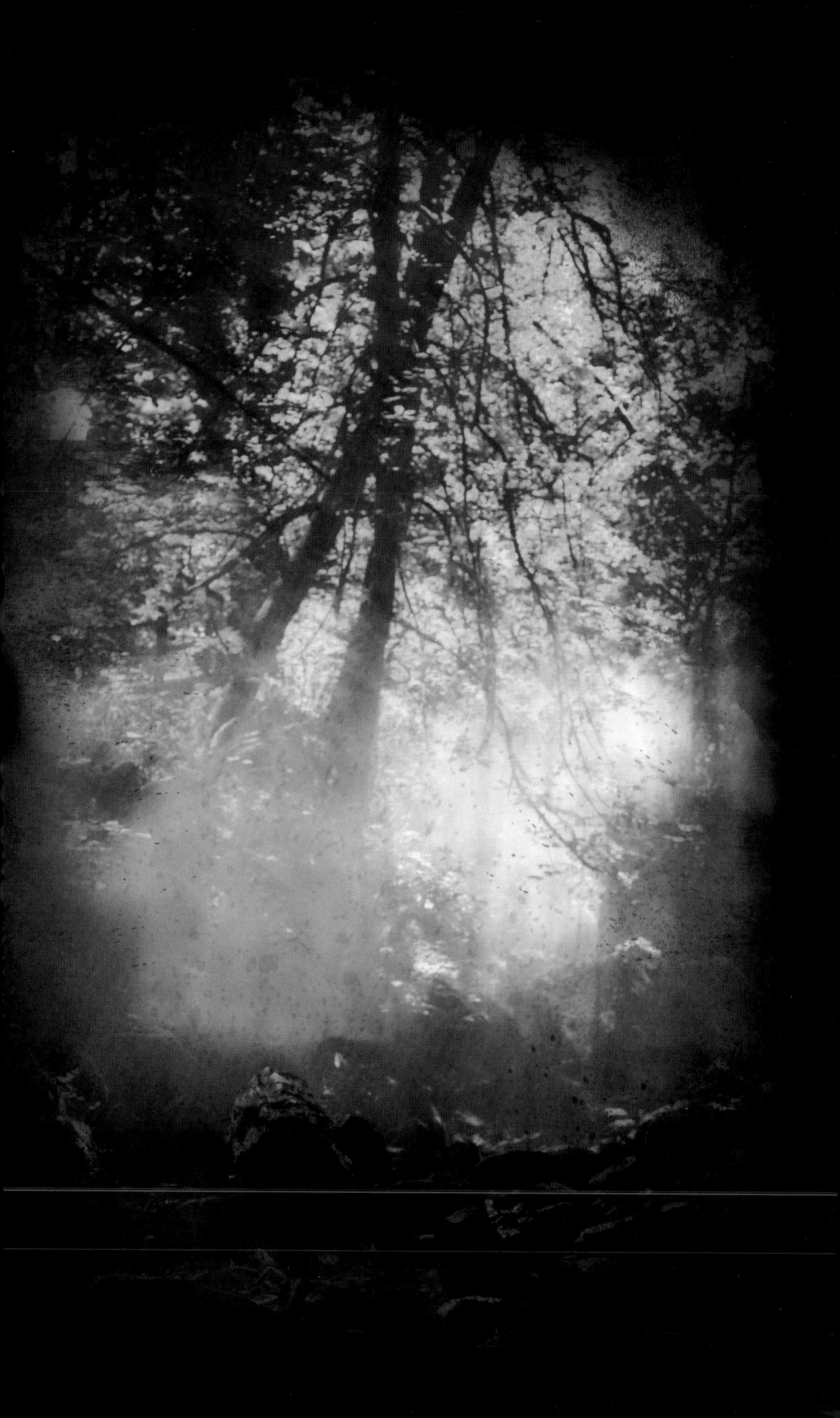

Ziegevolk

Die Ziegevolk, die man chmaz auch als Bluebeards, sind eine Ziege-wie geschopf, das san ich mit meinen eigenen Augen in Mnchen im winter 1305. Scheinen sie nicht gewalttatig.

Die Gefahr kommt aus ihre instinktiven Notwendigkeit der Rosse und scheinen sich nicht zu kommen. Menge uber die Qualitat.

Die Frauen schworen, wurden gegen trik llen und getrankt nen handlungsreisende Betrug, sie Ante Mag

Ziegevolk frauen, gut. Sobald die fra kleinste Berubrung n Dermaß sie fatzen chror Mütter

Ziegenvolk

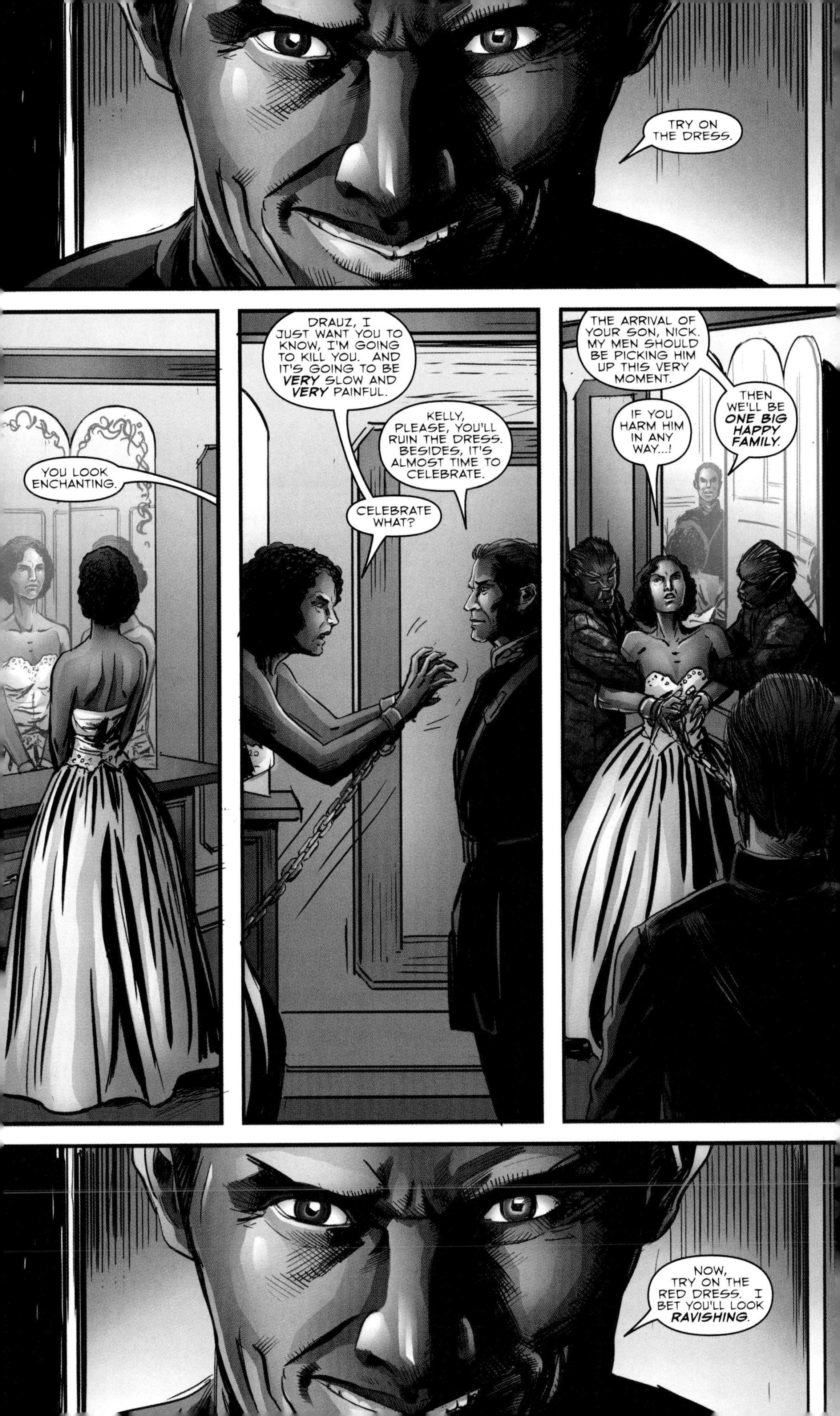
TRY ON THE DRESS.
YOU LOOK ENCHANTING.
DRAUZ, I JUST WANT YOU TO KNOW, I'M GOING TO KILL YOU. AND IT'S GOING TO BE **VERY** SLOW AND **VERY** PAINFUL.
KELLY, PLEASE, YOU'LL RUIN THE DRESS. BESIDES, IT'S ALMOST TIME TO CELEBRATE.
CELEBRATE WHAT?
THE ARRIVAL OF YOUR SON, NICK. MY MEN SHOULD BE PICKING HIM UP THIS VERY MOMENT.
IF YOU HARM HIM IN ANY WAY...!
THEN WE'LL BE **ONE BIG HAPPY FAMILY.**
NOW, TRY ON THE RED DRESS. I BET YOU'LL LOOK **RAVISHING**.

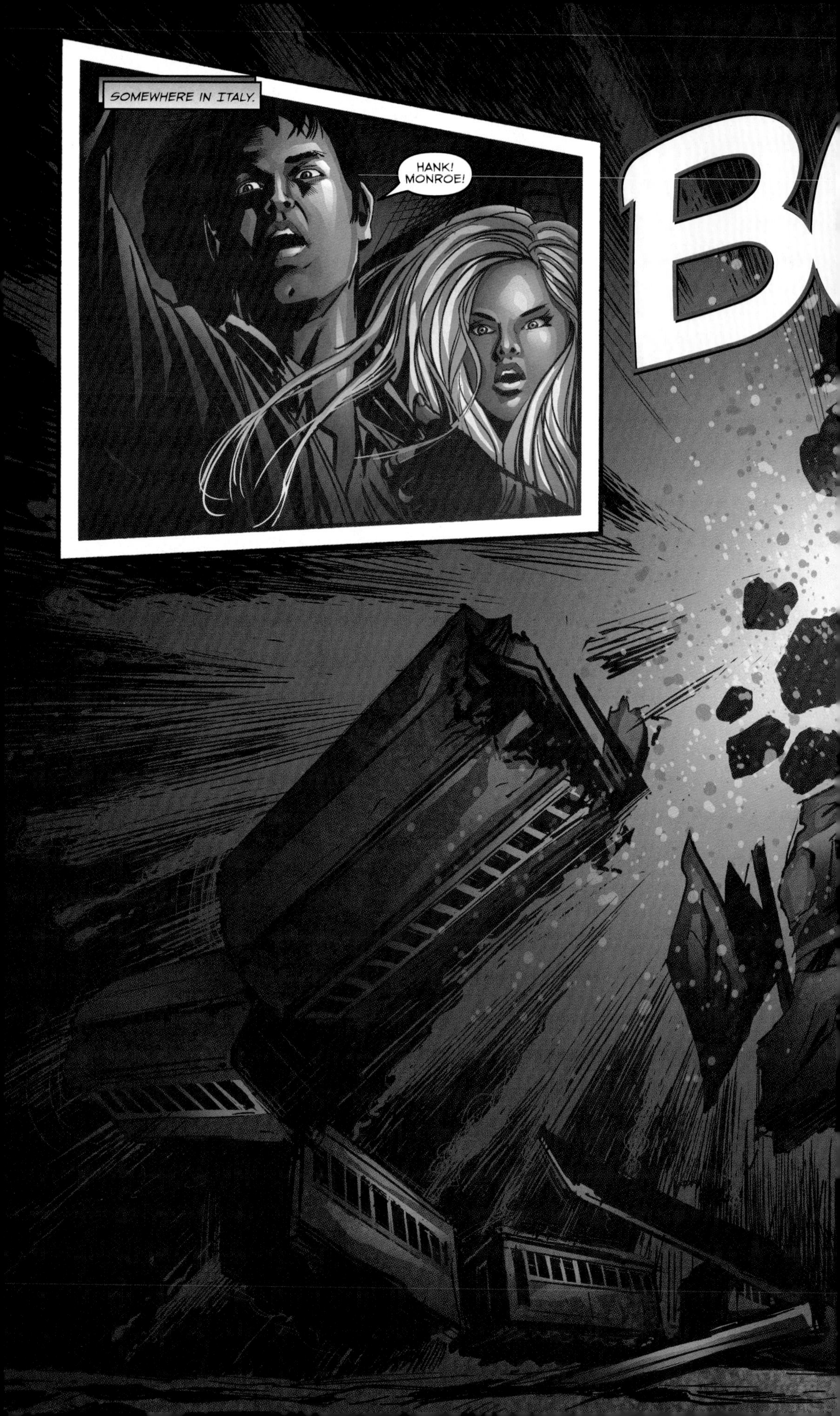
SOMEWHERE IN ITALY.
HANK! MONROE!

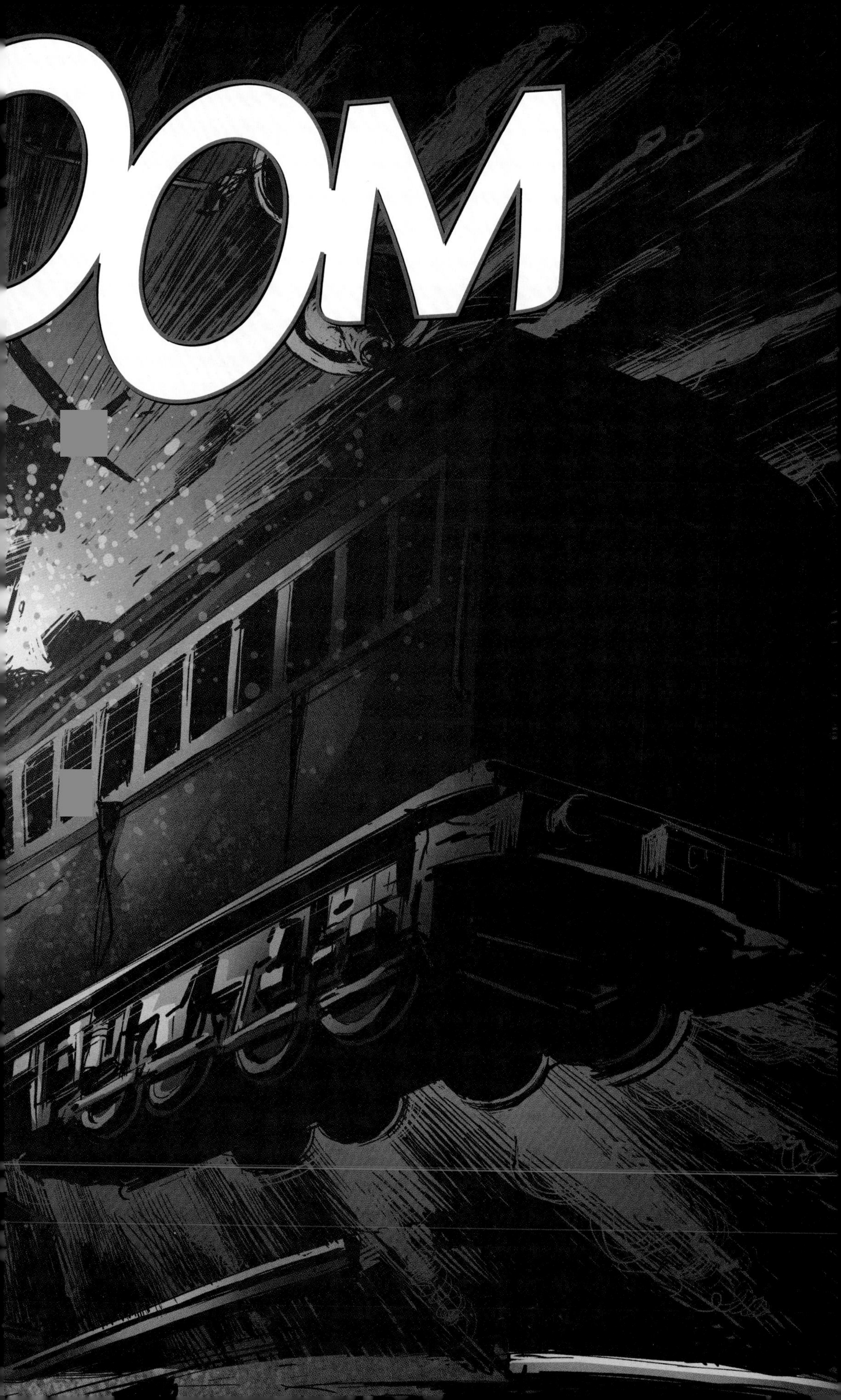
OOM

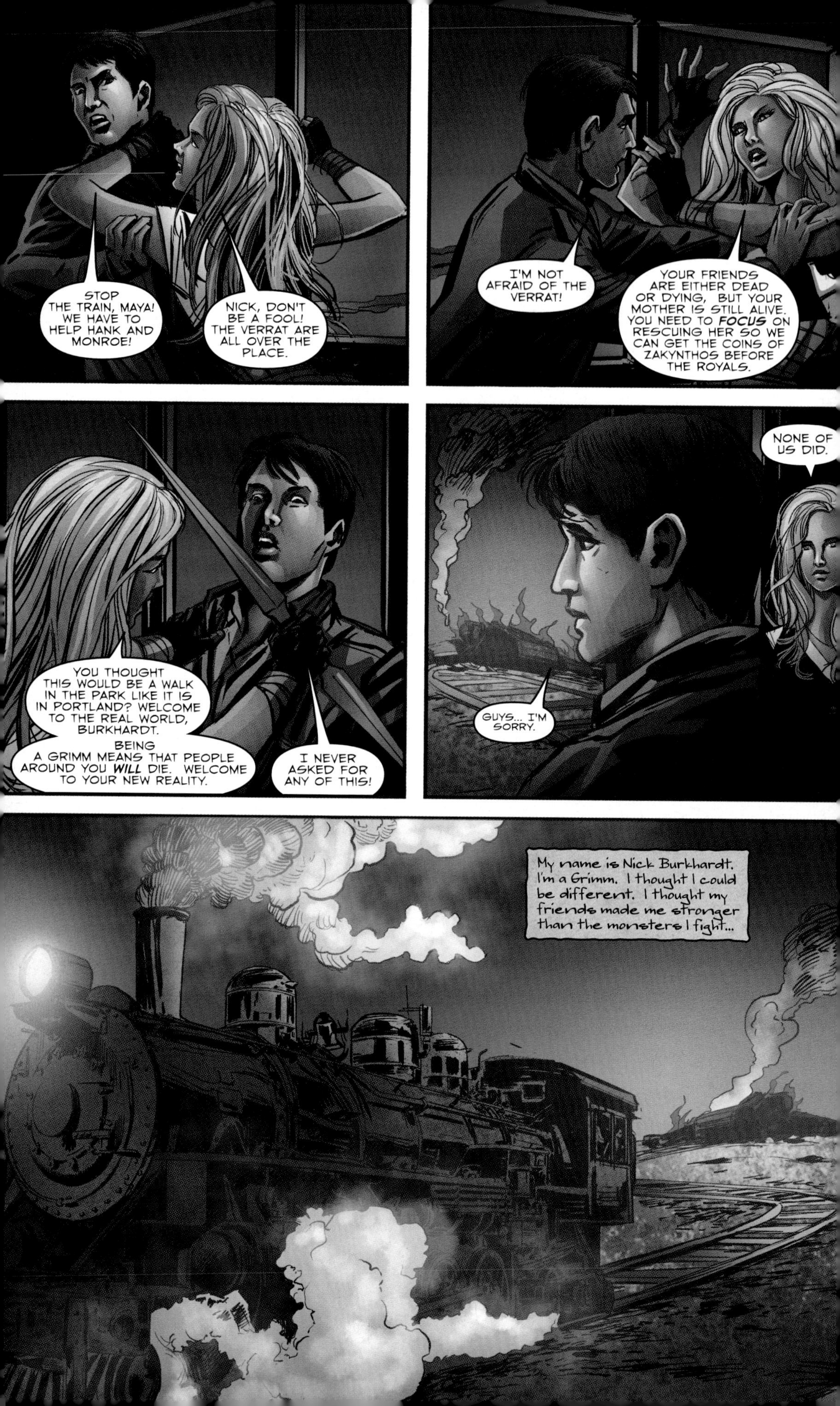
STOP THE TRAIN, MAYA! WE HAVE TO HELP HANK AND MONROE!
NICK, DON'T BE A FOOL! THE VERRAT ARE ALL OVER THE PLACE.
I'M NOT AFRAID OF THE VERRAT!
YOUR FRIENDS ARE EITHER DEAD OR DYING, BUT YOUR MOTHER IS STILL ALIVE. YOU NEED TO FOCUS ON RESCUING HER SO WE CAN GET THE COINS OF ZAKYNTHOS BEFORE THE ROYALS.
YOU THOUGHT THIS WOULD BE A WALK IN THE PARK LIKE IT IS IN PORTLAND? WELCOME TO THE REAL WORLD, BURKHARDT.
BEING A GRIMM MEANS THAT PEOPLE AROUND YOU WILL DIE. WELCOME TO YOUR NEW REALITY.
I NEVER ASKED FOR ANY OF THIS!
GUYS... I'M SORRY.
NONE OF US DID.
My name is Nick Burkhardt. I'm a Grimm. I thought I could be different. I thought my friends made me stronger than the monsters I fight...

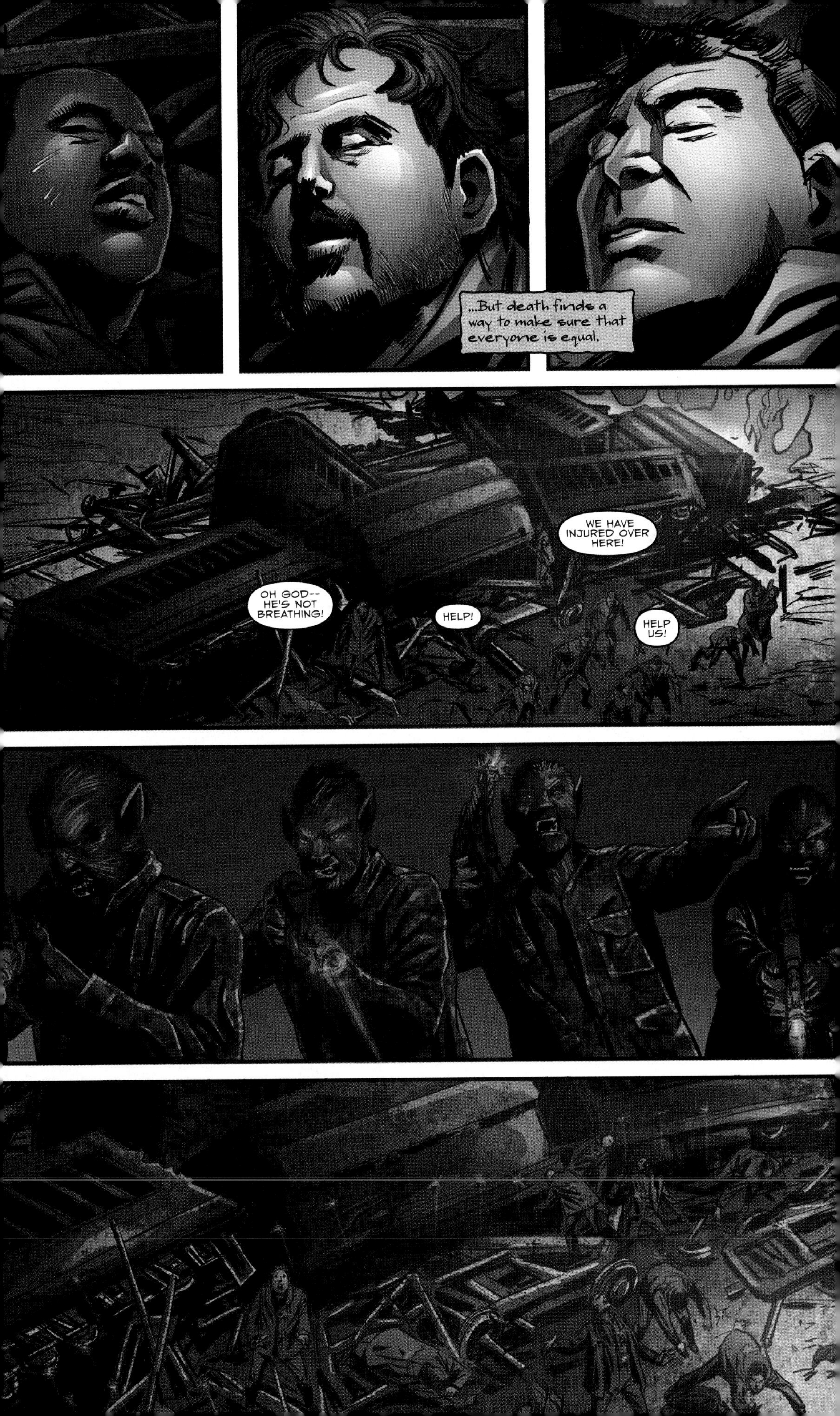
...But death finds a way to make sure that everyone is equal.
WE HAVE INJURED OVER HERE!
OH GOD-- HE'S NOT BREATHING!
HELP!
HELP US!

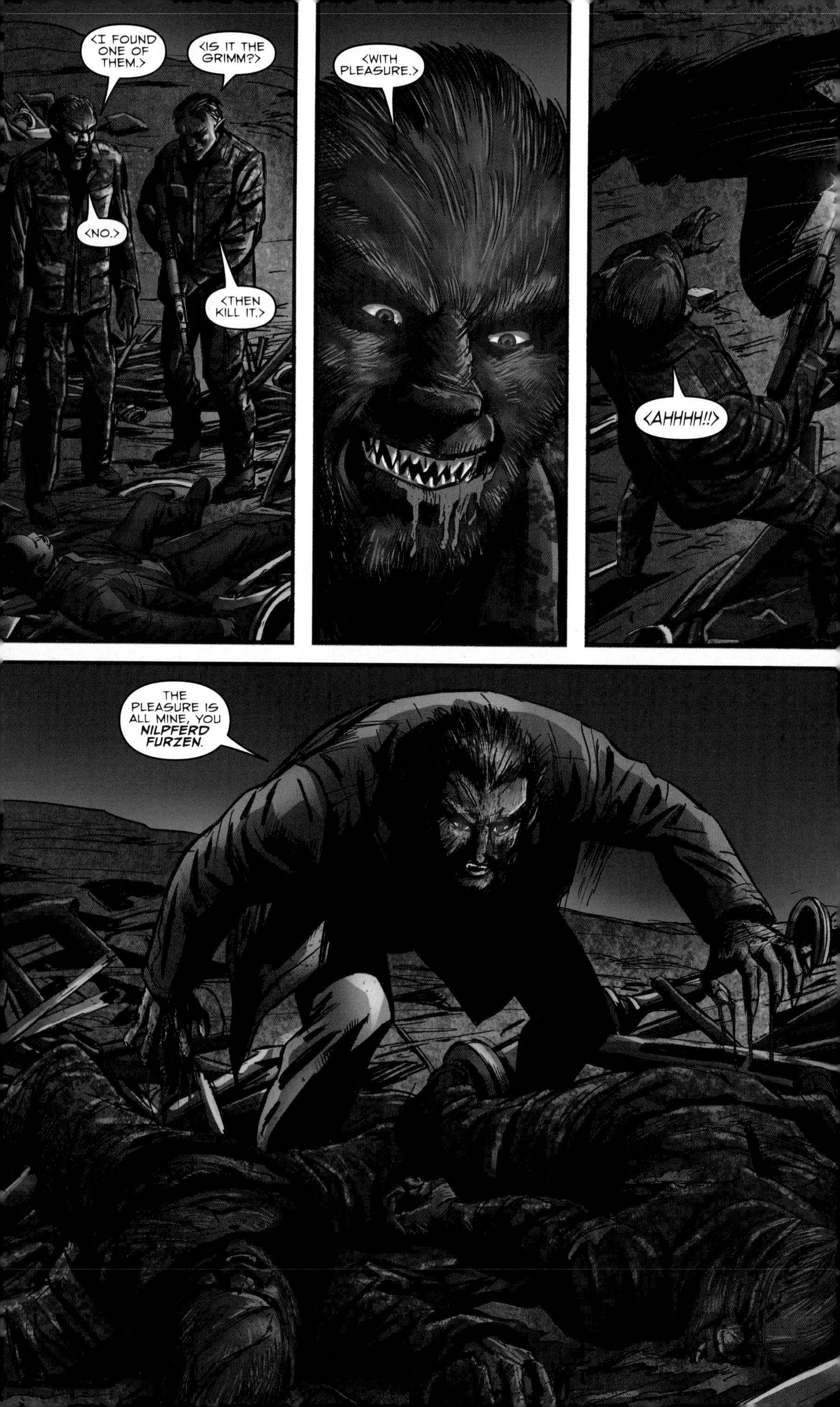
<I FOUND ONE OF THEM.>
<IS IT THE GRIMM?>
<NO.>
<THEN KILL IT.>
<WITH PLEASURE.>
<AHHHH!!>
THE PLEASURE IS ALL MINE, YOU ***NILPFERD FURZEN***.

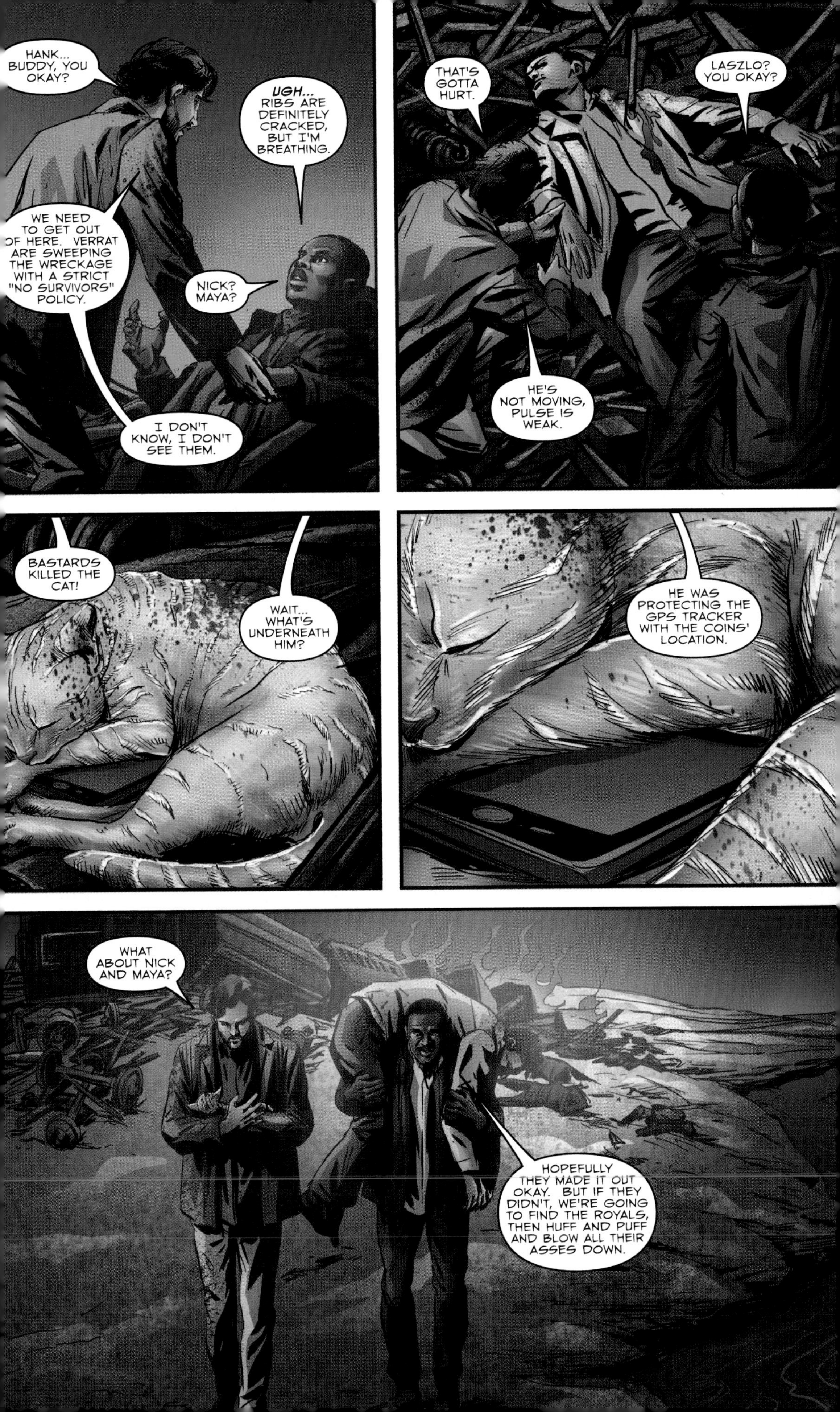
HANK... BUDDY, YOU OKAY?
UGH... RIBS ARE DEFINITELY CRACKED, BUT I'M BREATHING.
WE NEED TO GET OUT OF HERE. VERRAT ARE SWEEPING THE WRECKAGE WITH A STRICT "NO SURVIVORS" POLICY.
NICK? MAYA?
I DON'T KNOW, I DON'T SEE THEM.
THAT'S GOTTA HURT.
LASZLO? YOU OKAY?
HE'S NOT MOVING, PULSE IS WEAK.
BASTARDS KILLED THE CAT!
WAIT... WHAT'S UNDERNEATH HIM?
HE WAS PROTECTING THE GPS TRACKER WITH THE COINS' LOCATION.
WHAT ABOUT NICK AND MAYA?
HOPEFULLY THEY MADE IT OUT OKAY. BUT IF THEY DIDN'T, WE'RE GOING TO FIND THE ROYALS, THEN HUFF AND PUFF AND BLOW ALL THEIR ASSES DOWN.

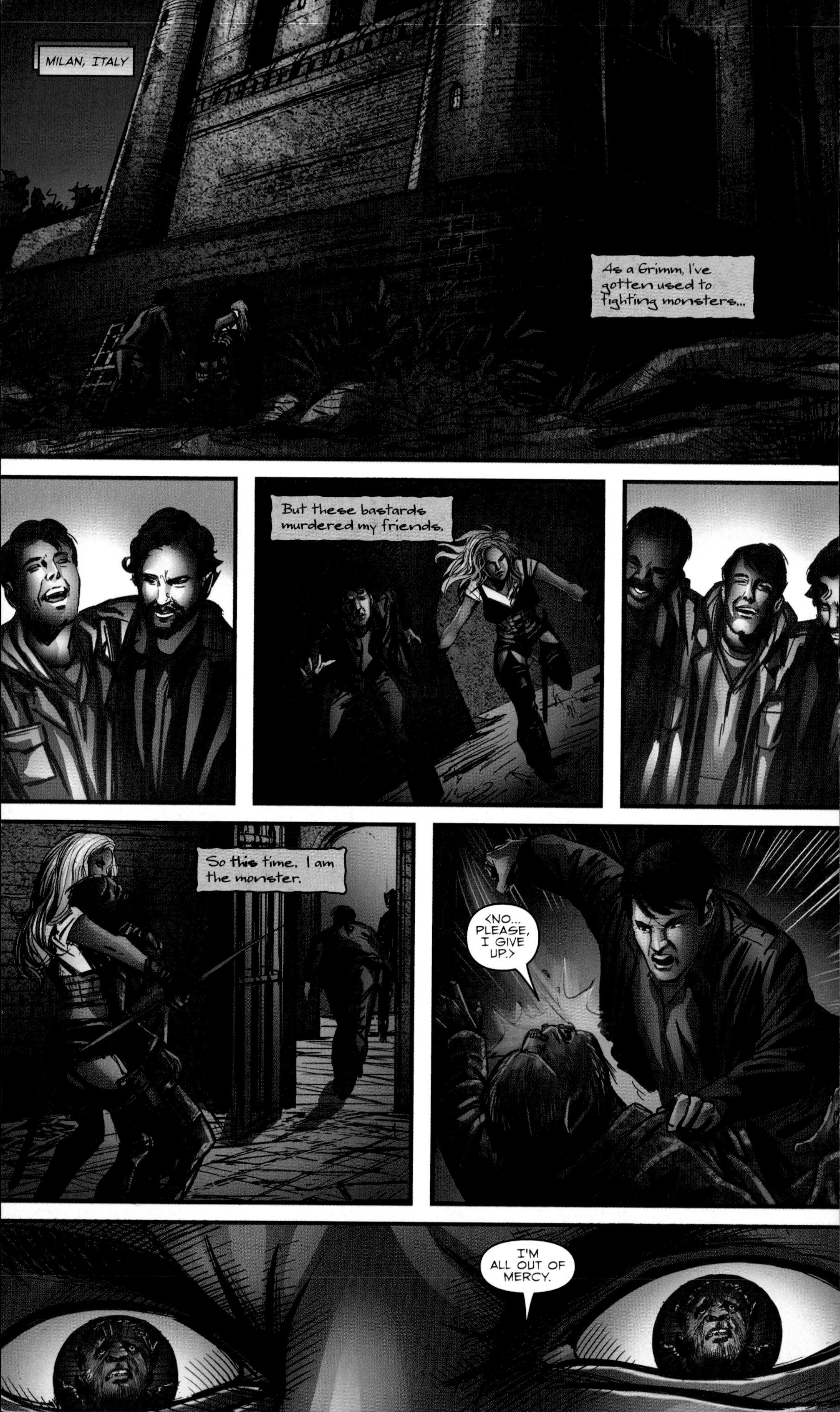
MILAN, ITALY
As a Grimm, I've gotten used to fighting monsters...
But these bastards murdered my friends.
So this time, I am the monster.
<NO... PLEASE, I GIVE UP.>
I'M ALL OUT OF MERCY.

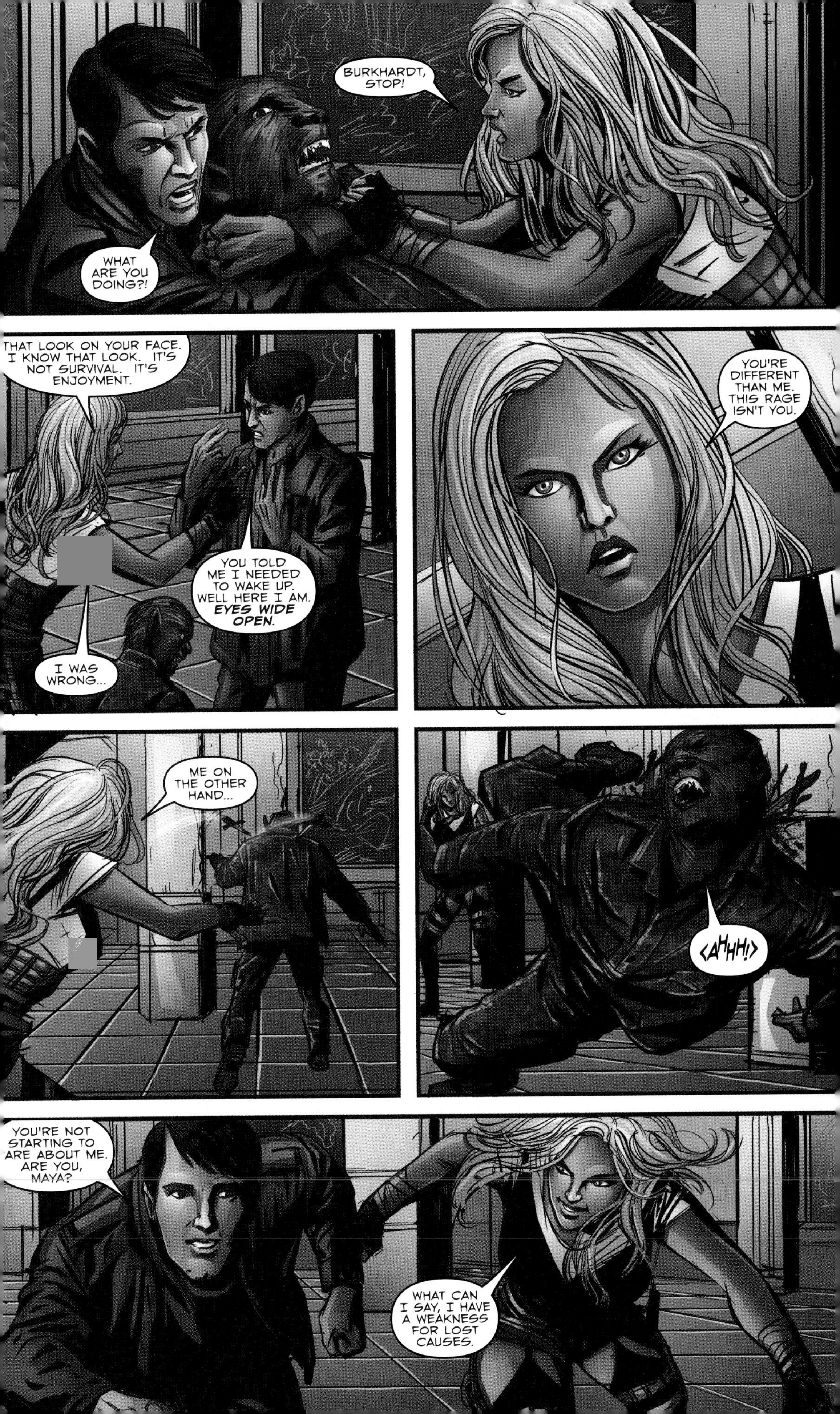
BURKHARDT, STOP!
WHAT ARE YOU DOING?!
THAT LOOK ON YOUR FACE. I KNOW THAT LOOK. IT'S NOT SURVIVAL. IT'S ENJOYMENT.
YOU TOLD ME I NEEDED TO WAKE UP. WELL HERE I AM. **EYES WIDE OPEN**.
I WAS WRONG...
YOU'RE DIFFERENT THAN ME. THIS RAGE ISN'T YOU.
ME ON THE OTHER HAND...
<AHHH!>
YOU'RE NOT STARTING TO ARE ABOUT ME. ARE YOU, MAYA?
WHAT CAN I SAY, I HAVE A WEAKNESS FOR LOST CAUSES.

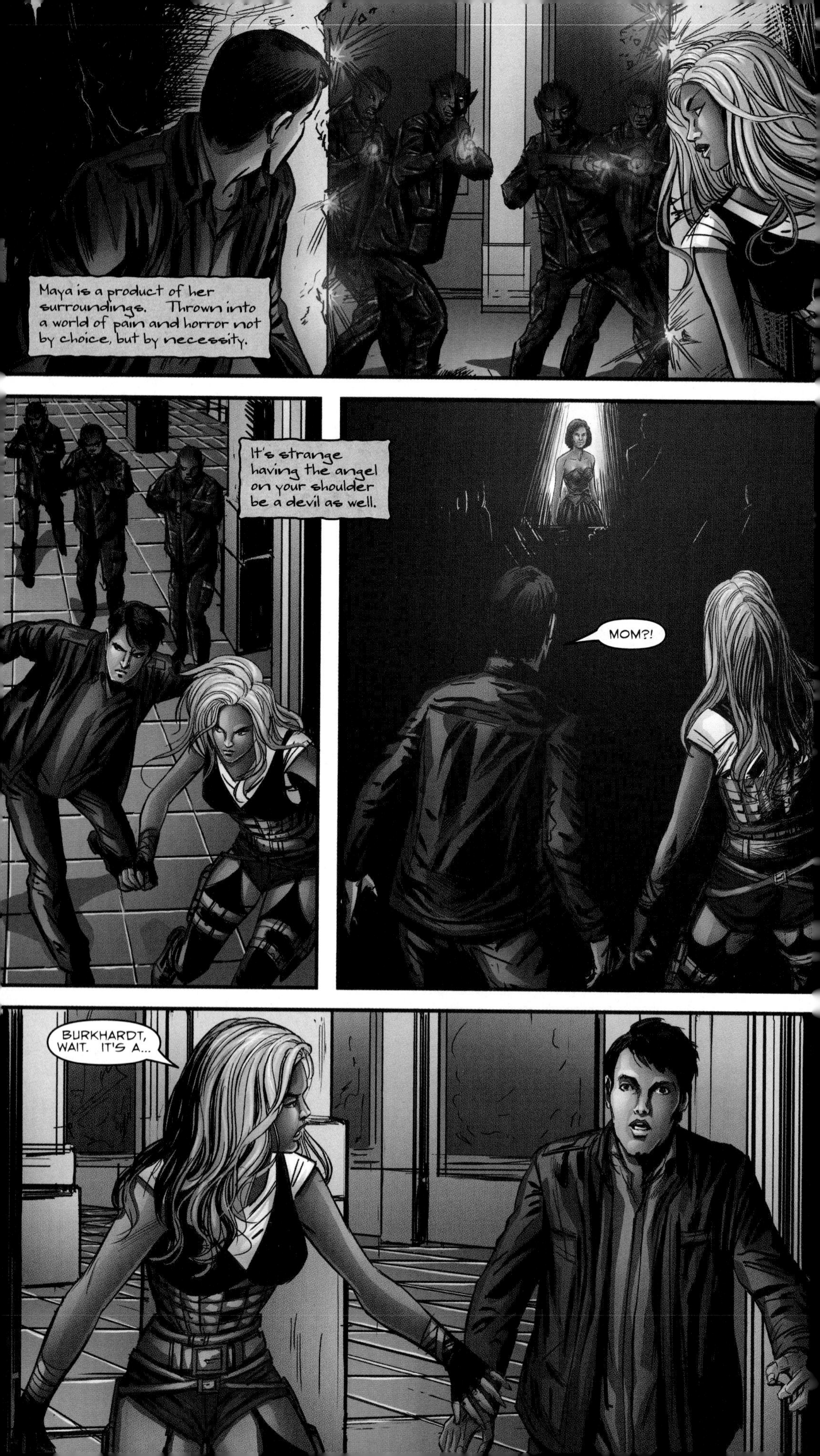
Maya is a product of her surroundings. Thrown into a world of pain and horror not by choice, but by necessity.
It's strange having the angel on your shoulder be a devil as well.
MOM?!
BURKHARDT, WAIT. IT'S A...

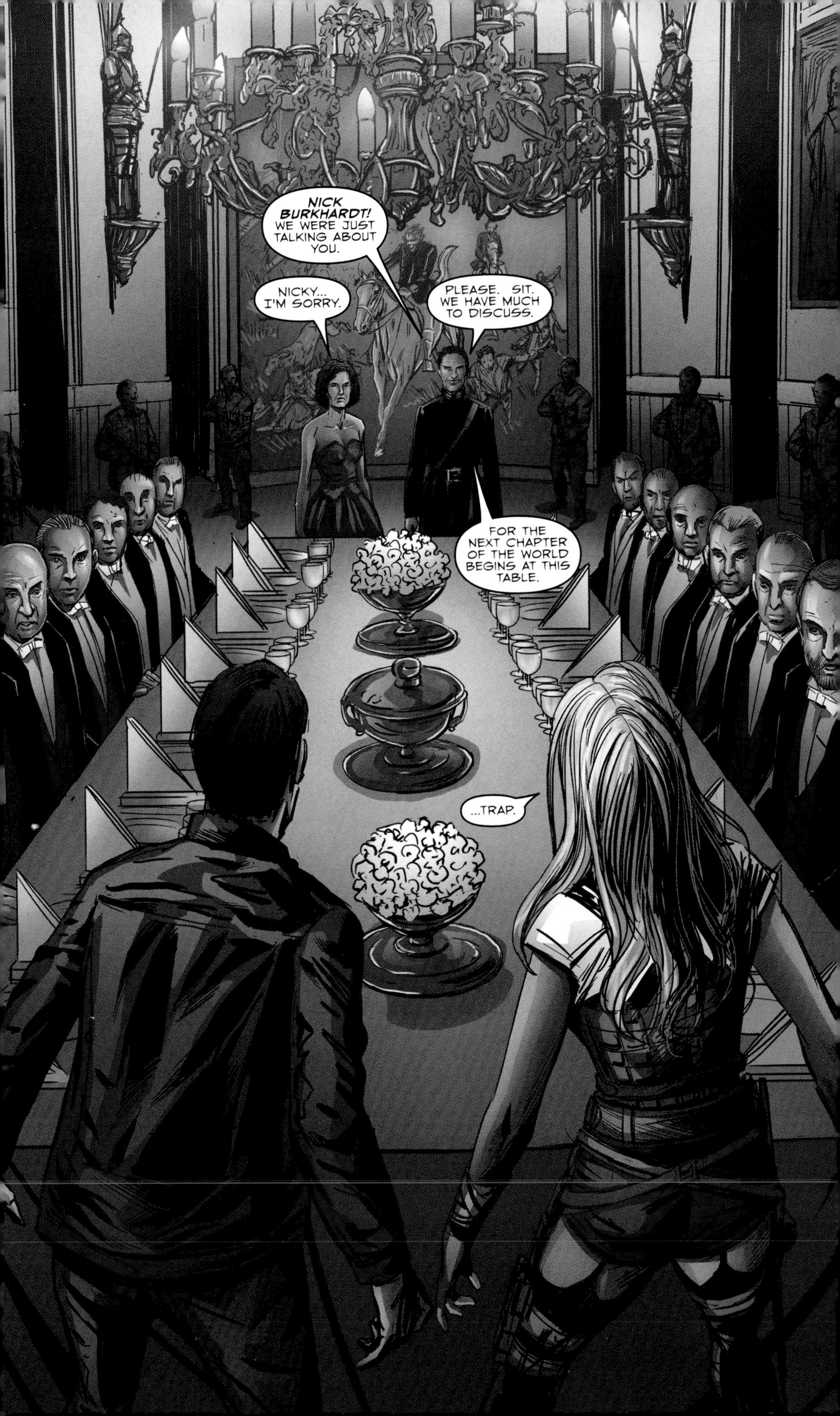

NICK BURKHARDT! WE WERE JUST TALKING ABOUT YOU.
NICKY... I'M SORRY.
PLEASE. SIT. WE HAVE MUCH TO DISCUSS.
FOR THE NEXT CHAPTER OF THE WORLD BEGINS AT THIS TABLE.
...TRAP.

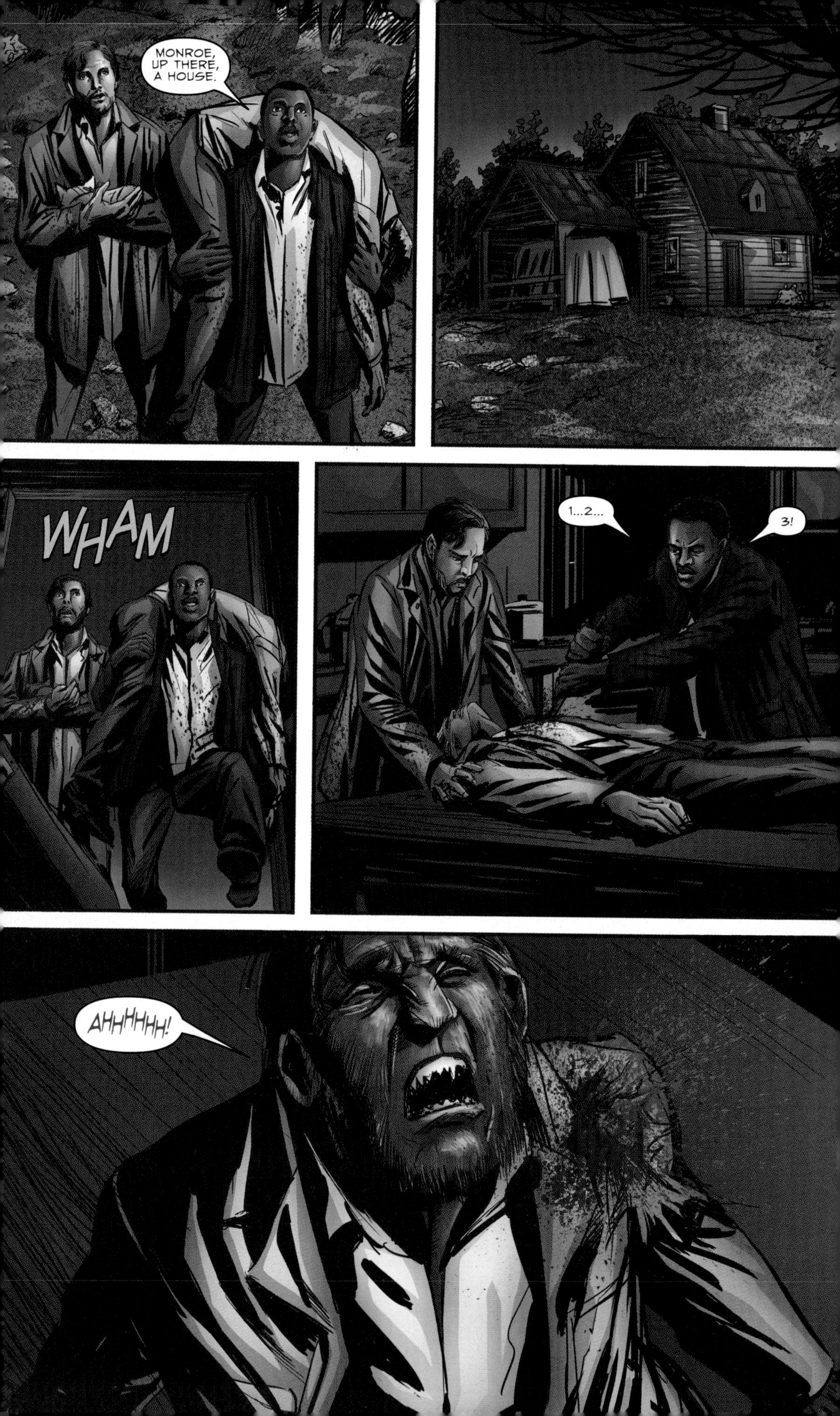
MONROE, UP THERE, A HOUSE.
WHAM
1...2...
3!
AHHHHHH!

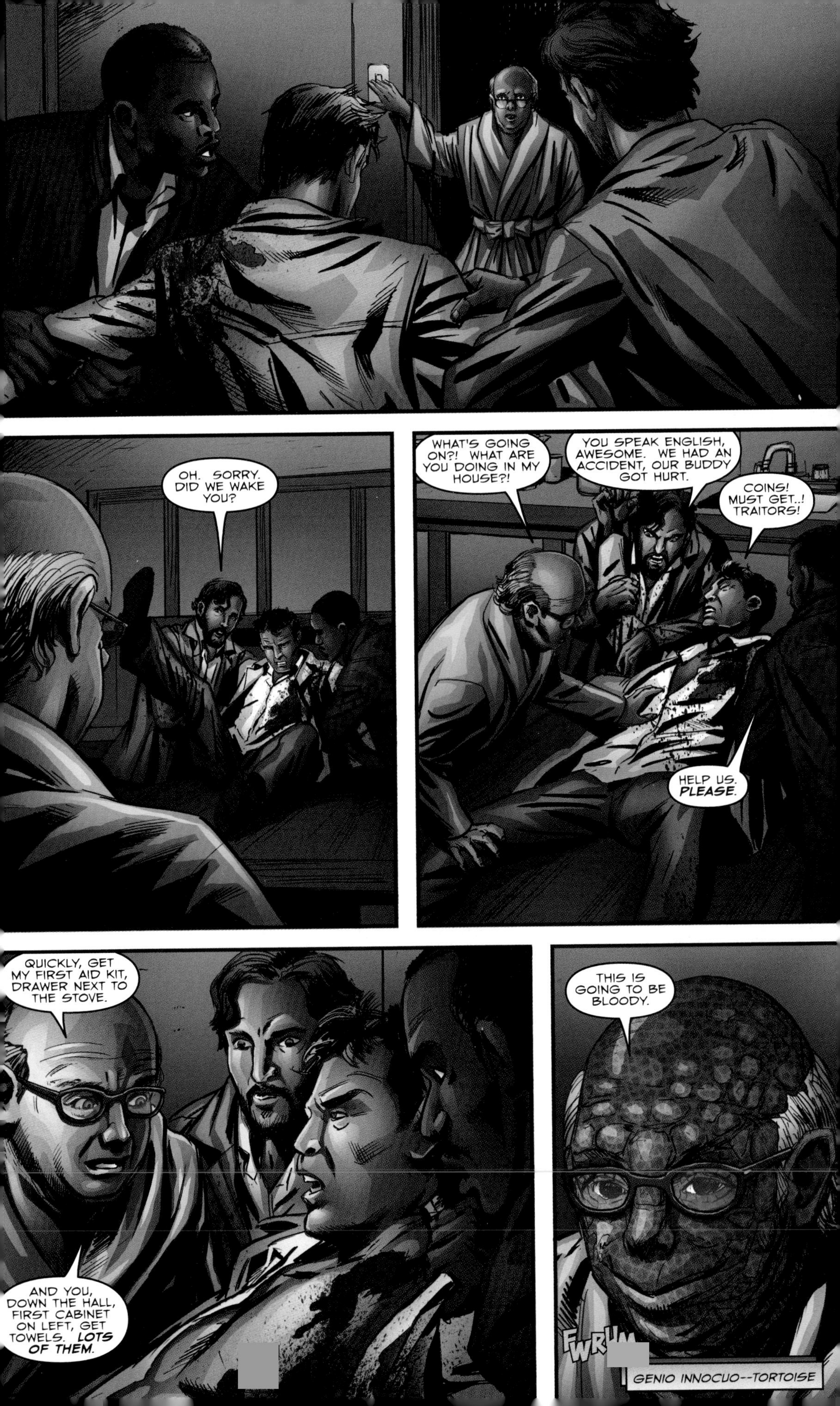
OH. SORRY. DID WE WAKE YOU?
WHAT'S GOING ON?! WHAT ARE YOU DOING IN MY HOUSE?!
YOU SPEAK ENGLISH, AWESOME. WE HAD AN ACCIDENT, OUR BUDDY GOT HURT.
COINS! MUST GET..! TRAITORS!
HELP US. *PLEASE*.
QUICKLY, GET MY FIRST AID KIT, DRAWER NEXT TO THE STOVE.
AND YOU, DOWN THE HALL, FIRST CABINET ON LEFT, GET TOWELS. *LOTS OF THEM*.
THIS IS GOING TO BE BLOODY.
FWRUM
GENIO INNOCUO--TORTOISE

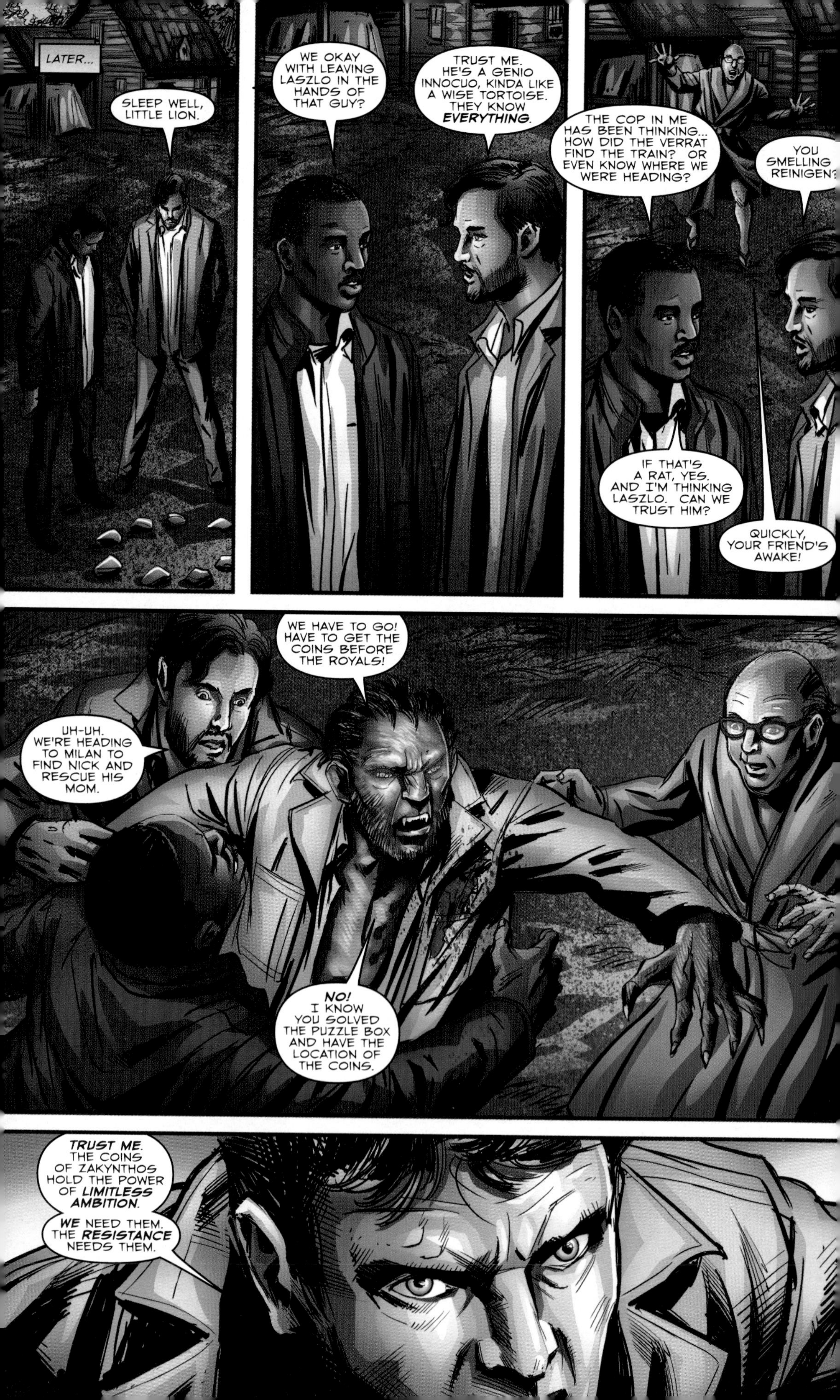
LATER...
SLEEP WELL, LITTLE LION.
WE OKAY WITH LEAVING LASZLO IN THE HANDS OF THAT GUY?
TRUST ME. HE'S A GENIO INNOCUO, KINDA LIKE A WISE TORTOISE. THEY KNOW ***EVERYTHING***.
THE COP IN ME HAS BEEN THINKING... HOW DID THE VERRAT FIND THE TRAIN? OR EVEN KNOW WHERE WE WERE HEADING?
YOU SMELLING REINIGEN?
IF THAT'S A RAT, YES. AND I'M THINKING LASZLO. CAN WE TRUST HIM?
QUICKLY, YOUR FRIEND'S AWAKE!
WE HAVE TO GO! HAVE TO GET THE COINS BEFORE THE ROYALS!
UH-UH. WE'RE HEADING TO MILAN TO FIND NICK AND RESCUE HIS MOM.
NO! I KNOW YOU SOLVED THE PUZZLE BOX AND HAVE THE LOCATION OF THE COINS.
TRUST ME. THE COINS OF ZAKYNTHOS HOLD THE POWER OF ***LIMITLESS AMBITION***.
WE NEED THEM. THE ***RESISTANCE*** NEEDS THEM.

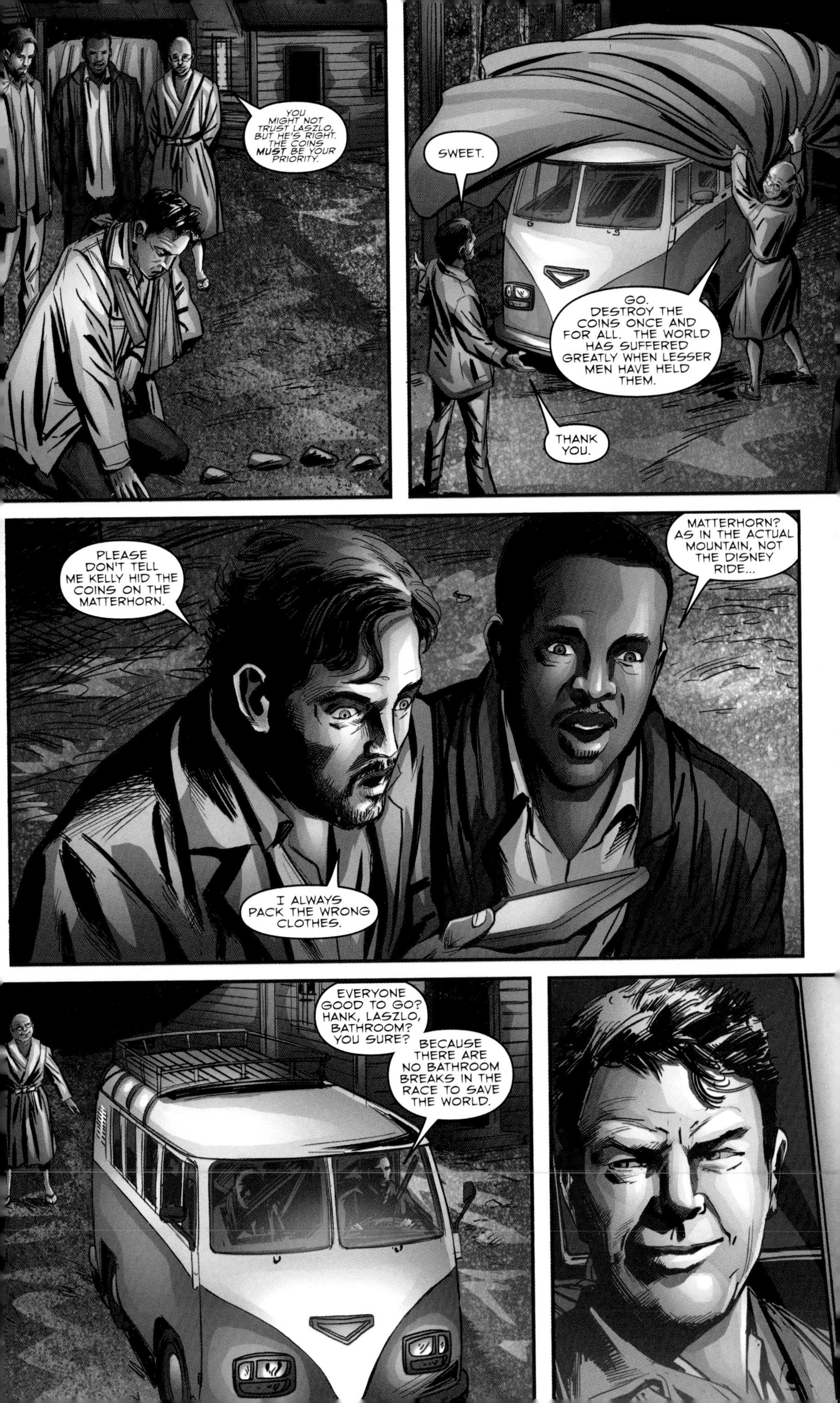
YOU MIGHT NOT TRUST LASZLO, BUT HE'S RIGHT. THE COINS **MUST** BE YOUR PRIORITY.
SWEET.
GO. DESTROY THE COINS ONCE AND FOR ALL. THE WORLD HAS SUFFERED GREATLY WHEN LESSER MEN HAVE HELD THEM.
THANK YOU.
PLEASE DON'T TELL ME KELLY HID THE COINS ON THE MATTERHORN.
MATTERHORN? AS IN THE ACTUAL MOUNTAIN, NOT THE DISNEY RIDE...
I ALWAYS PACK THE WRONG CLOTHES.
EVERYONE GOOD TO GO? HANK, LASZLO, BATHROOM? YOU SURE?
BECAUSE THERE ARE NO BATHROOM BREAKS IN THE RACE TO SAVE THE WORLD.

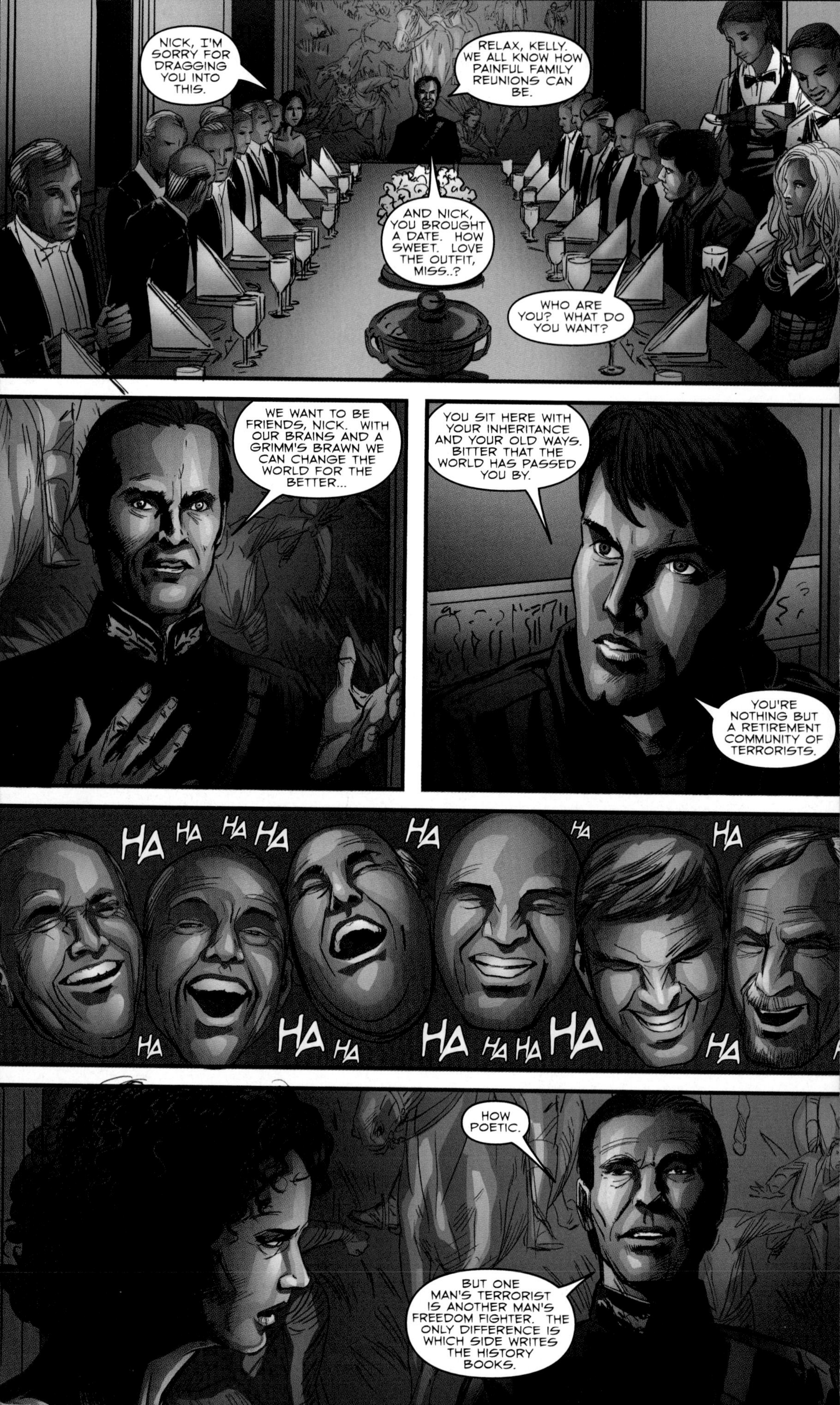
NICK, I'M SORRY FOR DRAGGING YOU INTO THIS.
RELAX, KELLY. WE ALL KNOW HOW PAINFUL FAMILY REUNIONS CAN BE.
AND NICK, YOU BROUGHT A DATE. HOW SWEET. LOVE THE OUTFIT, MISS..?
WHO ARE YOU? WHAT DO YOU WANT?
WE WANT TO BE FRIENDS, NICK. WITH OUR BRAINS AND A GRIMM'S BRAWN WE CAN CHANGE THE WORLD FOR THE BETTER...
YOU SIT HERE WITH YOUR INHERITANCE AND YOUR OLD WAYS. BITTER THAT THE WORLD HAS PASSED YOU BY.
YOU'RE NOTHING BUT A RETIREMENT COMMUNITY OF TERRORISTS.
HA HA HA HA HA HA HA
HA HA HA HA HA HA HA HA
HOW POETIC.
BUT ONE MAN'S TERRORIST IS ANOTHER MAN'S FREEDOM FIGHTER. THE ONLY DIFFERENCE IS WHICH SIDE WRITES THE HISTORY BOOKS.

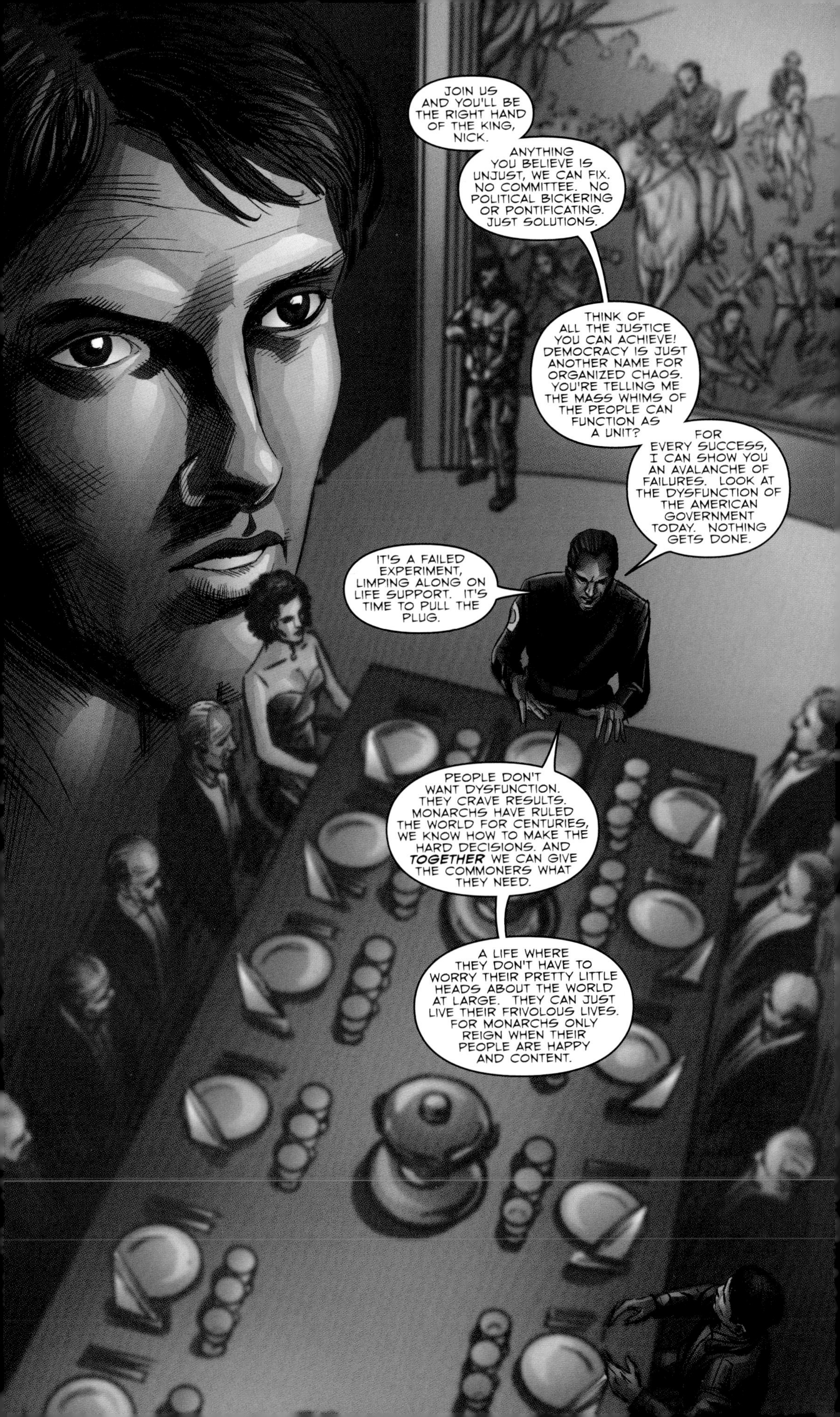
JOIN US AND YOU'LL BE THE RIGHT HAND OF THE KING, NICK.
ANYTHING YOU BELIEVE IS UNJUST, WE CAN FIX. NO COMMITTEE. NO POLITICAL BICKERING OR PONTIFICATING. JUST SOLUTIONS.
THINK OF ALL THE JUSTICE YOU CAN ACHIEVE! DEMOCRACY IS JUST ANOTHER NAME FOR ORGANIZED CHAOS. YOU'RE TELLING ME THE MASS WHIMS OF THE PEOPLE CAN FUNCTION AS A UNIT?
FOR EVERY SUCCESS, I CAN SHOW YOU AN AVALANCHE OF FAILURES. LOOK AT THE DYSFUNCTION OF THE AMERICAN GOVERNMENT TODAY. NOTHING GETS DONE.
IT'S A FAILED EXPERIMENT, LIMPING ALONG ON LIFE SUPPORT. IT'S TIME TO PULL THE PLUG.
PEOPLE DON'T WANT DYSFUNCTION. THEY CRAVE RESULTS. MONARCHS HAVE RULED THE WORLD FOR CENTURIES, WE KNOW HOW TO MAKE THE HARD DECISIONS. AND ***TOGETHER*** WE CAN GIVE THE COMMONERS WHAT THEY NEED.
A LIFE WHERE THEY DON'T HAVE TO WORRY THEIR PRETTY LITTLE HEADS ABOUT THE WORLD AT LARGE. THEY CAN JUST LIVE THEIR FRIVOLOUS LIVES. FOR MONARCHS ONLY REIGN WHEN THEIR PEOPLE ARE HAPPY AND CONTENT.

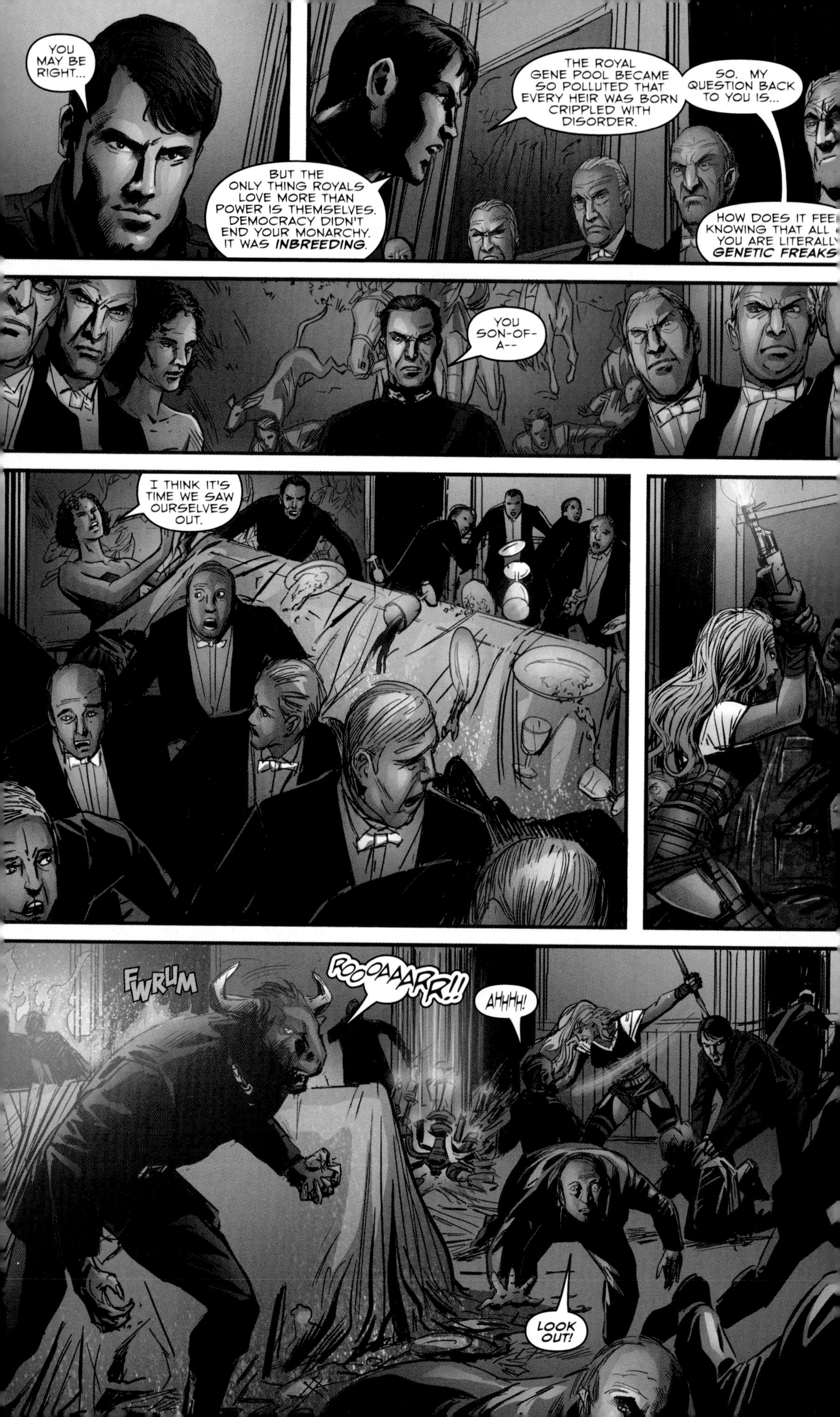
YOU MAY BE RIGHT...
BUT THE ONLY THING ROYALS LOVE MORE THAN POWER IS THEMSELVES. DEMOCRACY DIDN'T END YOUR MONARCHY. IT WAS *INBREEDING*.
THE ROYAL GENE POOL BECAME SO POLLUTED THAT EVERY HEIR WAS BORN CRIPPLED WITH DISORDER.
SO. MY QUESTION BACK TO YOU IS...
HOW DOES IT FEE KNOWING THAT ALL YOU ARE LITERALL *GENETIC FREAKS*
YOU SON-OF-A--
I THINK IT'S TIME WE SAW OURSELVES OUT.
FWRUM
ROOOAAARR!!
AHHHH!
LOOK OUT!

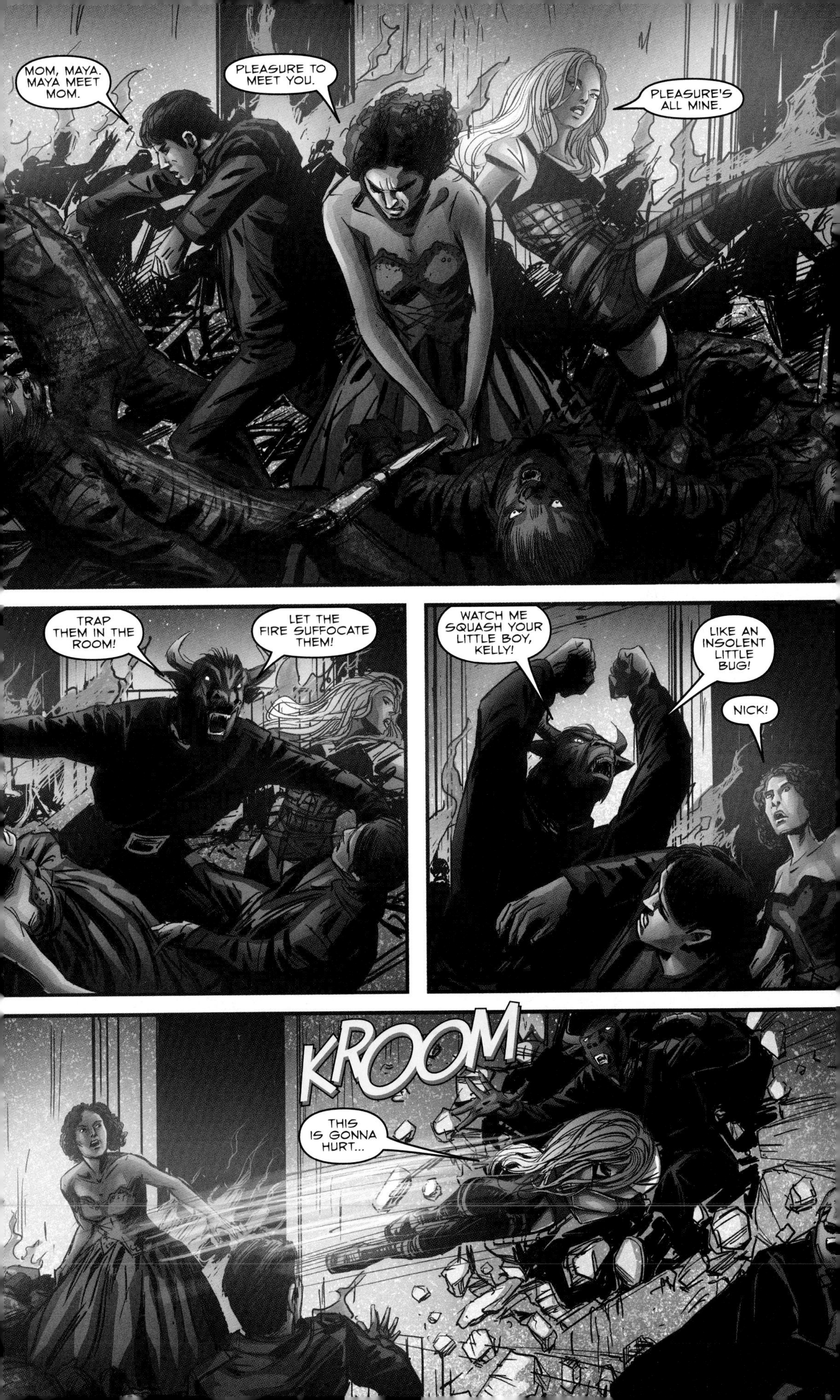
MOM, MAYA. MAYA MEET MOM.
PLEASURE TO MEET YOU.
PLEASURE'S ALL MINE.
TRAP THEM IN THE ROOM!
LET THE FIRE SUFFOCATE THEM!
WATCH ME SQUASH YOUR LITTLE BOY, KELLY!
LIKE AN INSOLENT LITTLE BUG!
NICK!
KROOM
THIS IS GONNA HURT...

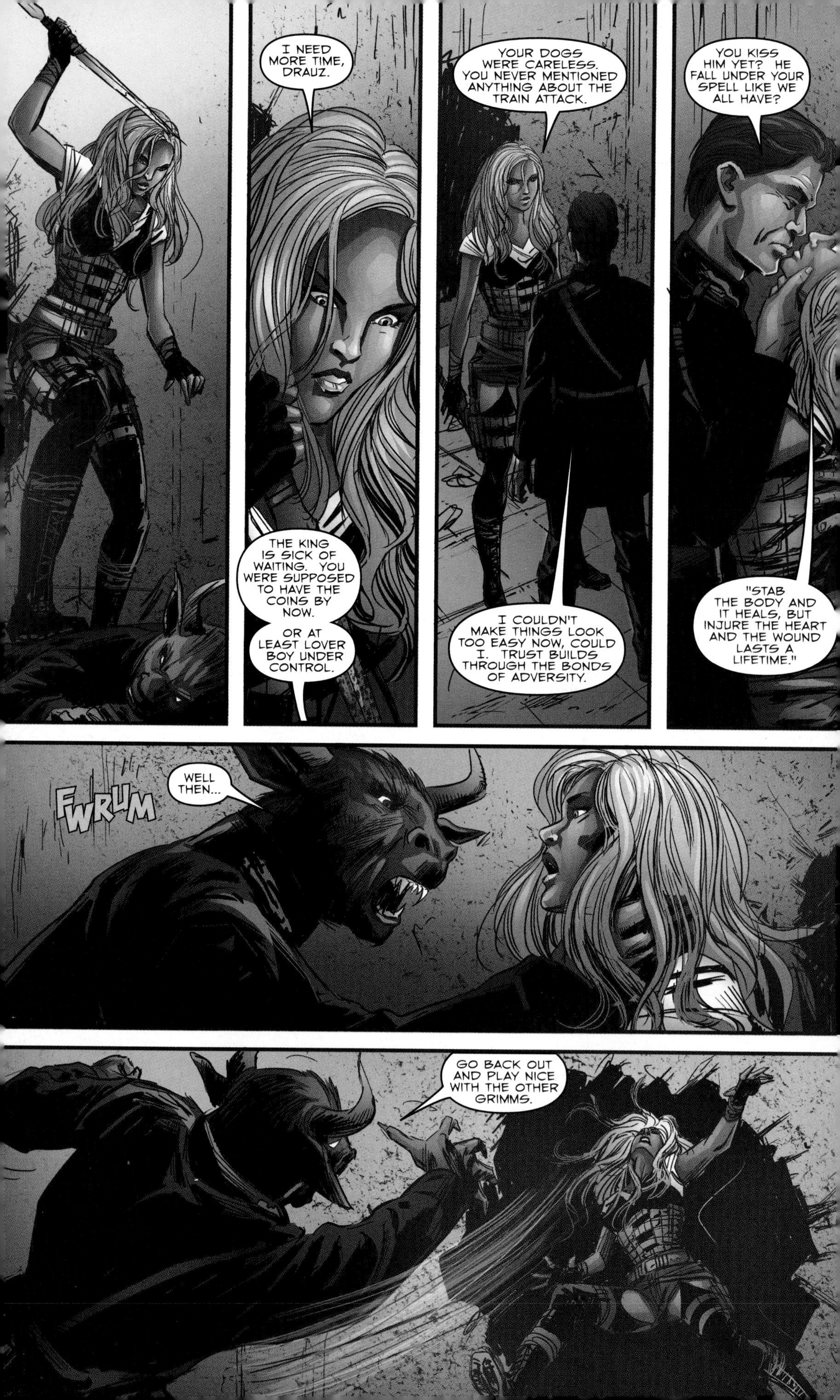
I NEED MORE TIME, DRAUZ.
THE KING IS SICK OF WAITING. YOU WERE SUPPOSED TO HAVE THE COINS BY NOW.
OR AT LEAST LOVER BOY UNDER CONTROL.
YOUR DOGS WERE CARELESS. YOU NEVER MENTIONED ANYTHING ABOUT THE TRAIN ATTACK.
I COULDN'T MAKE THINGS LOOK TOO EASY NOW, COULD I. TRUST BUILDS THROUGH THE BONDS OF ADVERSITY.
YOU KISS HIM YET? HE FALL UNDER YOUR SPELL LIKE WE ALL HAVE?
"STAB THE BODY AND IT HEALS, BUT INJURE THE HEART AND THE WOUND LASTS A LIFETIME."
FWRUM
WELL THEN...
GO BACK OUT AND PLAY NICE WITH THE OTHER GRIMMS.

I'VE JUST ABOUT HAD ENOUGH WITH THIS PLACE.

LET'S GET SOME AIR IN HERE.

KRASH

NEED TO BORROW YOUR JEEP.

VROOOM

HAHAHA, INBRED FREAKS...

COULDN'T HAVE DONE IT WITHOUT YOU, MAYA. THANKS.

YOU'RE NOT STARTING TO CARE ABOUT ME. ARE YOU, BURKHARDT?

WHAT CAN I SAY, I HAVE A WEAKNESS FOR LOST CAUSES.

LET'S GO DESTROY THOSE COINS BEFORE SOMEONE ELSE GETS TO THEM FIRST.

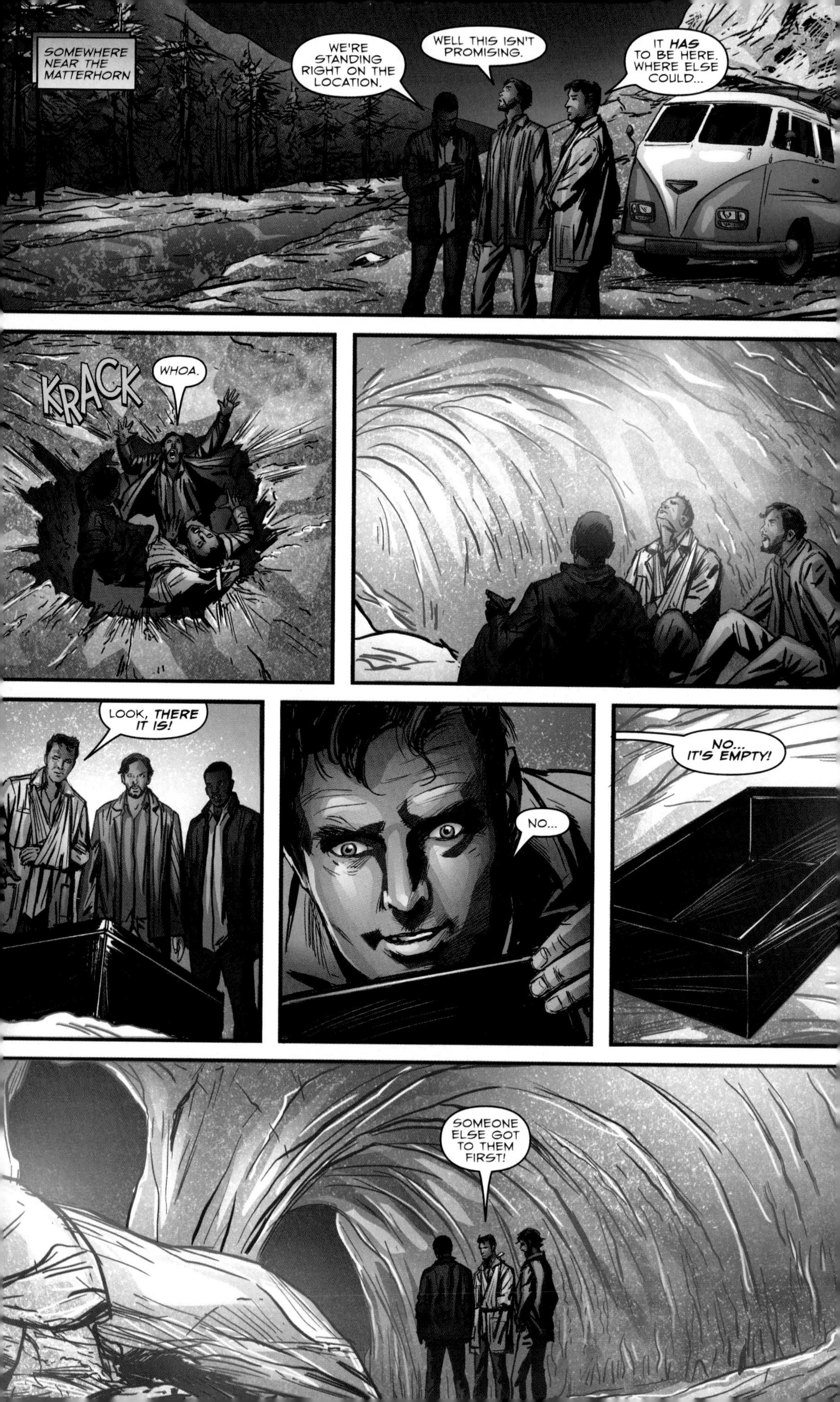
SOMEWHERE NEAR THE MATTERHORN
WE'RE STANDING RIGHT ON THE LOCATION.
WELL THIS ISN'T PROMISING.
IT HAS TO BE HERE. WHERE ELSE COULD...
KRACK
WHOA.
LOOK, THERE IT IS!
NO...
NO... IT'S EMPTY!
SOMEONE ELSE GOT TO THEM FIRST!

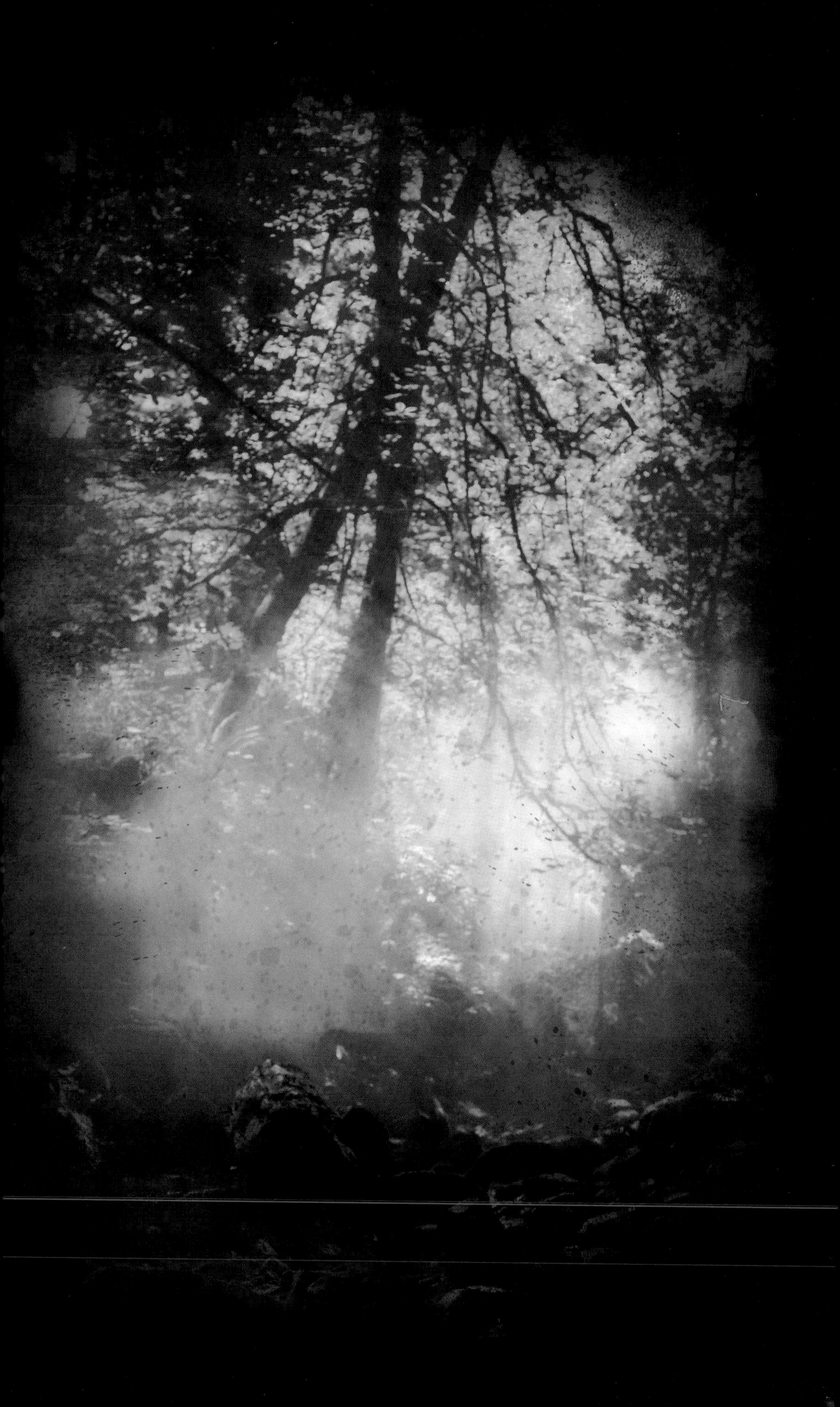

GEIERS ARE THE MOST VILE O...
WHILE THE VICTIMS ARE STILL...
IN THE SAVAGE PAIN THEY C...
CARNAGE ON THE FRONT...
A SEEMINGLY ENDLESS SU...
TERRIBLE TRADE.

3.1

Fig. 1

Fig. 2

Fig. 3

GEIERS HAVE AN INN...
ABILITY TO MOVE THR...
TREES, SEIZING ABO...
THEIR VICTIMS WHO...
BENEATH THEM UNA...

Geier

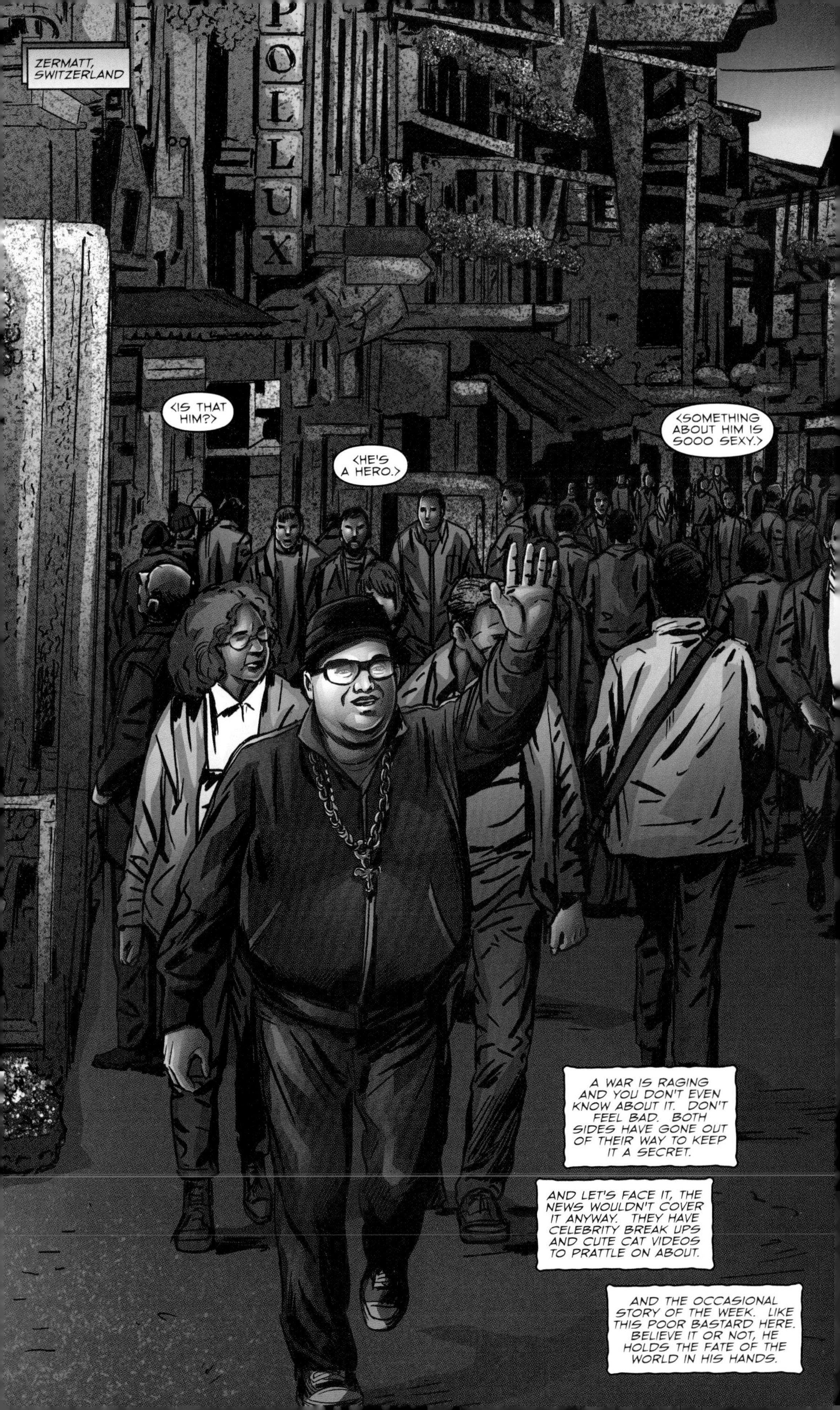

ZERMATT, SWITZERLAND
POLLUX
<IS THAT HIM?>
<HE'S A HERO.>
<SOMETHING ABOUT HIM IS SOOO SEXY.>
A WAR IS RAGING AND YOU DON'T EVEN KNOW ABOUT IT. DON'T FEEL BAD. BOTH SIDES HAVE GONE OUT OF THEIR WAY TO KEEP IT A SECRET.
AND LET'S FACE IT, THE NEWS WOULDN'T COVER IT ANYWAY. THEY HAVE CELEBRITY BREAK UPS AND CUTE CAT VIDEOS TO PRATTLE ON ABOUT.
AND THE OCCASIONAL STORY OF THE WEEK. LIKE THIS POOR BASTARD HERE. BELIEVE IT OR NOT, HE HOLDS THE FATE OF THE WORLD IN HIS HANDS.

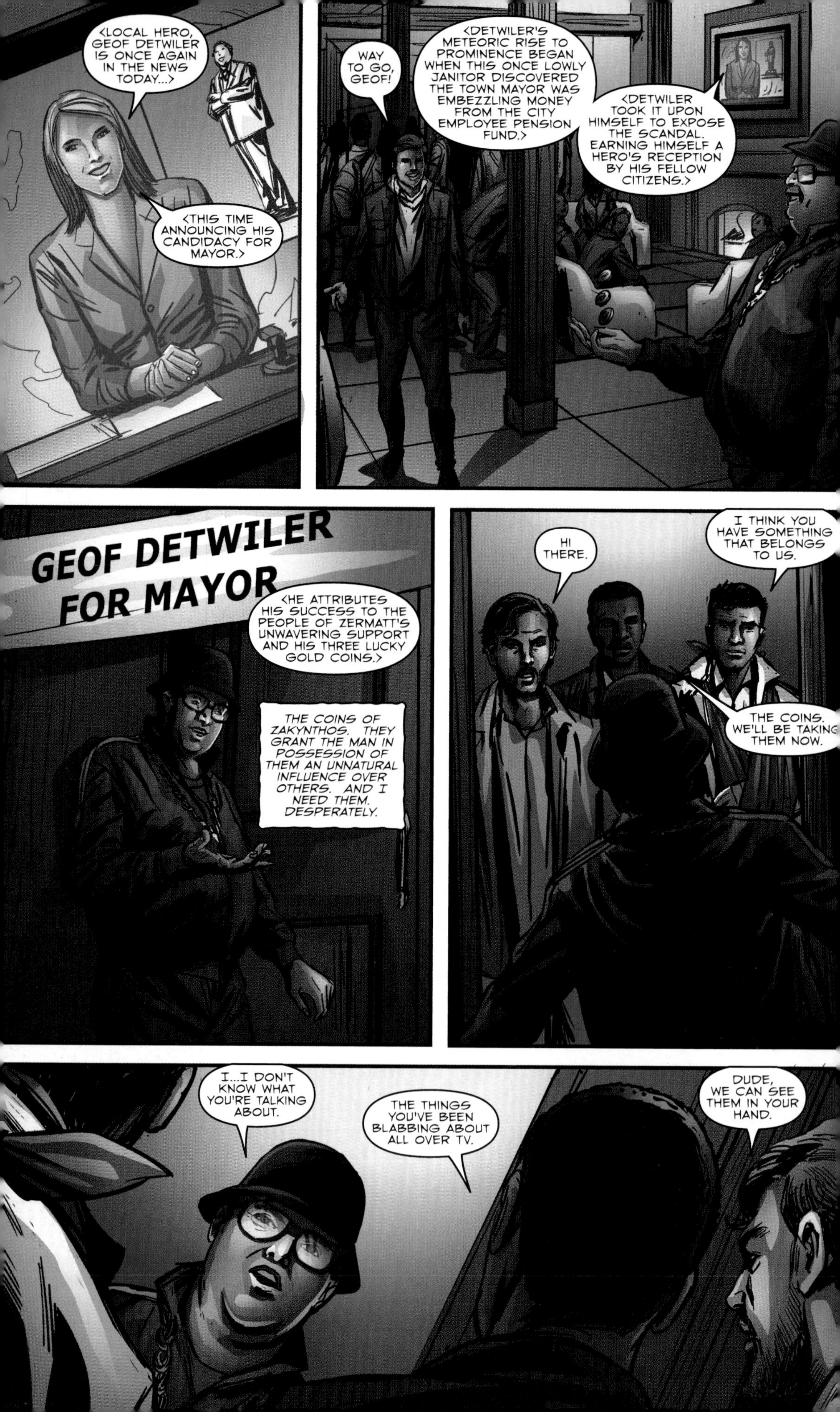
<LOCAL HERO, GEOF DETWILER IS ONCE AGAIN IN THE NEWS TODAY...>
<THIS TIME ANNOUNCING HIS CANDIDACY FOR MAYOR.>
WAY TO GO, GEOF!
<DETWILER'S METEORIC RISE TO PROMINENCE BEGAN WHEN THIS ONCE LOWLY JANITOR DISCOVERED THE TOWN MAYOR WAS EMBEZZLING MONEY FROM THE CITY EMPLOYEE PENSION FUND.>
<DETWILER TOOK IT UPON HIMSELF TO EXPOSE THE SCANDAL. EARNING HIMSELF A HERO'S RECEPTION BY HIS FELLOW CITIZENS.>
GEOF DETWILER FOR MAYOR
<HE ATTRIBUTES HIS SUCCESS TO THE PEOPLE OF ZERMATT'S UNWAVERING SUPPORT AND HIS THREE LUCKY GOLD COINS.>
THE COINS OF ZAKYNTHOS. THEY GRANT THE MAN IN POSSESSION OF THEM AN UNNATURAL INFLUENCE OVER OTHERS. AND I NEED THEM. DESPERATELY.
HI THERE.
I THINK YOU HAVE SOMETHING THAT BELONGS TO US.
THE COINS. WE'LL BE TAKING THEM NOW.
I...I DON'T KNOW WHAT YOU'RE TALKING ABOUT.
THE THINGS YOU'VE BEEN BLABBING ABOUT ALL OVER TV.
DUDE, WE CAN SEE THEM IN YOUR HAND.

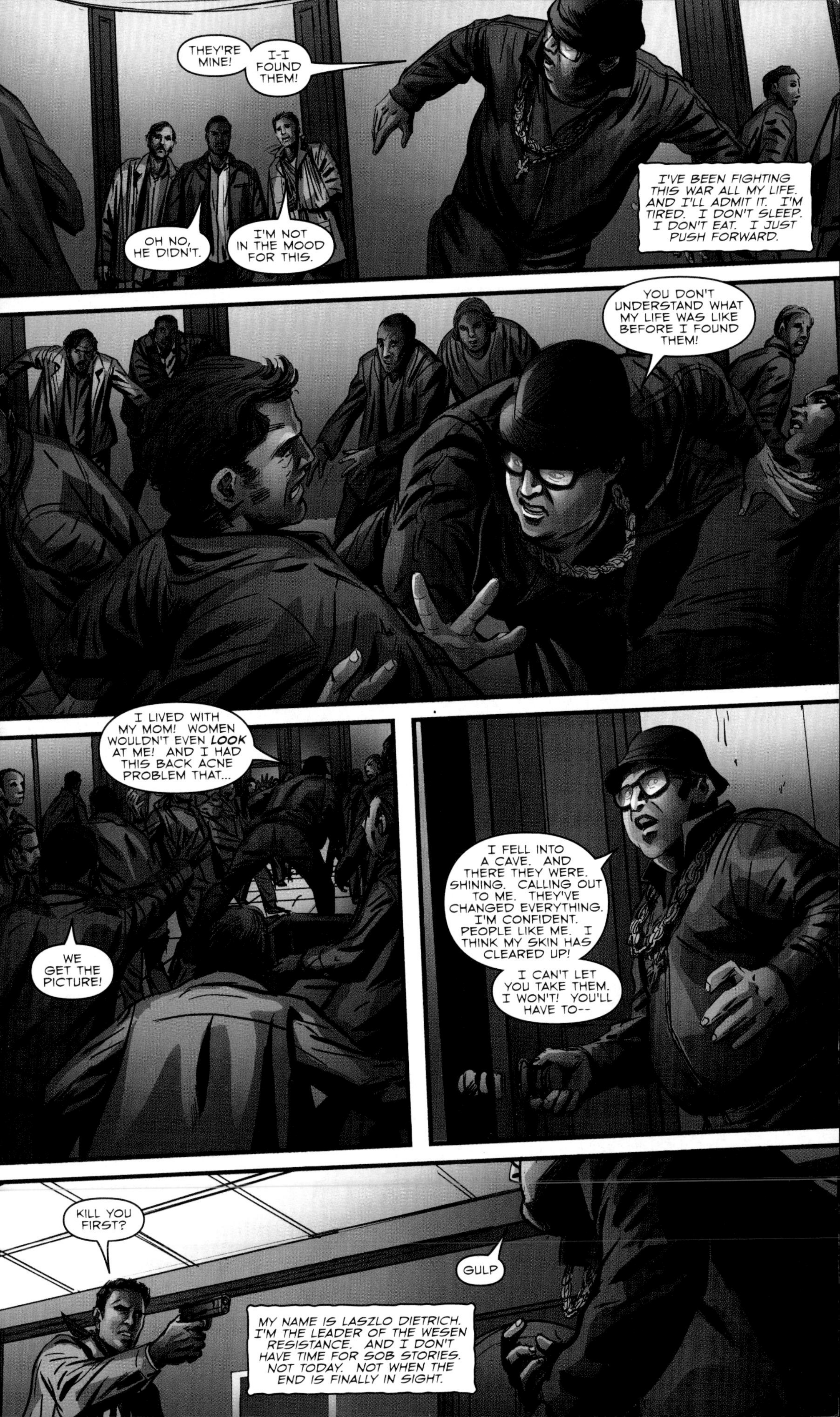

THEY'RE MINE!
I-I FOUND THEM!
OH NO, HE DIDN'T.
I'M NOT IN THE MOOD FOR THIS.
I'VE BEEN FIGHTING THIS WAR ALL MY LIFE. AND I'LL ADMIT IT. I'M TIRED. I DON'T SLEEP. I DON'T EAT. I JUST PUSH FORWARD.
YOU DON'T UNDERSTAND WHAT MY LIFE WAS LIKE BEFORE I FOUND THEM!
I LIVED WITH MY MOM! WOMEN WOULDN'T EVEN LOOK AT ME! AND I HAD THIS BACK ACNE PROBLEM THAT...
WE GET THE PICTURE!
I FELL INTO A CAVE. AND THERE THEY WERE. SHINING. CALLING OUT TO ME. THEY'VE CHANGED EVERYTHING. I'M CONFIDENT. PEOPLE LIKE ME. I THINK MY SKIN HAS CLEARED UP!
I CAN'T LET YOU TAKE THEM. I WON'T! YOU'LL HAVE TO--
KILL YOU FIRST?
GULP
MY NAME IS LASZLO DIETRICH. I'M THE LEADER OF THE WESEN RESISTANCE. AND I DON'T HAVE TIME FOR SOB STORIES. NOT TODAY. NOT WHEN THE END IS FINALLY IN SIGHT.

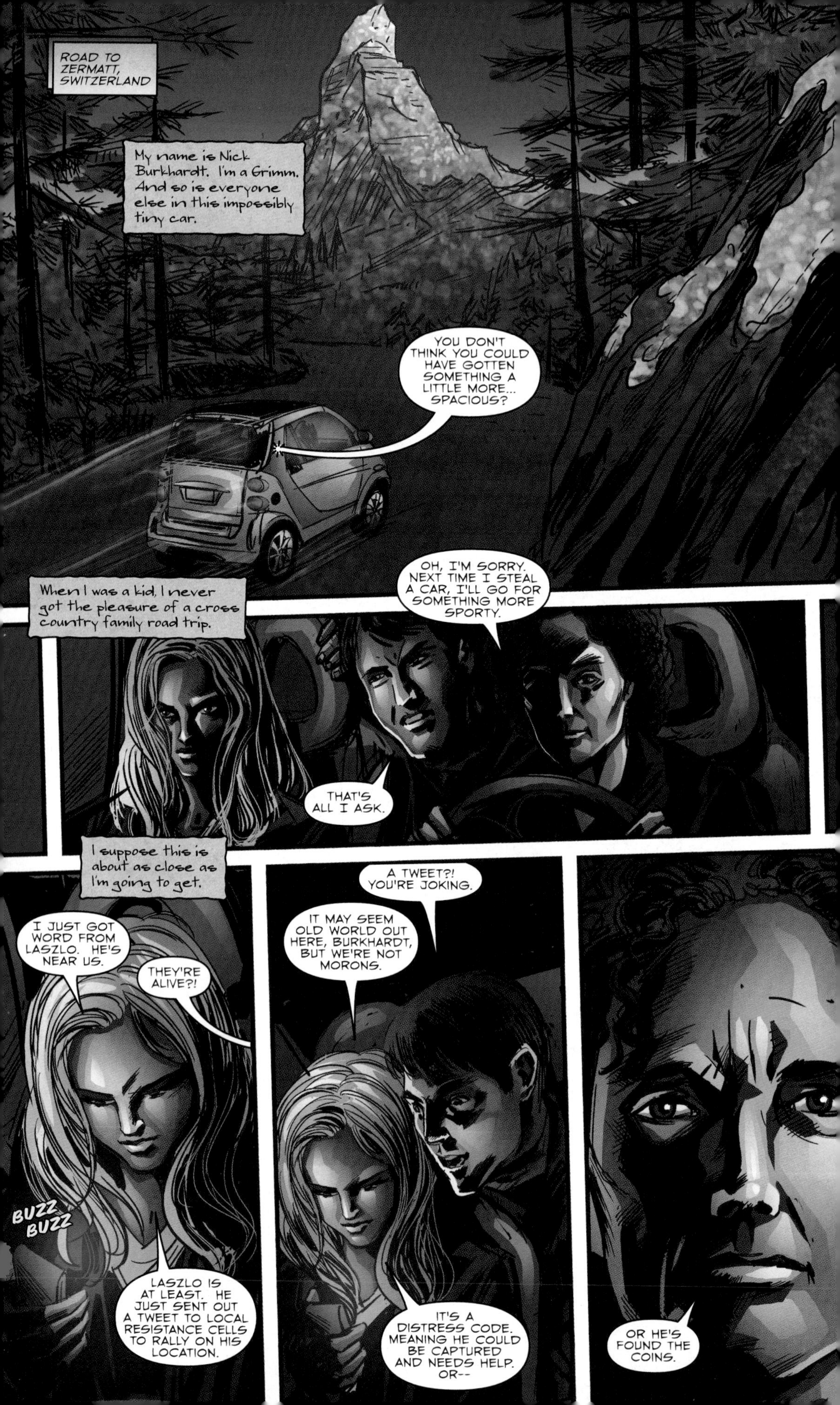
ROAD TO ZERMATT, SWITZERLAND
My name is Nick Burkhardt. I'm a Grimm. And so is everyone else in this impossibly tiny car.
YOU DON'T THINK YOU COULD HAVE GOTTEN SOMETHING A LITTLE MORE... SPACIOUS?
When I was a kid, I never got the pleasure of a cross country family road trip.
OH, I'M SORRY. NEXT TIME I STEAL A CAR, I'LL GO FOR SOMETHING MORE SPORTY.
THAT'S ALL I ASK.
I suppose this is about as close as I'm going to get.
I JUST GOT WORD FROM LASZLO. HE'S NEAR US.
THEY'RE ALIVE?!
BUZZ BUZZ
LASZLO IS AT LEAST. HE JUST SENT OUT A TWEET TO LOCAL RESISTANCE CELLS TO RALLY ON HIS LOCATION.
A TWEET?! YOU'RE JOKING.
IT MAY SEEM OLD WORLD OUT HERE, BURKHARDT, BUT WE'RE NOT MORONS.
IT'S A DISTRESS CODE. MEANING HE COULD BE CAPTURED AND NEEDS HELP. OR--
OR HE'S FOUND THE COINS.

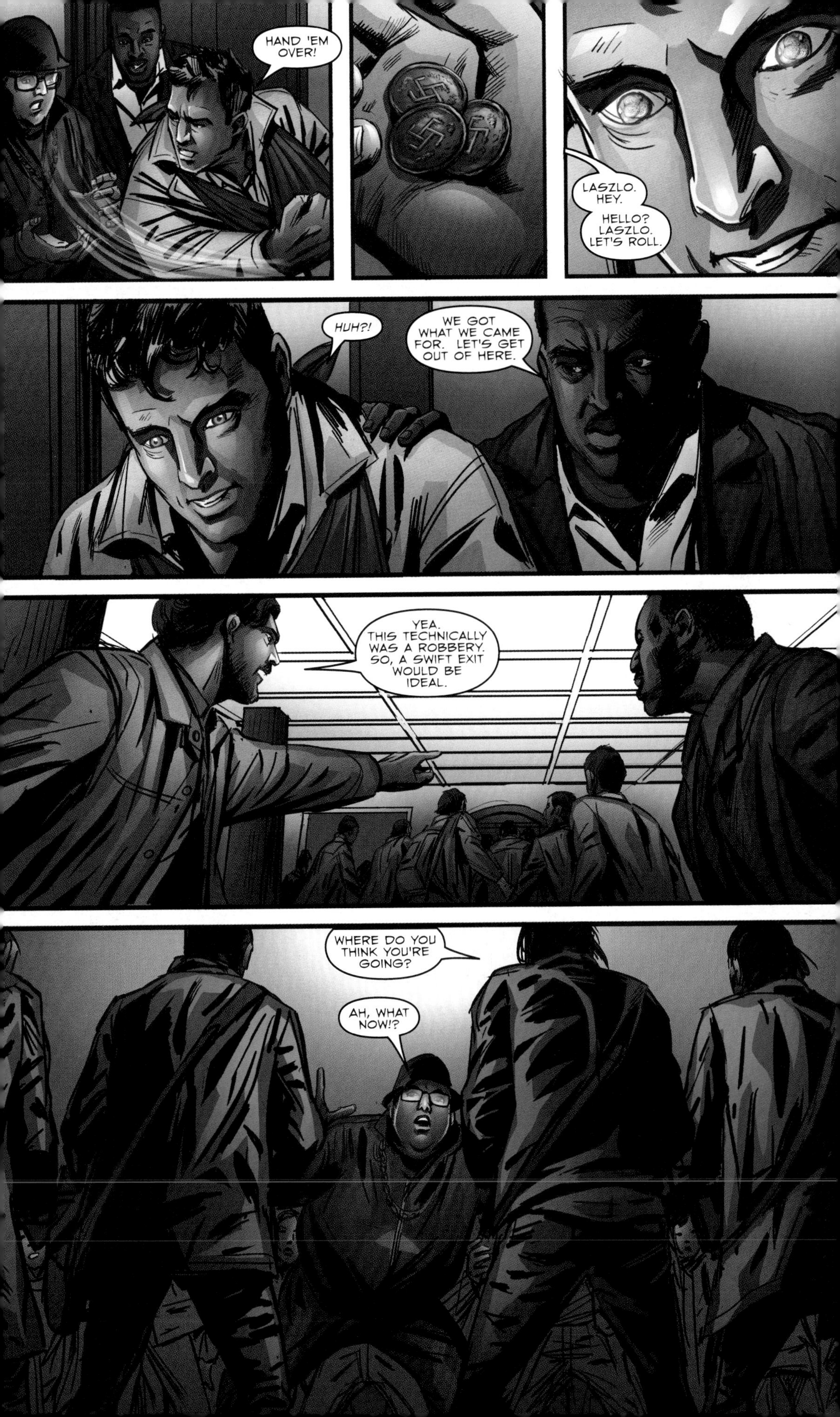
HAND 'EM OVER!
LASZLO. HEY.
HELLO? LASZLO. LET'S ROLL.
HUH?!
WE GOT WHAT WE CAME FOR. LET'S GET OUT OF HERE.
YEA. THIS TECHNICALLY WAS A ROBBERY. SO, A SWIFT EXIT WOULD BE IDEAL.
WHERE DO YOU THINK YOU'RE GOING?
AH, WHAT NOW!?

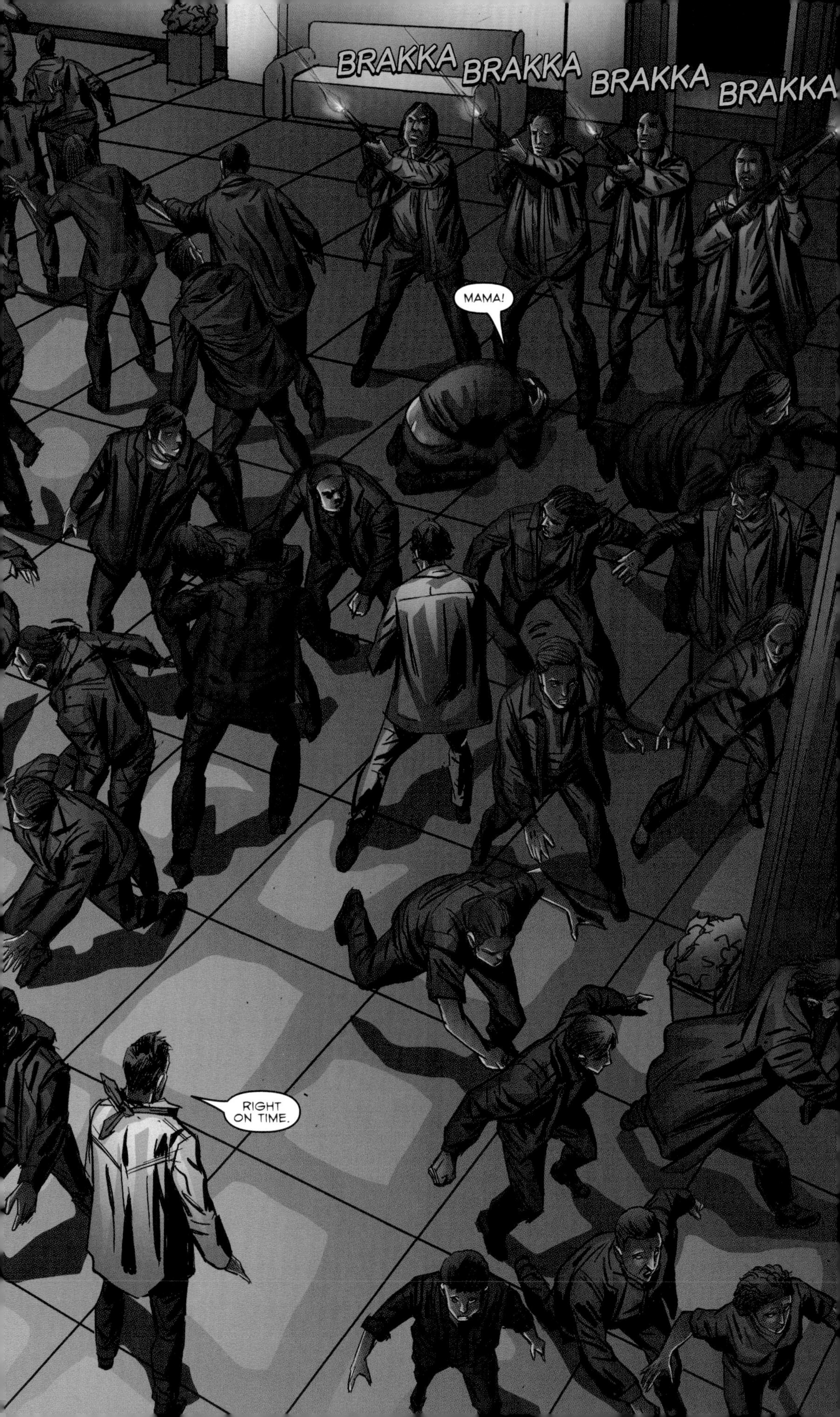
BRAKKA BRAKKA BRAKKA BRAKKA
MAMA!
RIGHT ON TIME.

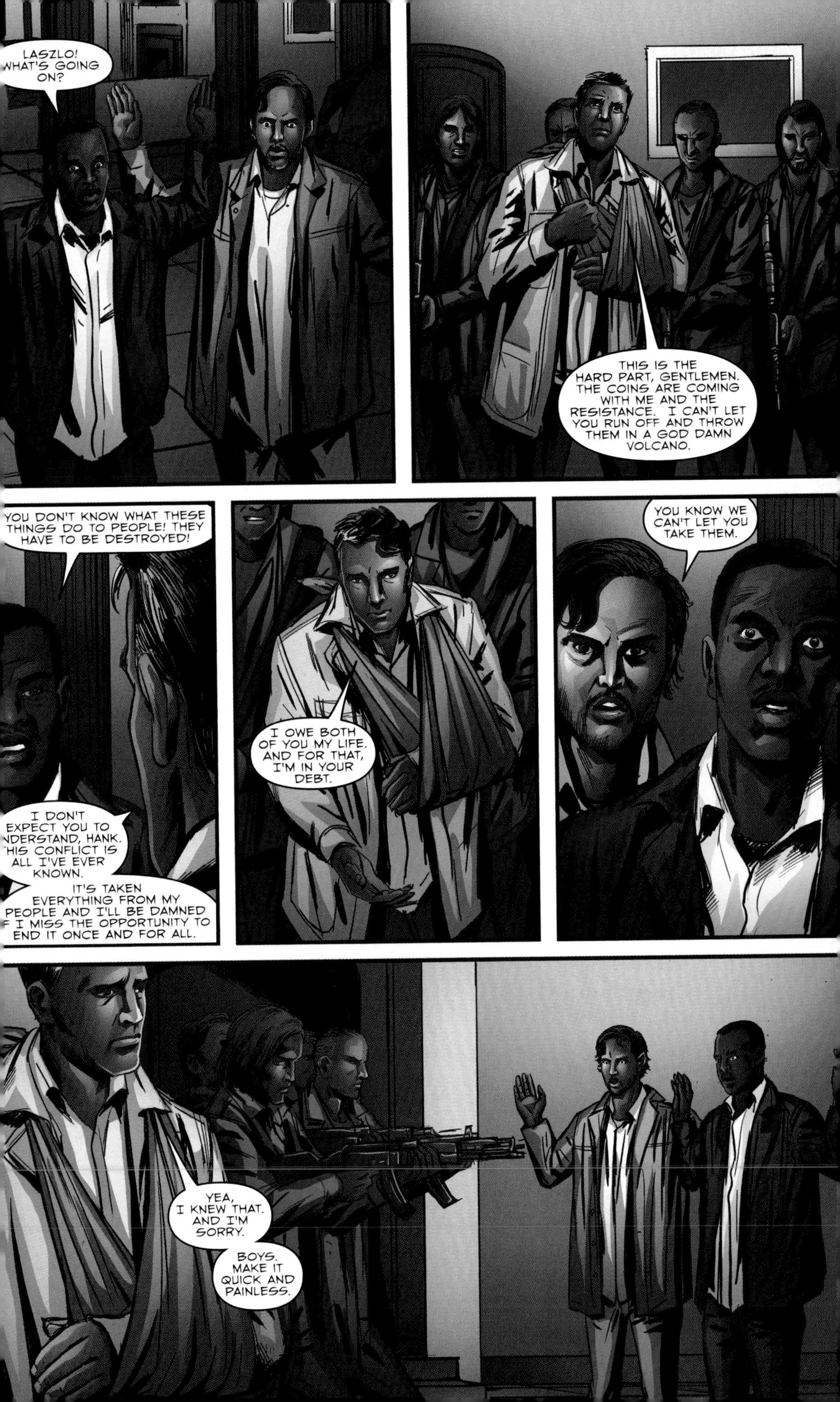
LASZLO! WHAT'S GOING ON?
THIS IS THE HARD PART, GENTLEMEN. THE COINS ARE COMING WITH ME AND THE RESISTANCE. I CAN'T LET YOU RUN OFF AND THROW THEM IN A GOD DAMN VOLCANO.
YOU DON'T KNOW WHAT THESE THINGS DO TO PEOPLE! THEY HAVE TO BE DESTROYED!
I DON'T EXPECT YOU TO NDERSTAND, HANK. THIS CONFLICT IS ALL I'VE EVER KNOWN.
IT'S TAKEN EVERYTHING FROM MY PEOPLE AND I'LL BE DAMNED F I MISS THE OPPORTUNITY TO END IT ONCE AND FOR ALL.
I OWE BOTH OF YOU MY LIFE. AND FOR THAT, I'M IN YOUR DEBT.
YOU KNOW WE CAN'T LET YOU TAKE THEM.
YEA, I KNEW THAT. AND I'M SORRY.
BOYS. MAKE IT QUICK AND PAINLESS.

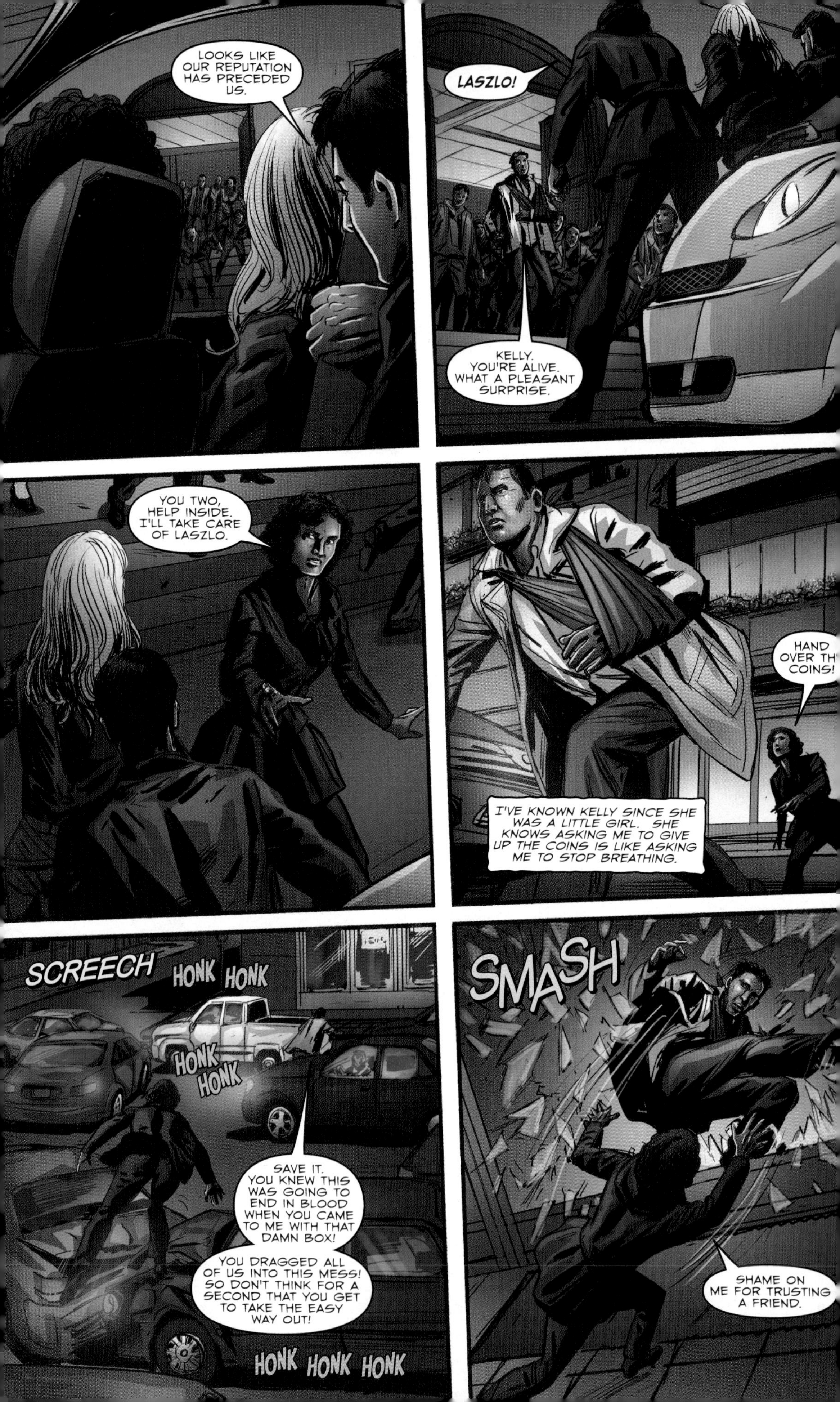
LOOKS LIKE OUR REPUTATION HAS PRECEDED US.
LASZLO!
KELLY. YOU'RE ALIVE. WHAT A PLEASANT SURPRISE.
YOU TWO, HELP INSIDE. I'LL TAKE CARE OF LASZLO.
HAND OVER TH COINS!
I'VE KNOWN KELLY SINCE SHE WAS A LITTLE GIRL. SHE KNOWS ASKING ME TO GIVE UP THE COINS IS LIKE ASKING ME TO STOP BREATHING.
SCREECH
HONK HONK
HONK HONK
SAVE IT. YOU KNEW THIS WAS GOING TO END IN BLOOD WHEN YOU CAME TO ME WITH THAT DAMN BOX!
YOU DRAGGED ALL OF US INTO THIS MESS! SO DON'T THINK FOR A SECOND THAT YOU GET TO TAKE THE EASY WAY OUT!
HONK HONK HONK
SMASH
SHAME ON ME FOR TRUSTING A FRIEND.

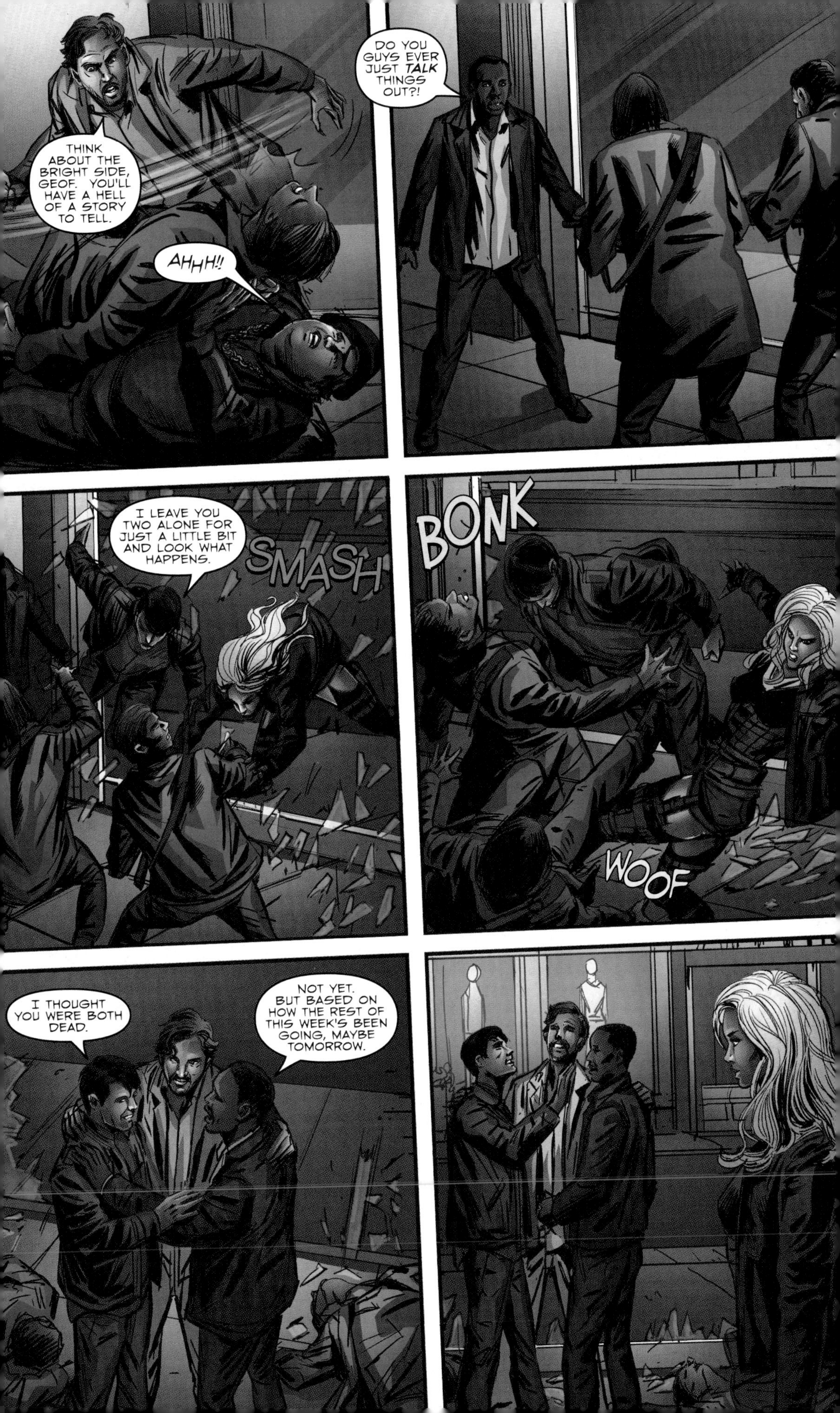
THINK ABOUT THE BRIGHT SIDE, GEOF. YOU'LL HAVE A HELL OF A STORY TO TELL.
AHHH!!
DO YOU GUYS EVER JUST TALK THINGS OUT?!
I LEAVE YOU TWO ALONE FOR JUST A LITTLE BIT AND LOOK WHAT HAPPENS.
SMASH
BONK
WOOF
I THOUGHT YOU WERE BOTH DEAD.
NOT YET. BUT BASED ON HOW THE REST OF THIS WEEK'S BEEN GOING, MAYBE TOMORROW.

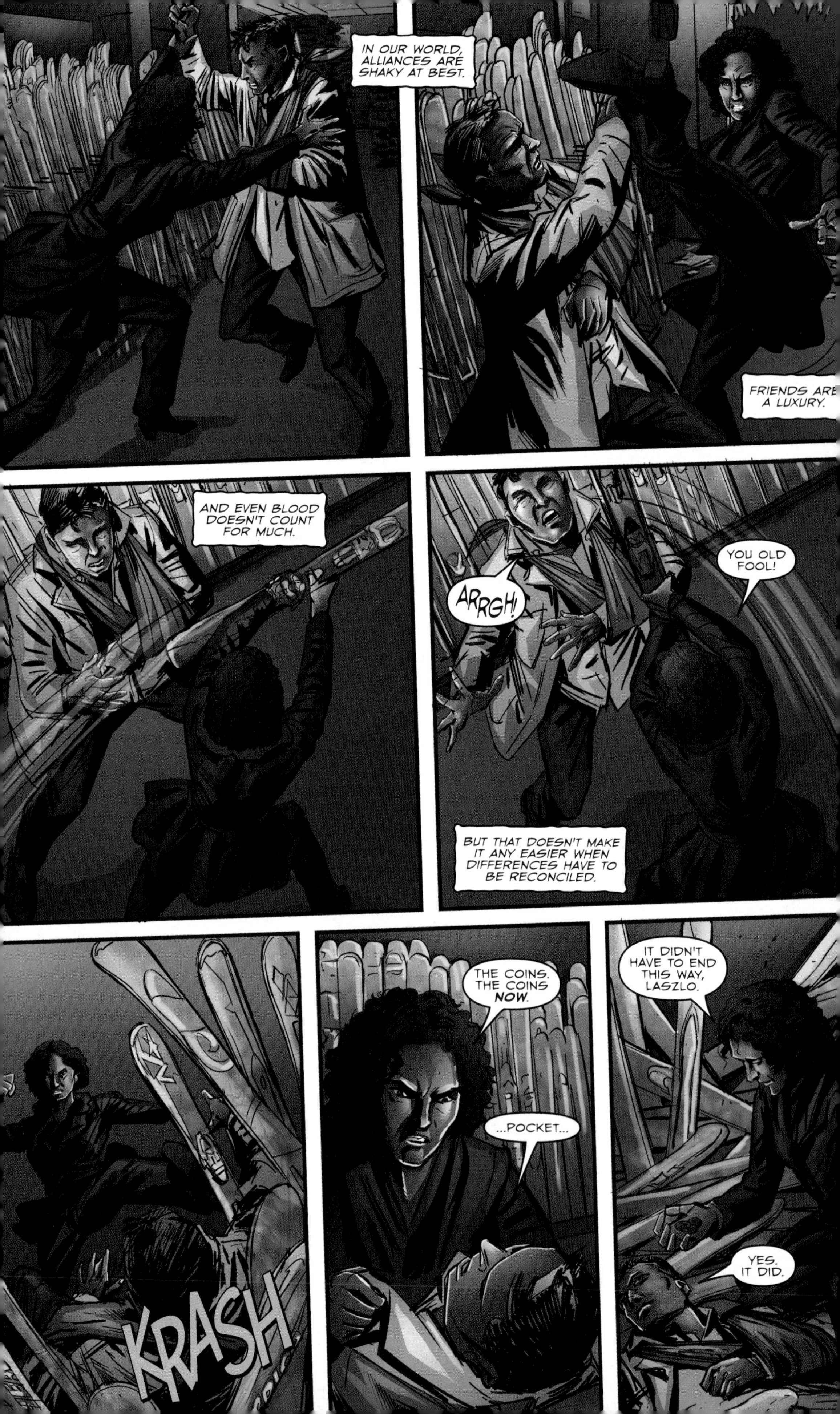
IN OUR WORLD, ALLIANCES ARE SHAKY AT BEST.
FRIENDS ARE A LUXURY.
AND EVEN BLOOD DOESN'T COUNT FOR MUCH.
ARRGH!
YOU OLD FOOL!
BUT THAT DOESN'T MAKE IT ANY EASIER WHEN DIFFERENCES HAVE TO BE RECONCILED.
KRASH
THE COINS. THE COINS NOW.
...POCKET...
IT DIDN'T HAVE TO END THIS WAY, LASZLO.
YES. IT DID.

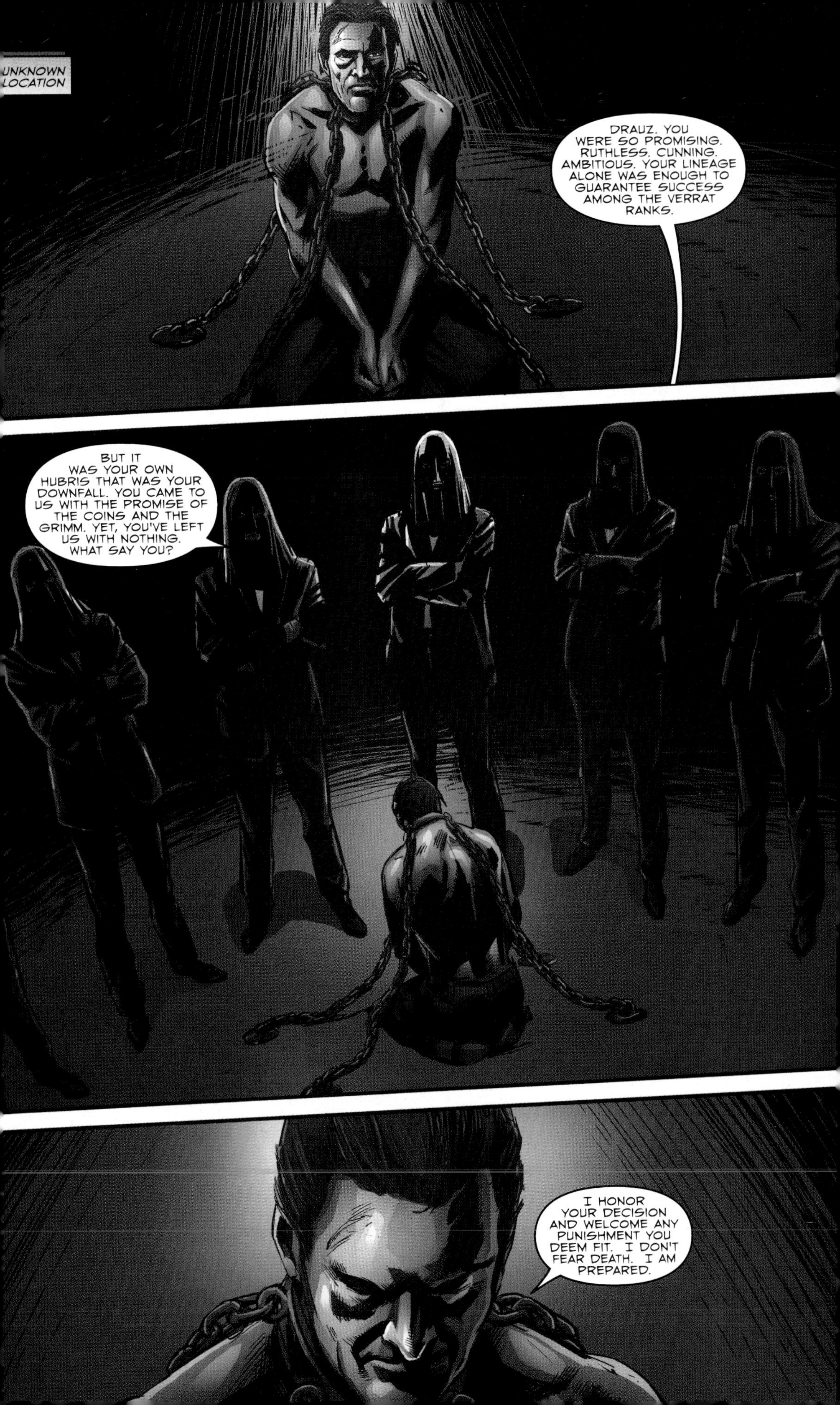
UNKNOWN LOCATION
DRAUZ. YOU WERE SO PROMISING. RUTHLESS. CUNNING. AMBITIOUS. YOUR LINEAGE ALONE WAS ENOUGH TO GUARANTEE SUCCESS AMONG THE VERRAT RANKS.
BUT IT WAS YOUR OWN HUBRIS THAT WAS YOUR DOWNFALL. YOU CAME TO US WITH THE PROMISE OF THE COINS AND THE GRIMM. YET, YOU'VE LEFT US WITH NOTHING. WHAT SAY YOU?
I HONOR YOUR DECISION AND WELCOME ANY PUNISHMENT YOU DEEM FIT. I DON'T FEAR DEATH. I AM PREPARED.

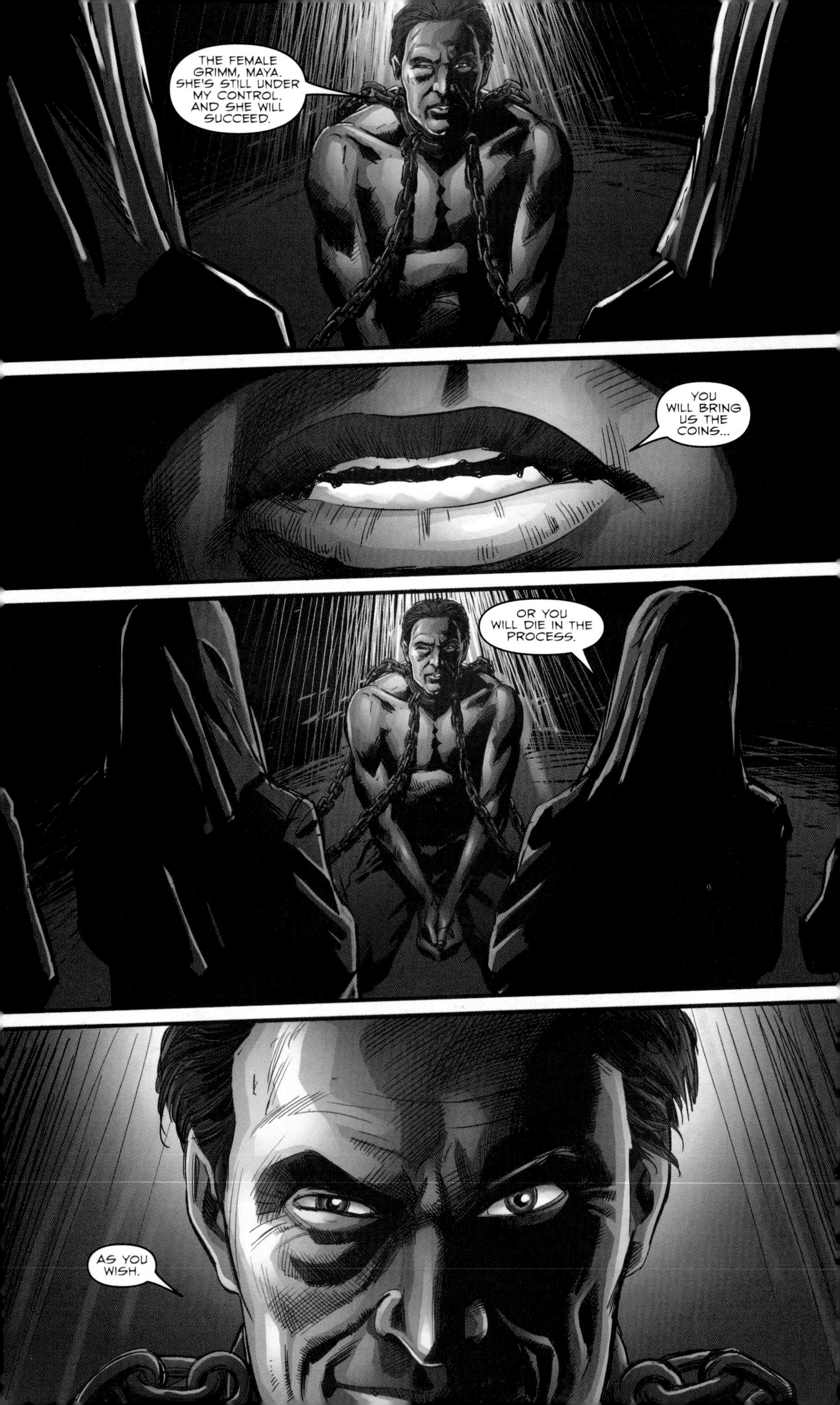
THE FEMALE GRIMM, MAYA. SHE'S STILL UNDER MY CONTROL. AND SHE WILL SUCCEED.
YOU WILL BRING US THE COINS...
OR YOU WILL DIE IN THE PROCESS.
AS YOU WISH.

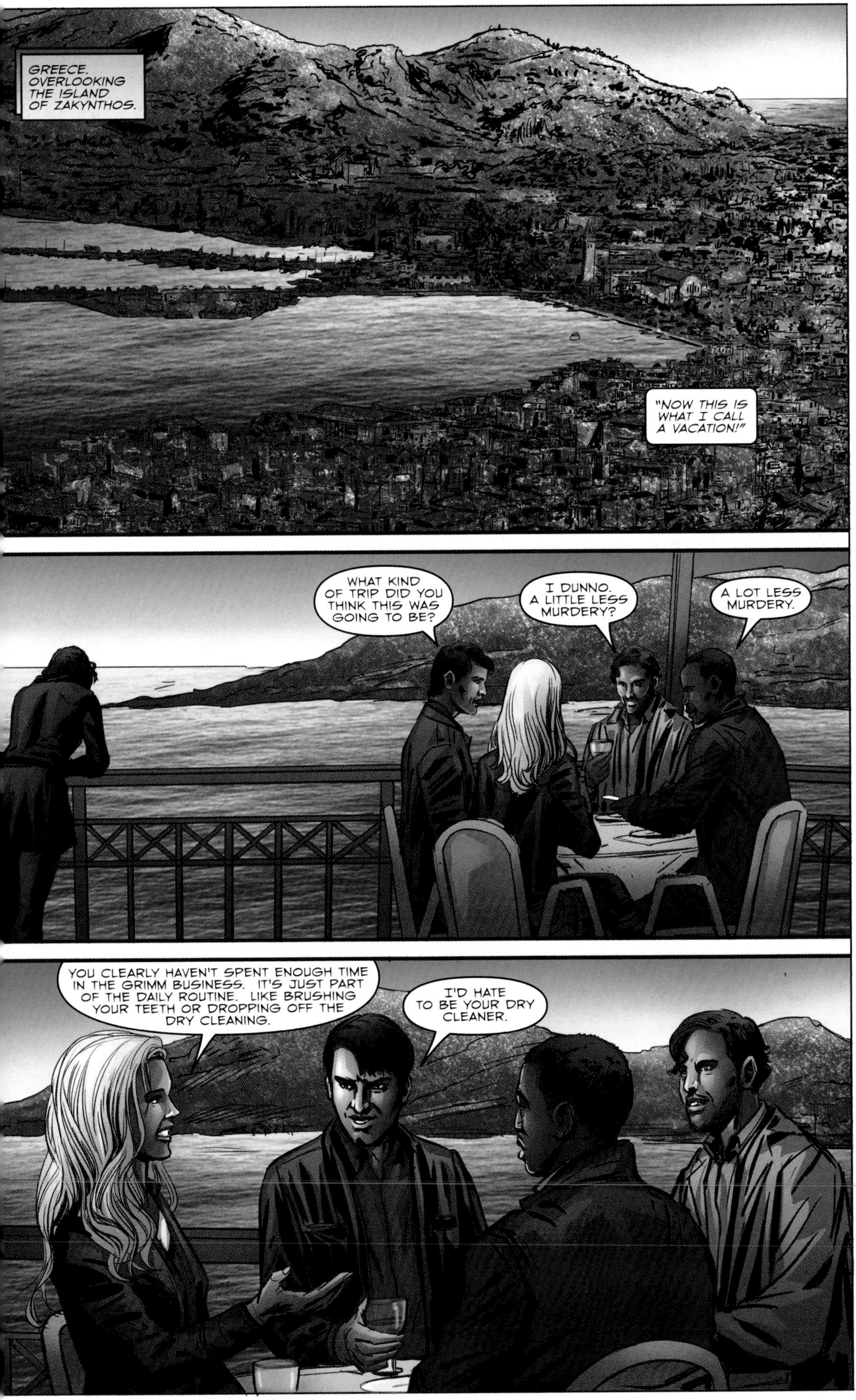
GREECE. OVERLOOKING THE ISLAND OF ZAKYNTHOS.
"NOW THIS IS WHAT I CALL A VACATION!"
WHAT KIND OF TRIP DID YOU THINK THIS WAS GOING TO BE?
I DUNNO. A LITTLE LESS MURDERY?
A LOT LESS MURDERY.
YOU CLEARLY HAVEN'T SPENT ENOUGH TIME IN THE GRIMM BUSINESS. IT'S JUST PART OF THE DAILY ROUTINE. LIKE BRUSHING YOUR TEETH OR DROPPING OFF THE DRY CLEANING.
I'D HATE TO BE YOUR DRY CLEANER.

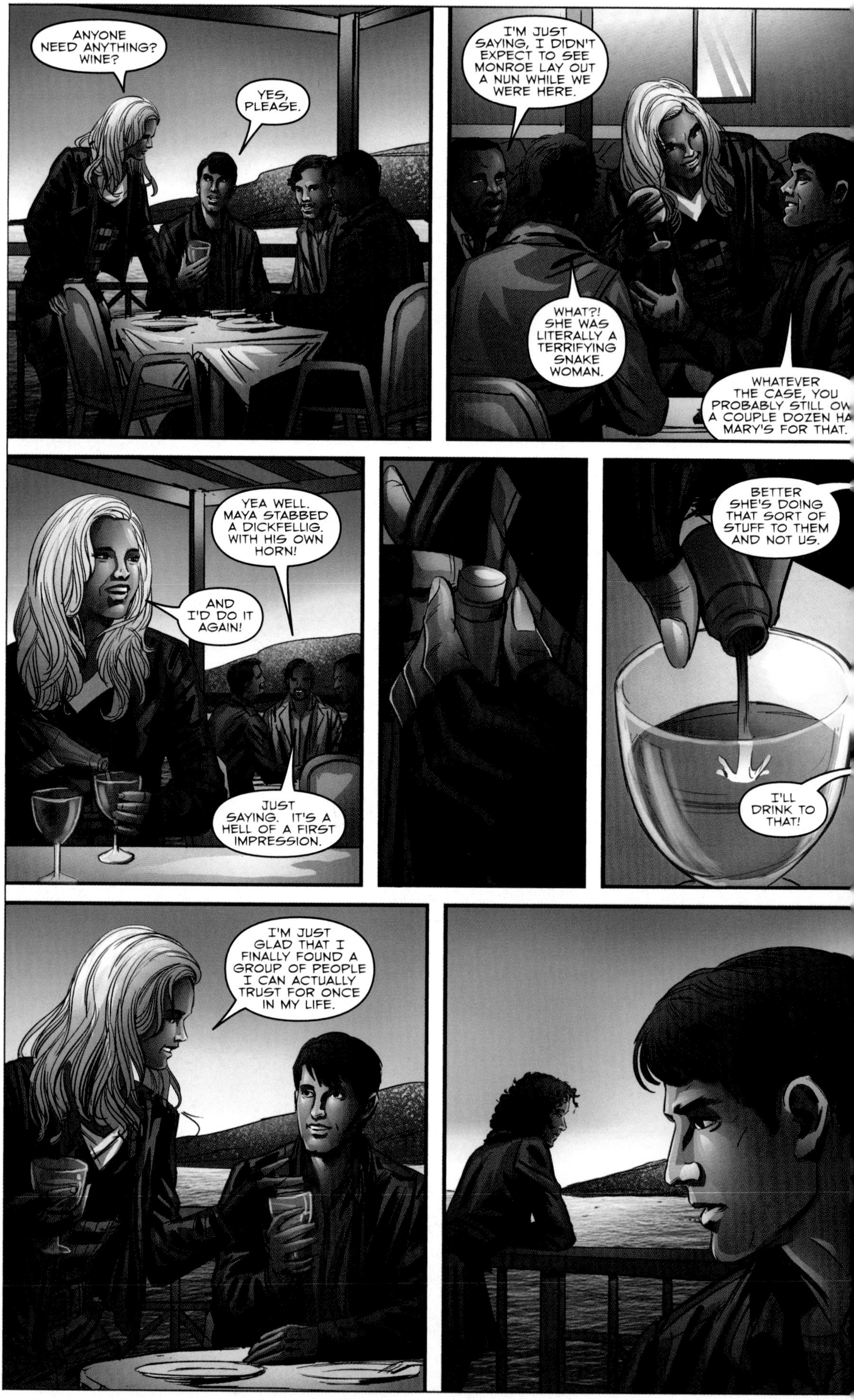
ANYONE NEED ANYTHING? WINE?
YES, PLEASE.
I'M JUST SAYING, I DIDN'T EXPECT TO SEE MONROE LAY OUT A NUN WHILE WE WERE HERE.
WHAT?! SHE WAS LITERALLY A TERRIFYING SNAKE WOMAN.
WHATEVER THE CASE, YOU PROBABLY STILL OW A COUPLE DOZEN HA MARY'S FOR THAT.
YEA WELL. MAYA STABBED A DICKFELLIG. WITH HIS OWN HORN!
AND I'D DO IT AGAIN!
JUST SAYING. IT'S A HELL OF A FIRST IMPRESSION.
BETTER SHE'S DOING THAT SORT OF STUFF TO THEM AND NOT US.
I'LL DRINK TO THAT!
I'M JUST GLAD THAT I FINALLY FOUND A GROUP OF PEOPLE I CAN ACTUALLY TRUST FOR ONCE IN MY LIFE.

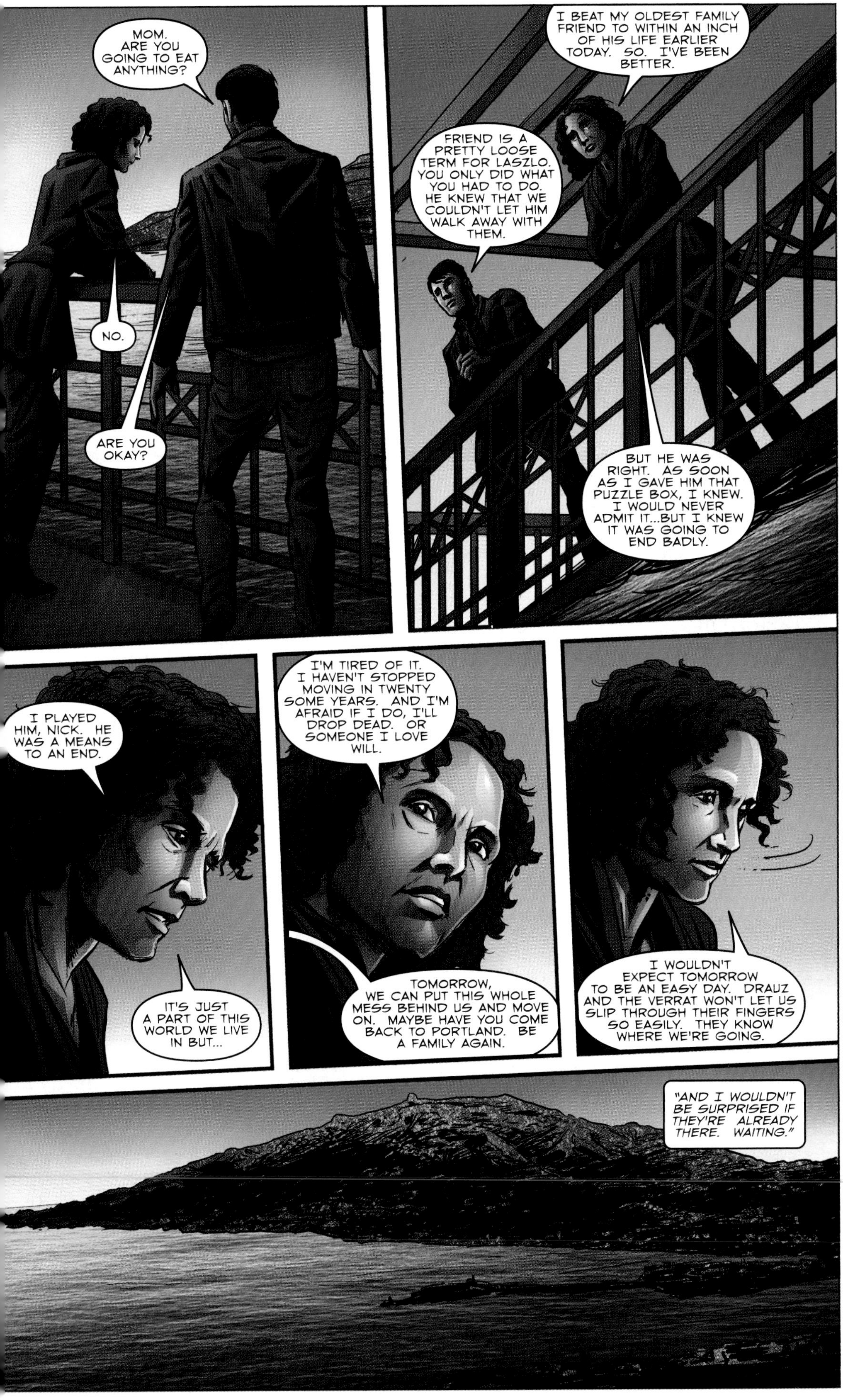
MOM. ARE YOU GOING TO EAT ANYTHING?
NO.
ARE YOU OKAY?
I BEAT MY OLDEST FAMILY FRIEND TO WITHIN AN INCH OF HIS LIFE EARLIER TODAY. SO. I'VE BEEN BETTER.
FRIEND IS A PRETTY LOOSE TERM FOR LASZLO. YOU ONLY DID WHAT YOU HAD TO DO. HE KNEW THAT WE COULDN'T LET HIM WALK AWAY WITH THEM.
BUT HE WAS RIGHT. AS SOON AS I GAVE HIM THAT PUZZLE BOX, I KNEW. I WOULD NEVER ADMIT IT...BUT I KNEW IT WAS GOING TO END BADLY.
I PLAYED HIM, NICK. HE WAS A MEANS TO AN END.
IT'S JUST A PART OF THIS WORLD WE LIVE IN BUT...
I'M TIRED OF IT. I HAVEN'T STOPPED MOVING IN TWENTY SOME YEARS. AND I'M AFRAID IF I DO, I'LL DROP DEAD. OR SOMEONE I LOVE WILL.
TOMORROW, WE CAN PUT THIS WHOLE MESS BEHIND US AND MOVE ON. MAYBE HAVE YOU COME BACK TO PORTLAND. BE A FAMILY AGAIN.
I WOULDN'T EXPECT TOMORROW TO BE AN EASY DAY. DRAUZ AND THE VERRAT WON'T LET US SLIP THROUGH THEIR FINGERS SO EASILY. THEY KNOW WHERE WE'RE GOING.
"AND I WOULDN'T BE SURPRISED IF THEY'RE ALREADY THERE. WAITING."

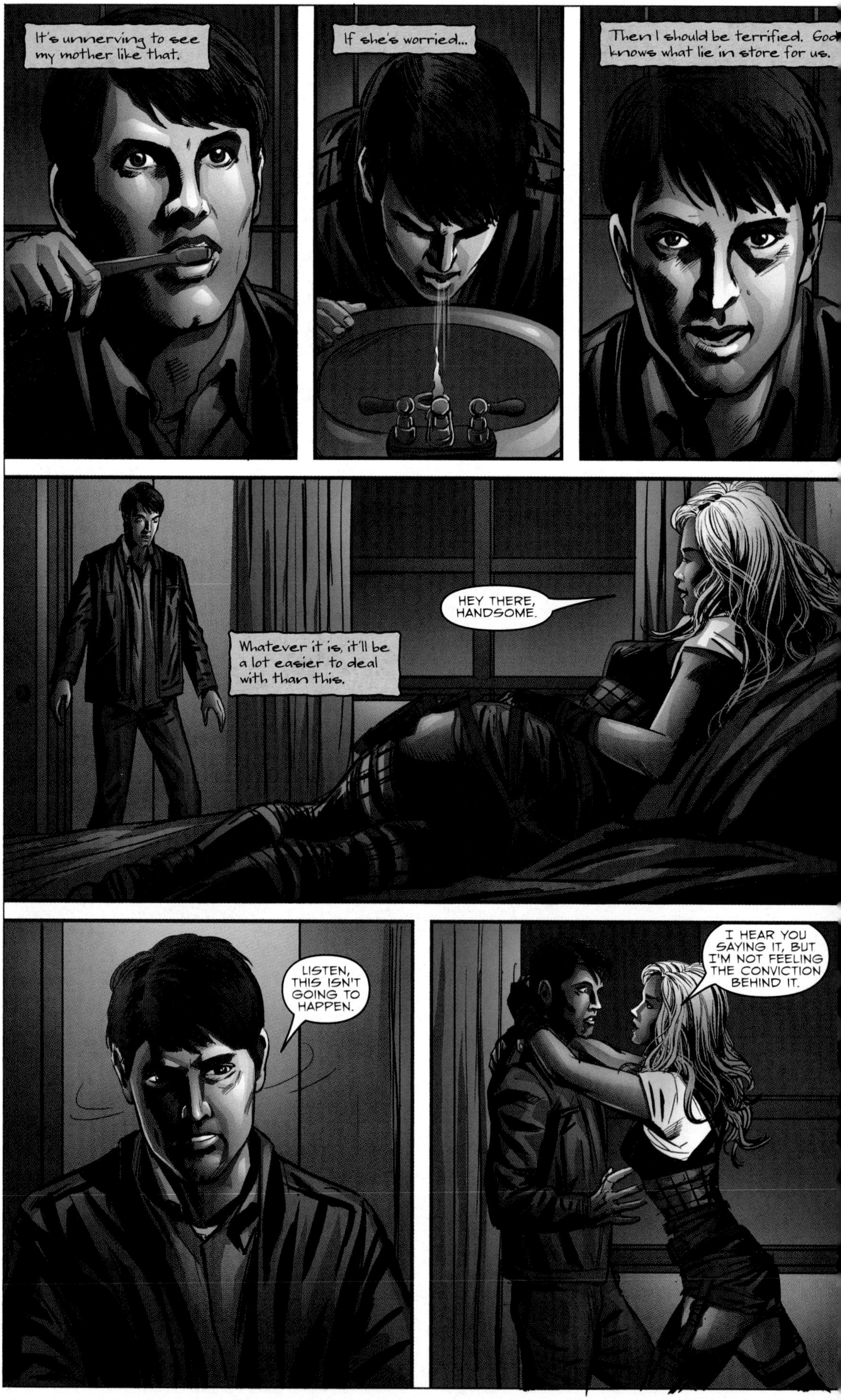
It's unnerving to see my mother like that.
If she's worried...
Then I should be terrified. God knows what lie in store for us.
Whatever it is, it'll be a lot easier to deal with than this.
HEY THERE, HANDSOME.
LISTEN, THIS ISN'T GOING TO HAPPEN.
I HEAR YOU SAYING IT, BUT I'M NOT FEELING THE CONVICTION BEHIND IT.

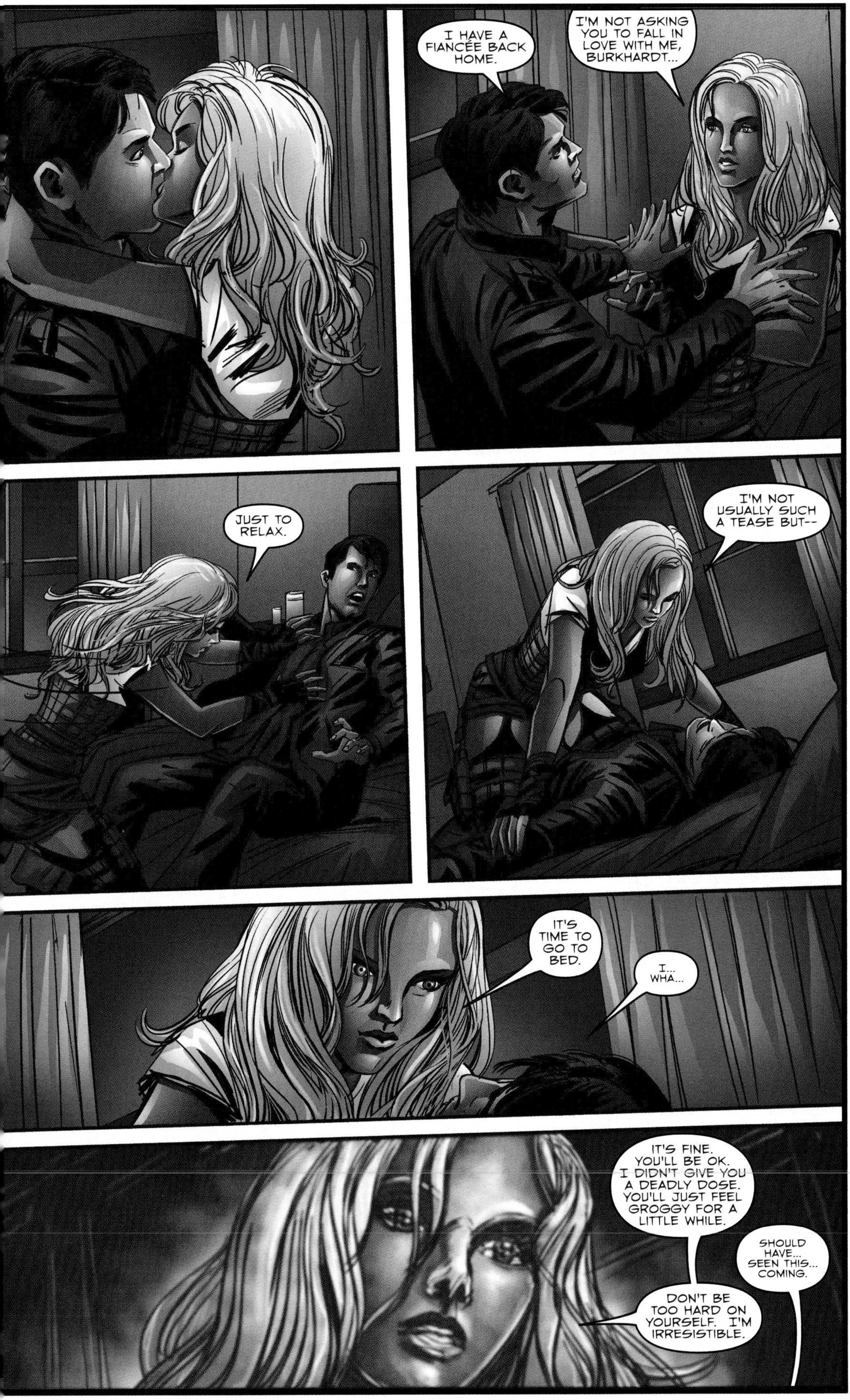
I HAVE A FIANCÉE BACK HOME.
I'M NOT ASKING YOU TO FALL IN LOVE WITH ME, BURKHARDT...
JUST TO RELAX.
I'M NOT USUALLY SUCH A TEASE BUT--
IT'S TIME TO GO TO BED.
I... WHA...
IT'S FINE. YOU'LL BE OK. I DIDN'T GIVE YOU A DEADLY DOSE. YOU'LL JUST FEEL GROGGY FOR A LITTLE WHILE.
SHOULD HAVE... SEEN THIS... COMING.
DON'T BE TOO HARD ON YOURSELF. I'M IRRESISTIBLE.

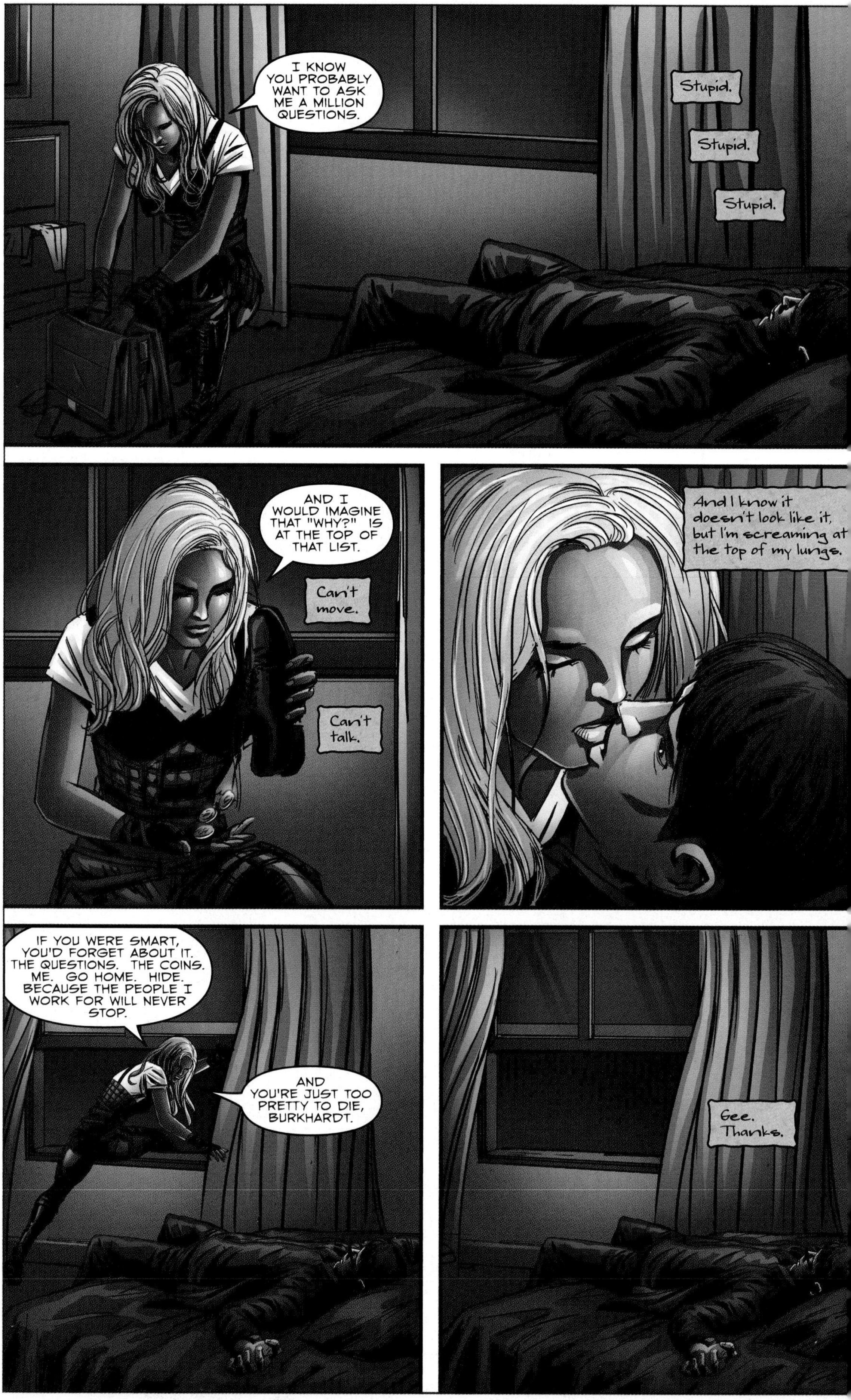
I KNOW YOU PROBABLY WANT TO ASK ME A MILLION QUESTIONS.
Stupid.
Stupid.
Stupid.
AND I WOULD IMAGINE THAT "WHY?" IS AT THE TOP OF THAT LIST.
Can't move.
Can't talk.
And I know it doesn't look like it, but I'm screaming at the top of my lungs.
IF YOU WERE SMART, YOU'D FORGET ABOUT IT. THE QUESTIONS. THE COINS. ME. GO HOME. HIDE. BECAUSE THE PEOPLE I WORK FOR WILL NEVER STOP.
AND YOU'RE JUST TOO PRETTY TO DIE, BURKHARDT.
Gee. Thanks.

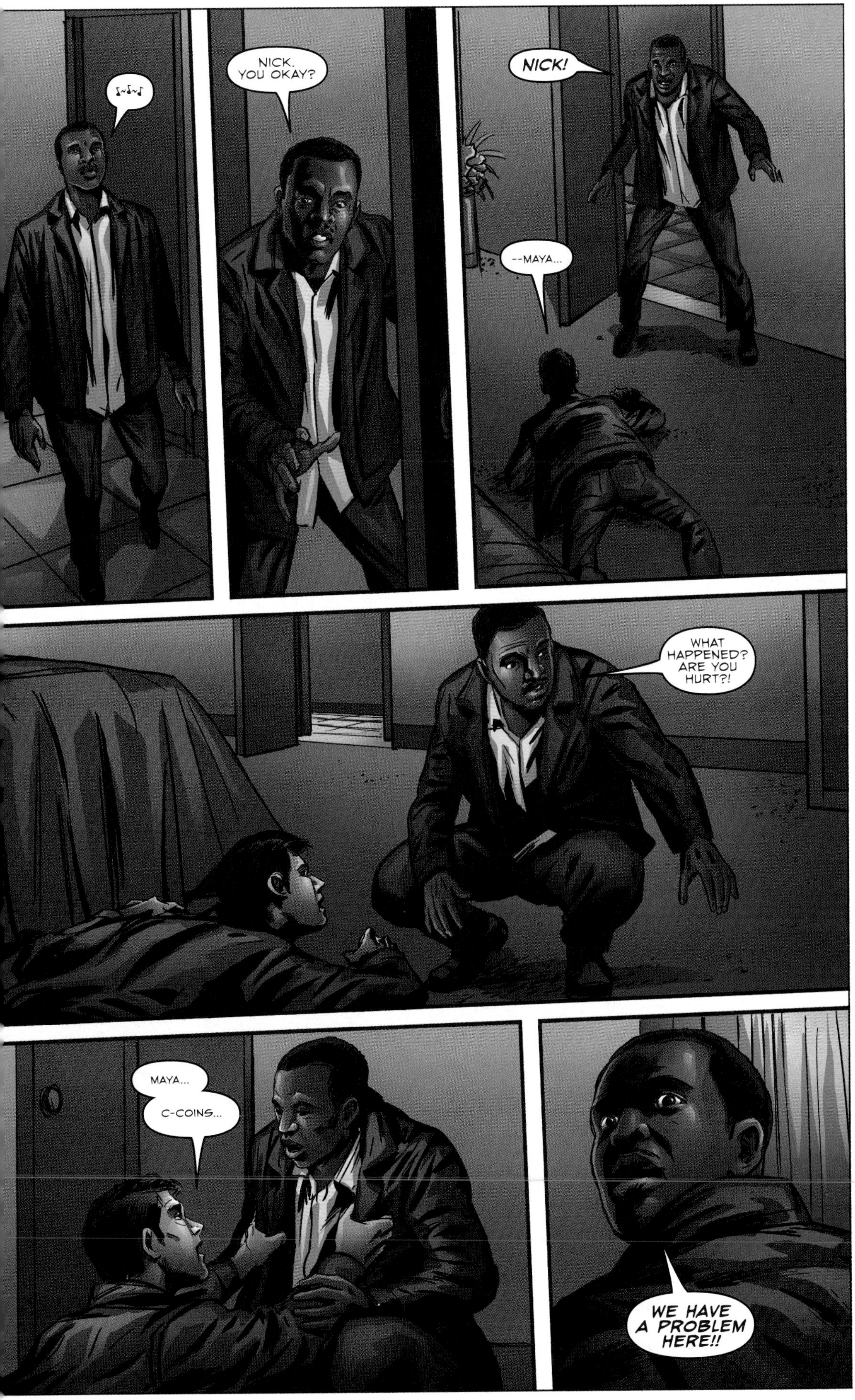

NICK. YOU OKAY?
NICK!
--MAYA...
WHAT HAPPENED? ARE YOU HURT?!
MAYA...
C-COINS...
WE HAVE A PROBLEM HERE!!

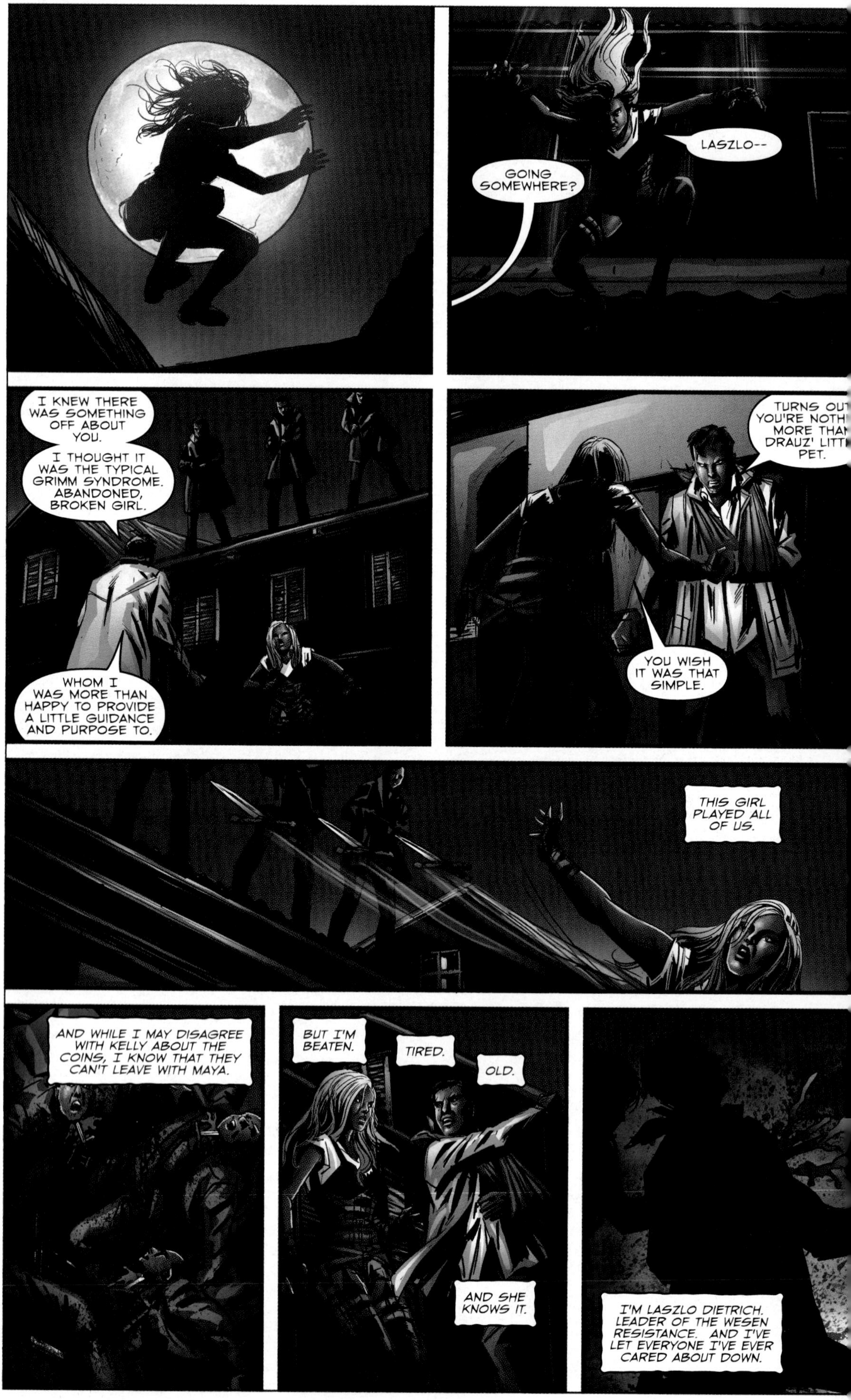
LASZLO--
GOING SOMEWHERE?
I KNEW THERE WAS SOMETHING OFF ABOUT YOU.
I THOUGHT IT WAS THE TYPICAL GRIMM SYNDROME. ABANDONED, BROKEN GIRL.
WHOM I WAS MORE THAN HAPPY TO PROVIDE A LITTLE GUIDANCE AND PURPOSE TO.
TURNS OUT YOU'RE NOTH MORE THAN DRAUZ' LITT PET.
YOU WISH IT WAS THAT SIMPLE.
THIS GIRL PLAYED ALL OF US.
AND WHILE I MAY DISAGREE WITH KELLY ABOUT THE COINS, I KNOW THAT THEY CAN'T LEAVE WITH MAYA.
BUT I'M BEATEN.
TIRED.
OLD.
AND SHE KNOWS IT.
I'M LASZLO DIETRICH. LEADER OF THE WESEN RESISTANCE. AND I'VE LET EVERYONE I'VE EVER CARED ABOUT DOWN.

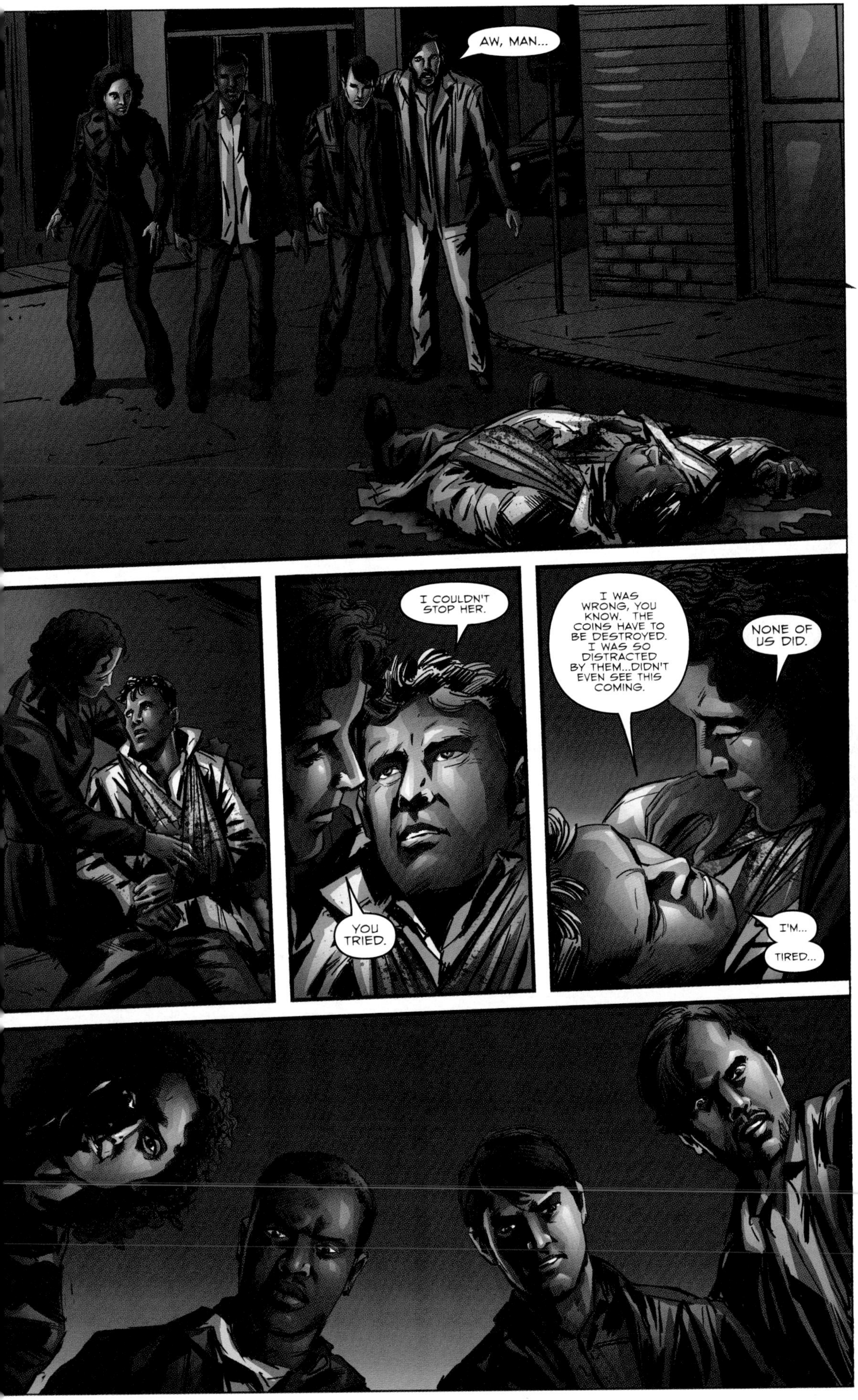
AW, MAN...
I COULDN'T STOP HER.
YOU TRIED.
I WAS WRONG, YOU KNOW. THE COINS HAVE TO BE DESTROYED. I WAS SO DISTRACTED BY THEM...DIDN'T EVEN SEE THIS COMING.
NONE OF US DID.
I'M...
TIRED...

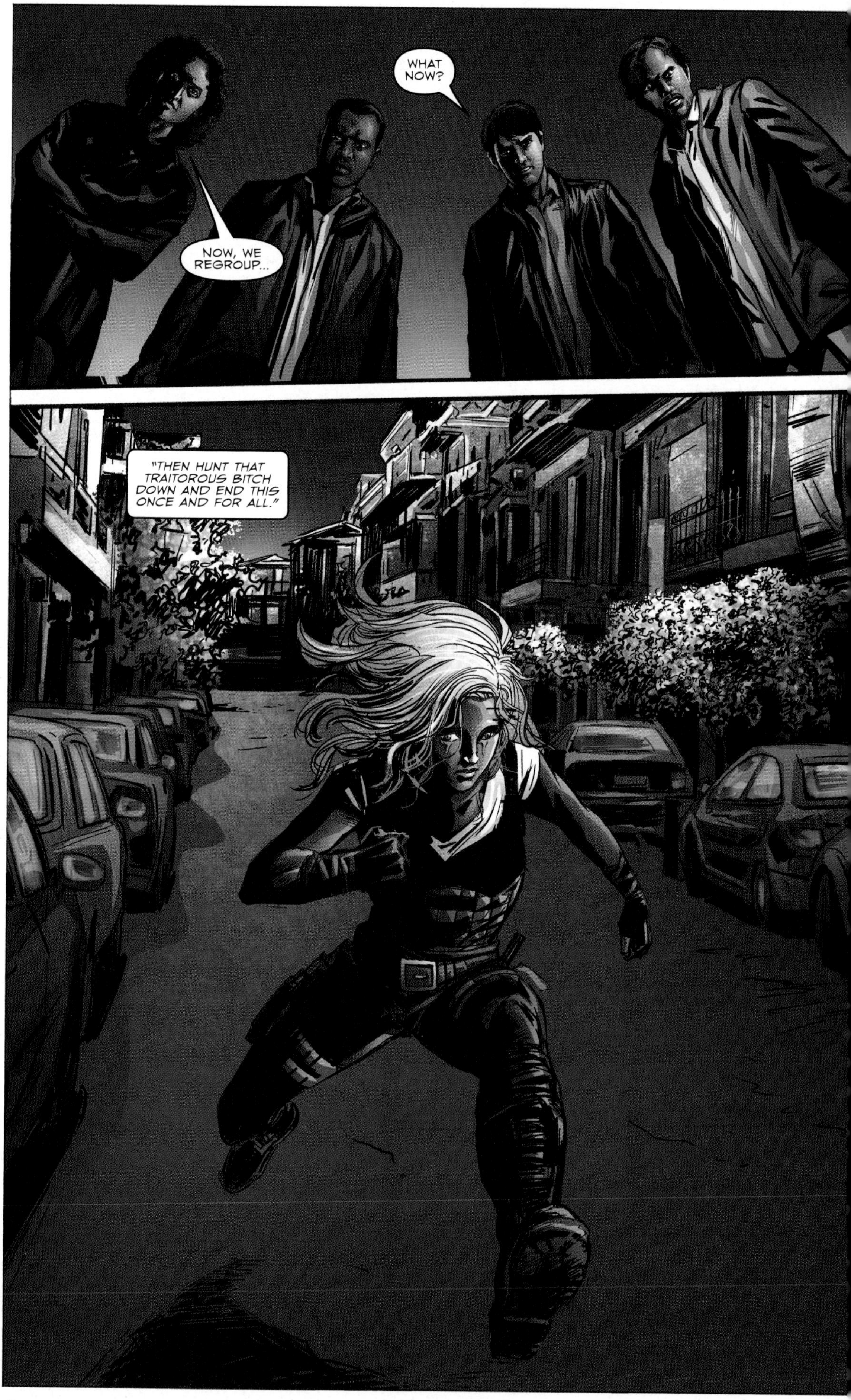
WHAT NOW?
NOW, WE REGROUP...
"THEN HUNT THAT TRAITOROUS BITCH DOWN AND END THIS ONCE AND FOR ALL."

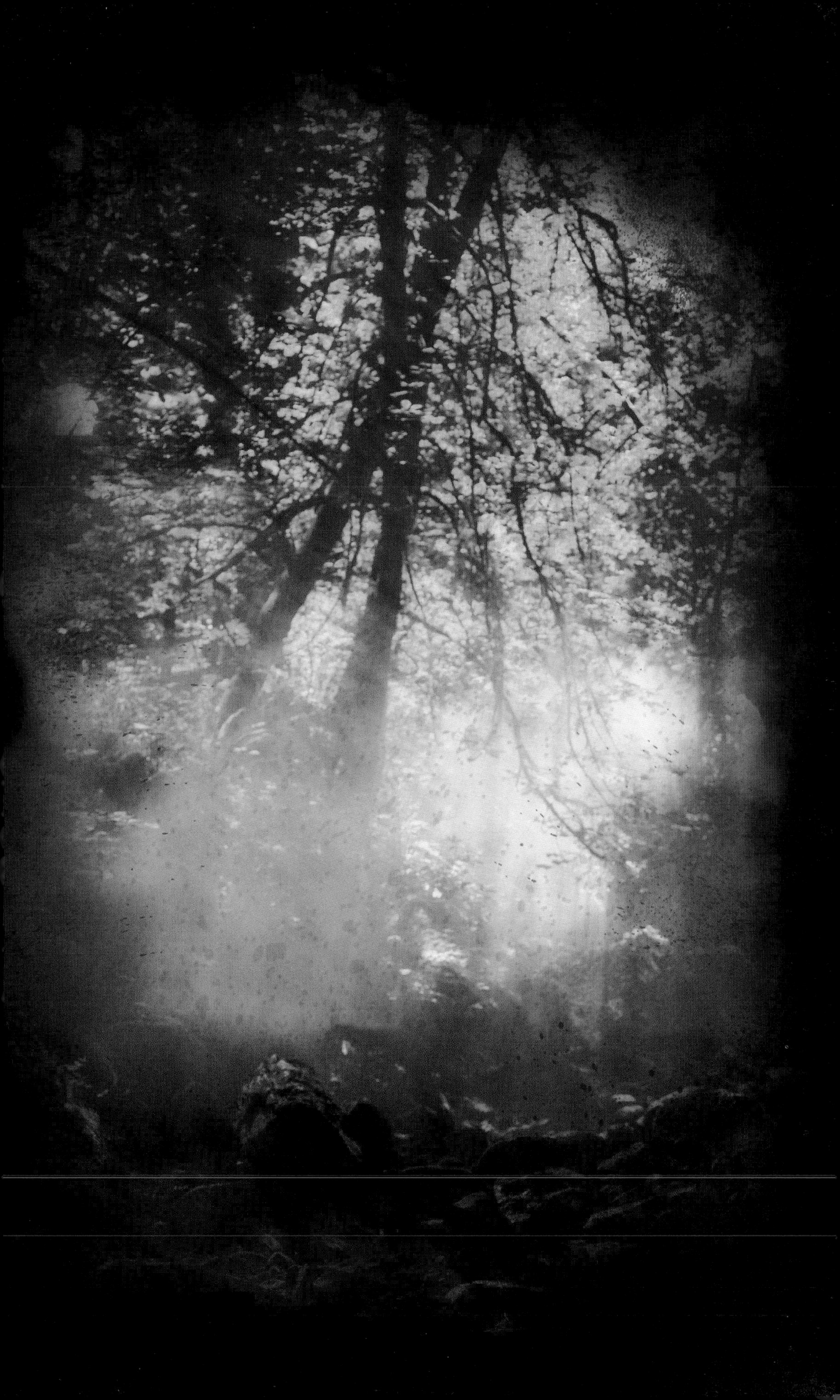

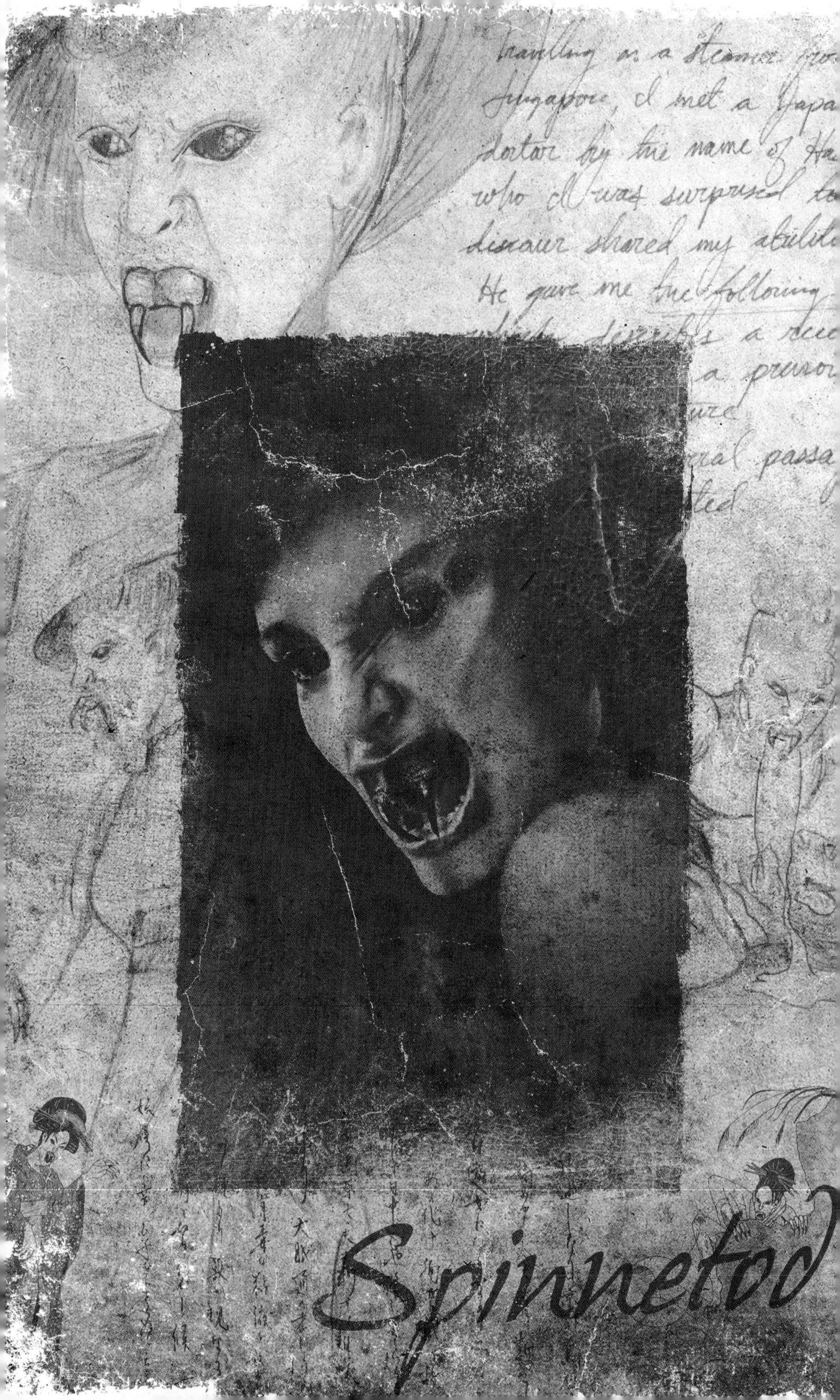
travelling on a steamer fro
Singapore, I met a Japa
doctor by the name of Ha
who I was surprised to
discover shared my abiliti
He gave me the following
Spinnetod

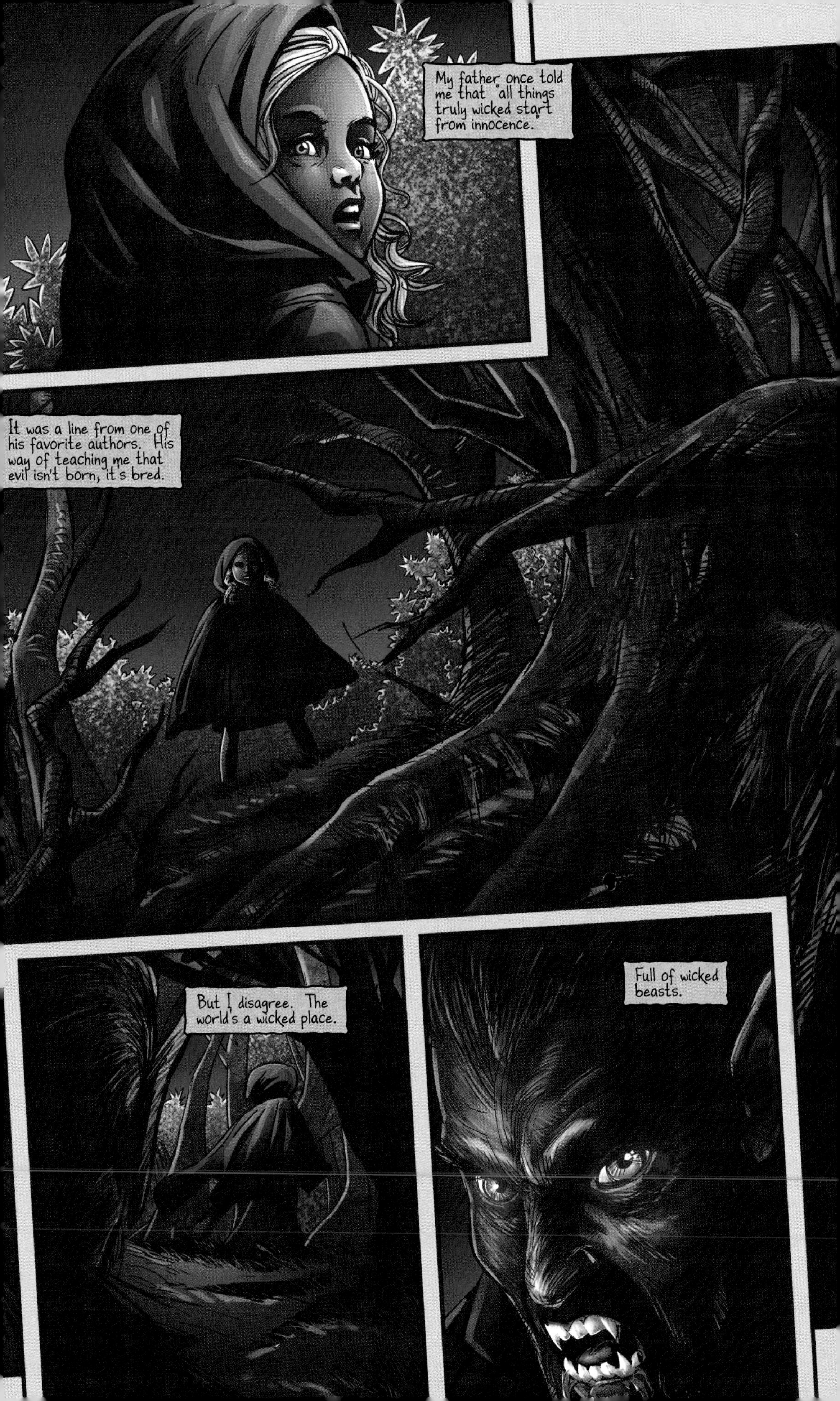
My father once told me that "all things truly wicked start from innocence."
It was a line from one of his favorite authors. His way of teaching me that evil isn't born, it's bred.
But I disagree. The world's a wicked place.
Full of wicked beasts.

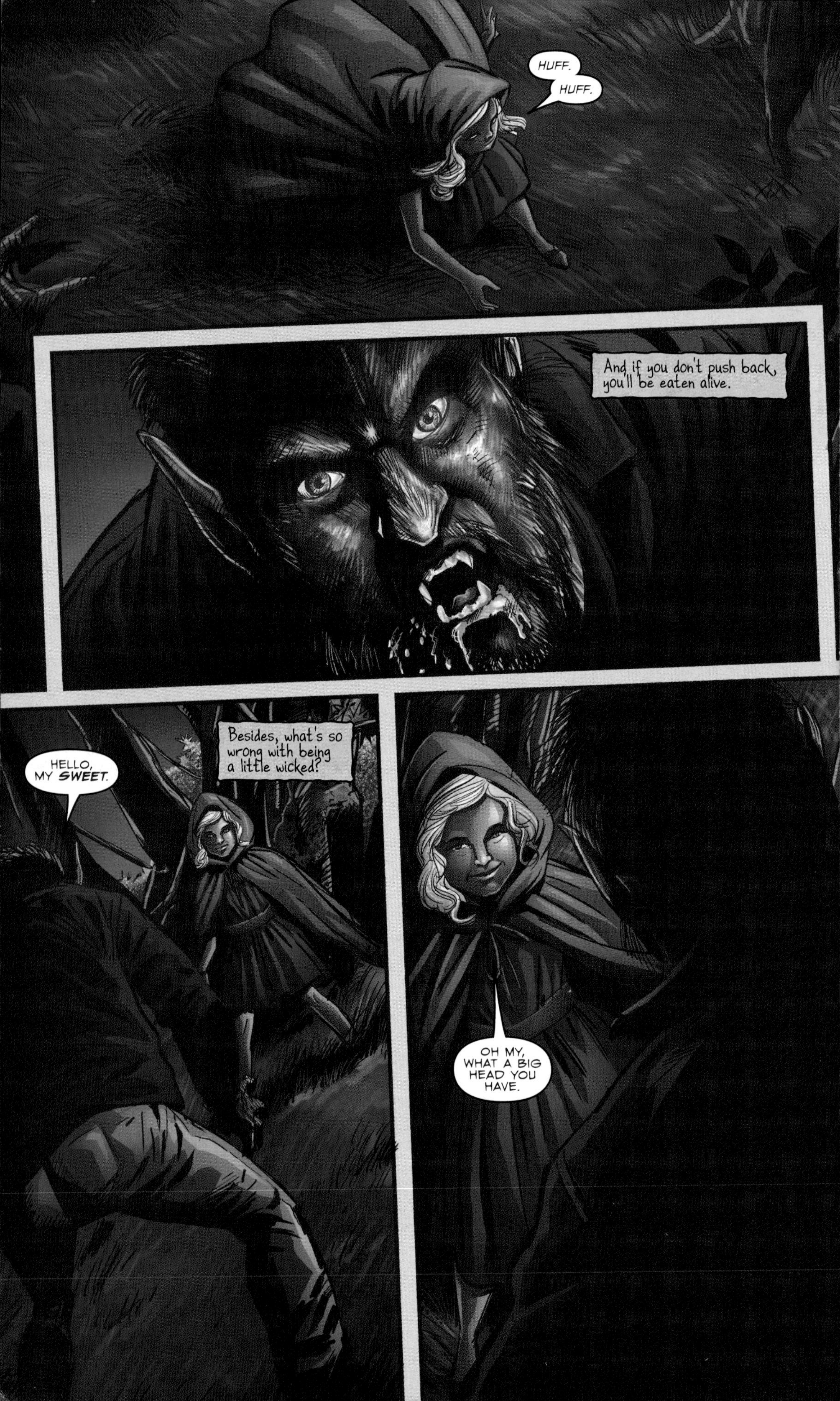
HUFF.
HUFF.
And if you don't push back, you'll be eaten alive.
Besides, what's so wrong with being a little wicked?
HELLO, MY SWEET.
OH MY, WHAT A BIG HEAD YOU HAVE.

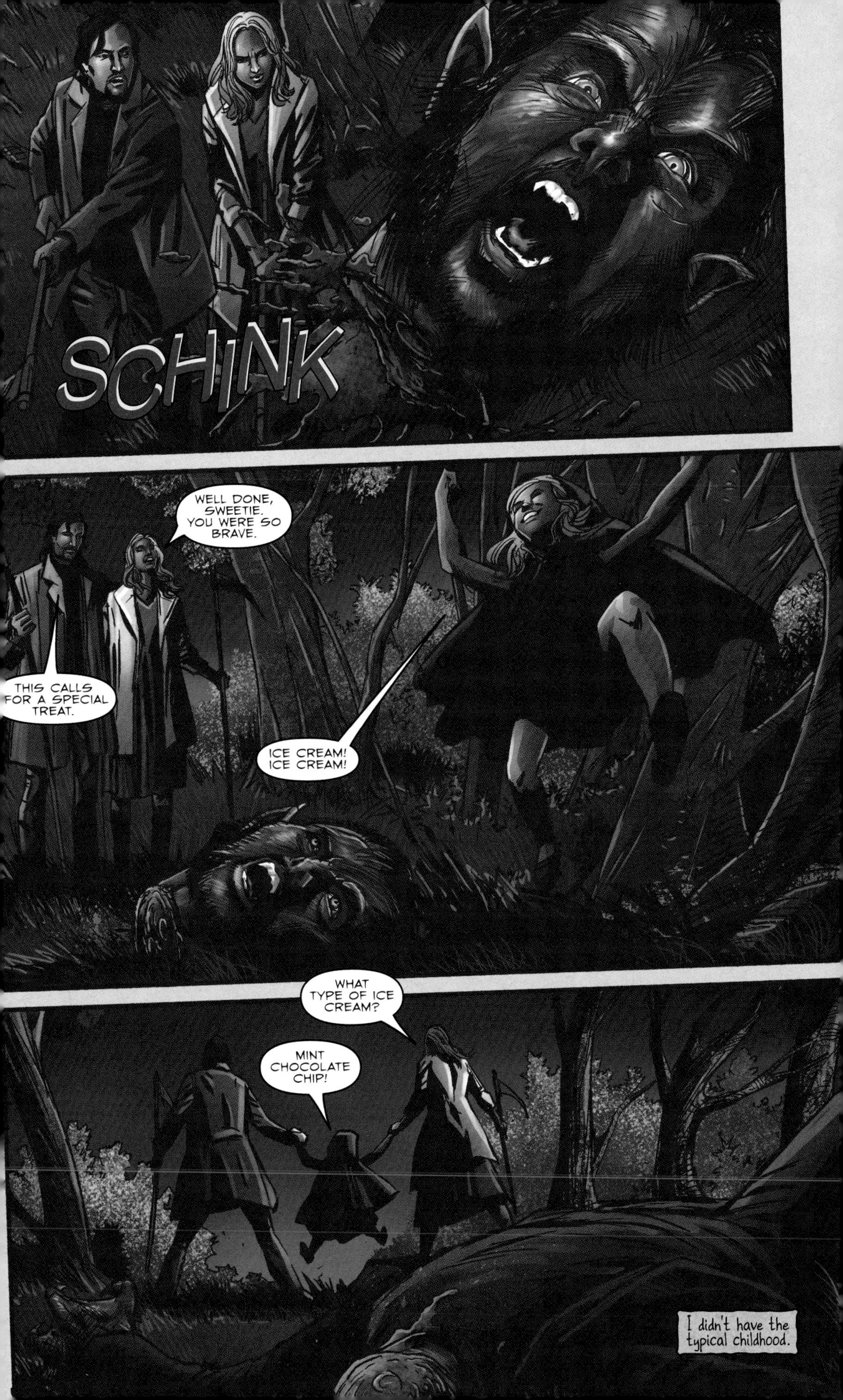
SCHINK
WELL DONE, SWEETIE. YOU WERE SO BRAVE.
THIS CALLS FOR A SPECIAL TREAT.
ICE CREAM! ICE CREAM!
WHAT TYPE OF ICE CREAM?
MINT CHOCOLATE CHIP!
I didn't have the typical childhood.

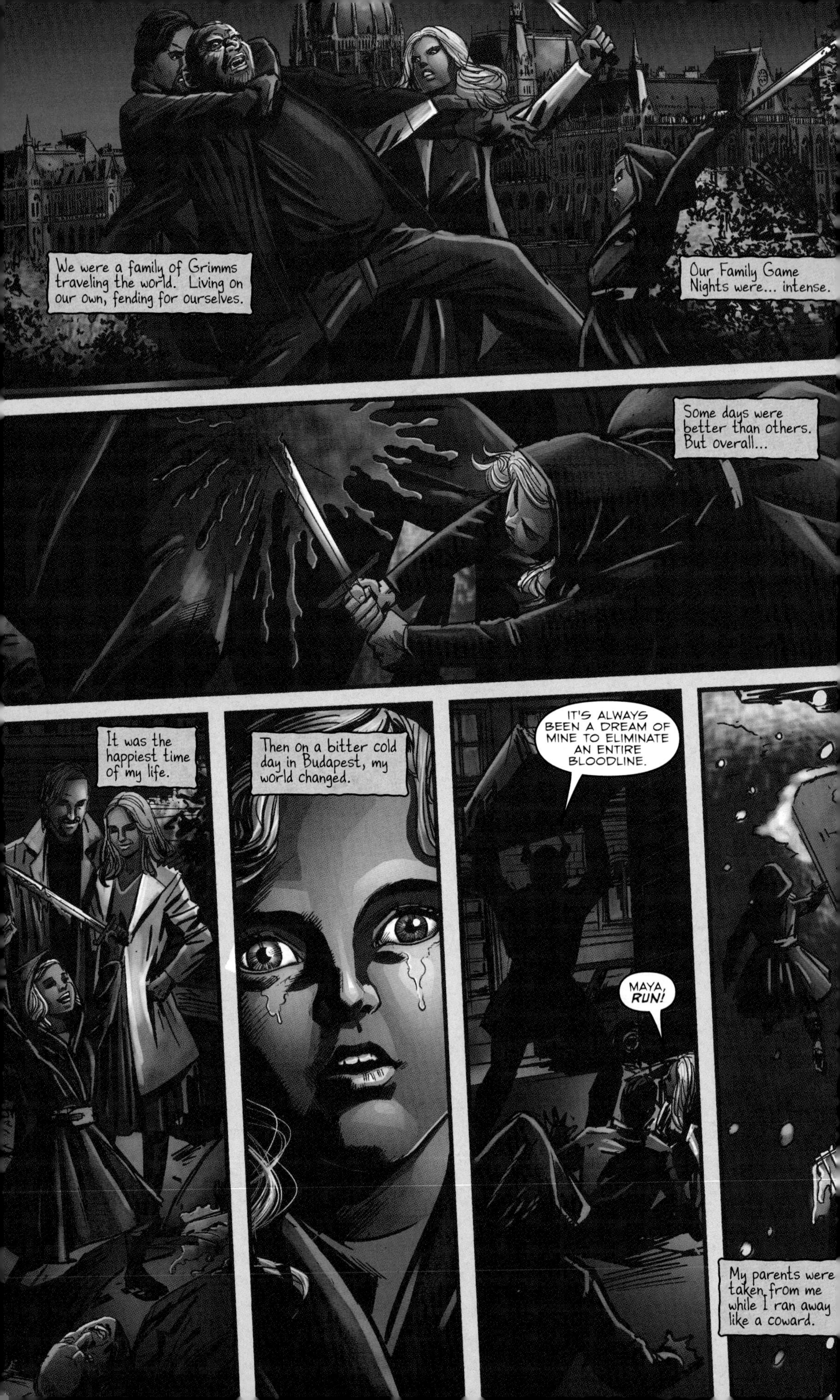
We were a family of Grimms traveling the world. Living on our own, fending for ourselves.
Our Family Game Nights were... intense.
Some days were better than others. But overall...
It was the happiest time of my life.
Then on a bitter cold day in Budapest, my world changed.
IT'S ALWAYS BEEN A DREAM OF MINE TO ELIMINATE AN ENTIRE BLOODLINE.
MAYA, RUN!
My parents were taken from me while I ran away like a coward.

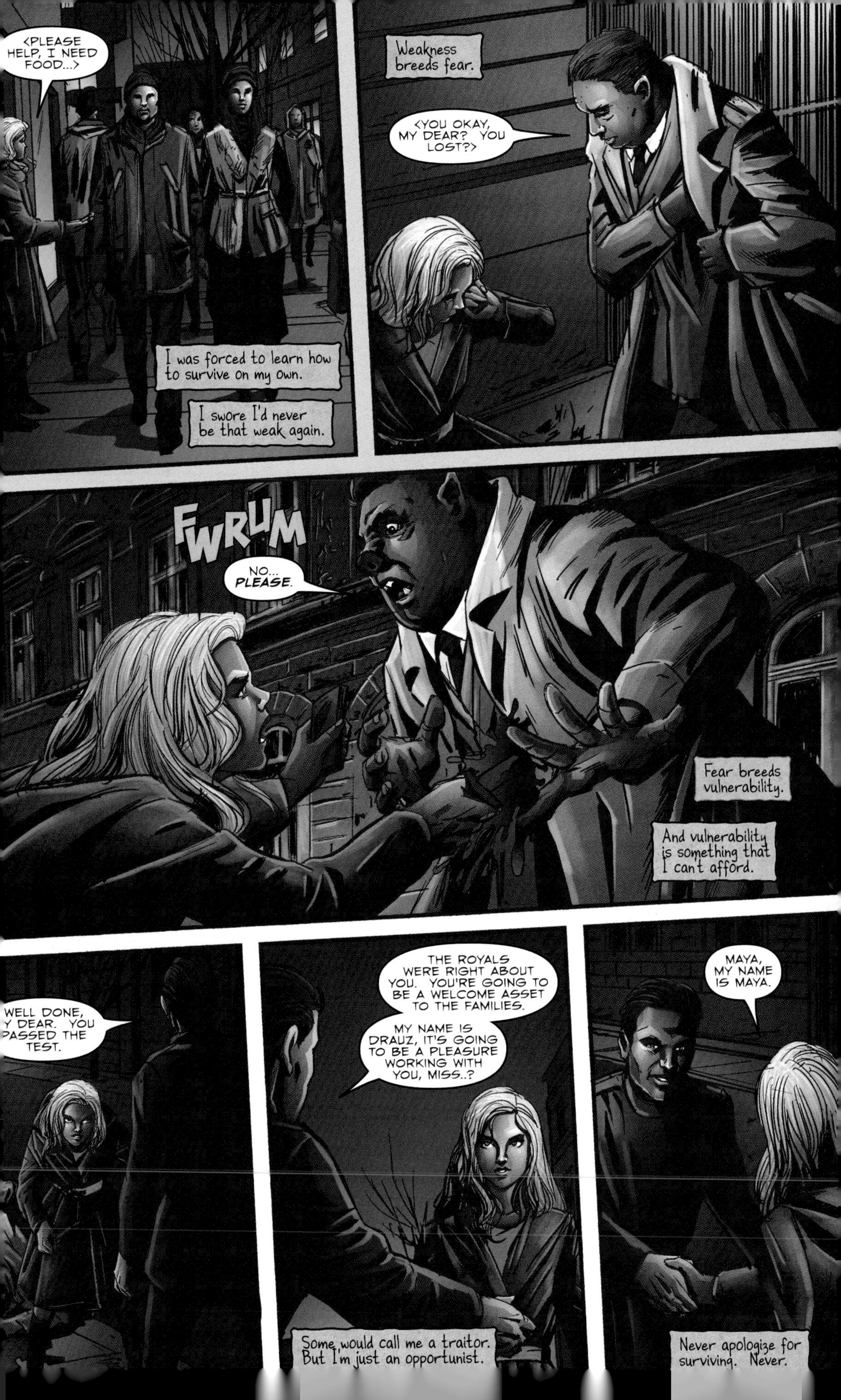

<PLEASE HELP, I NEED FOOD...>
I was forced to learn how to survive on my own.
I swore I'd never be that weak again.
Weakness breeds fear.
<YOU OKAY, MY DEAR? YOU LOST?>
FWRUM
NO... PLEASE.
Fear breeds vulnerability.
And vulnerability is something that I can't afford.
WELL DONE, Y DEAR. YOU PASSED THE TEST.
THE ROYALS WERE RIGHT ABOUT YOU. YOU'RE GOING TO BE A WELCOME ASSET TO THE FAMILIES.
MY NAME IS DRAUZ, IT'S GOING TO BE A PLEASURE WORKING WITH YOU, MISS..?
Some would call me a traitor. But I'm just an opportunist.
MAYA, MY NAME IS MAYA.
Never apologize for surviving. Never.

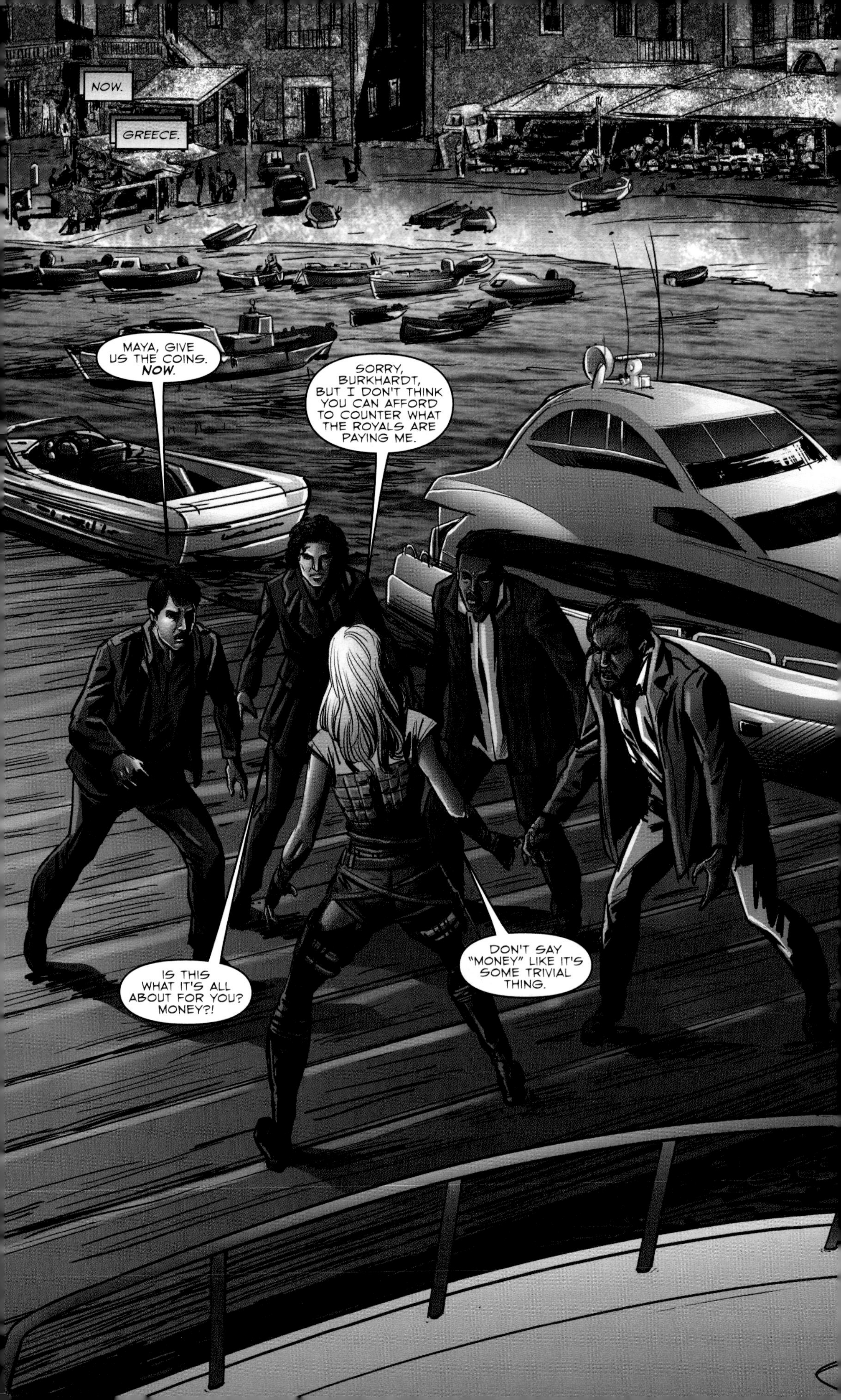
NOW.
GREECE.
MAYA, GIVE US THE COINS. **NOW**.
SORRY, BURKHARDT, BUT I DON'T THINK YOU CAN AFFORD TO COUNTER WHAT THE ROYALS ARE PAYING ME.
IS THIS WHAT IT'S ALL ABOUT FOR YOU? MONEY?!
DON'T SAY "MONEY" LIKE IT'S SOME TRIVIAL THING.

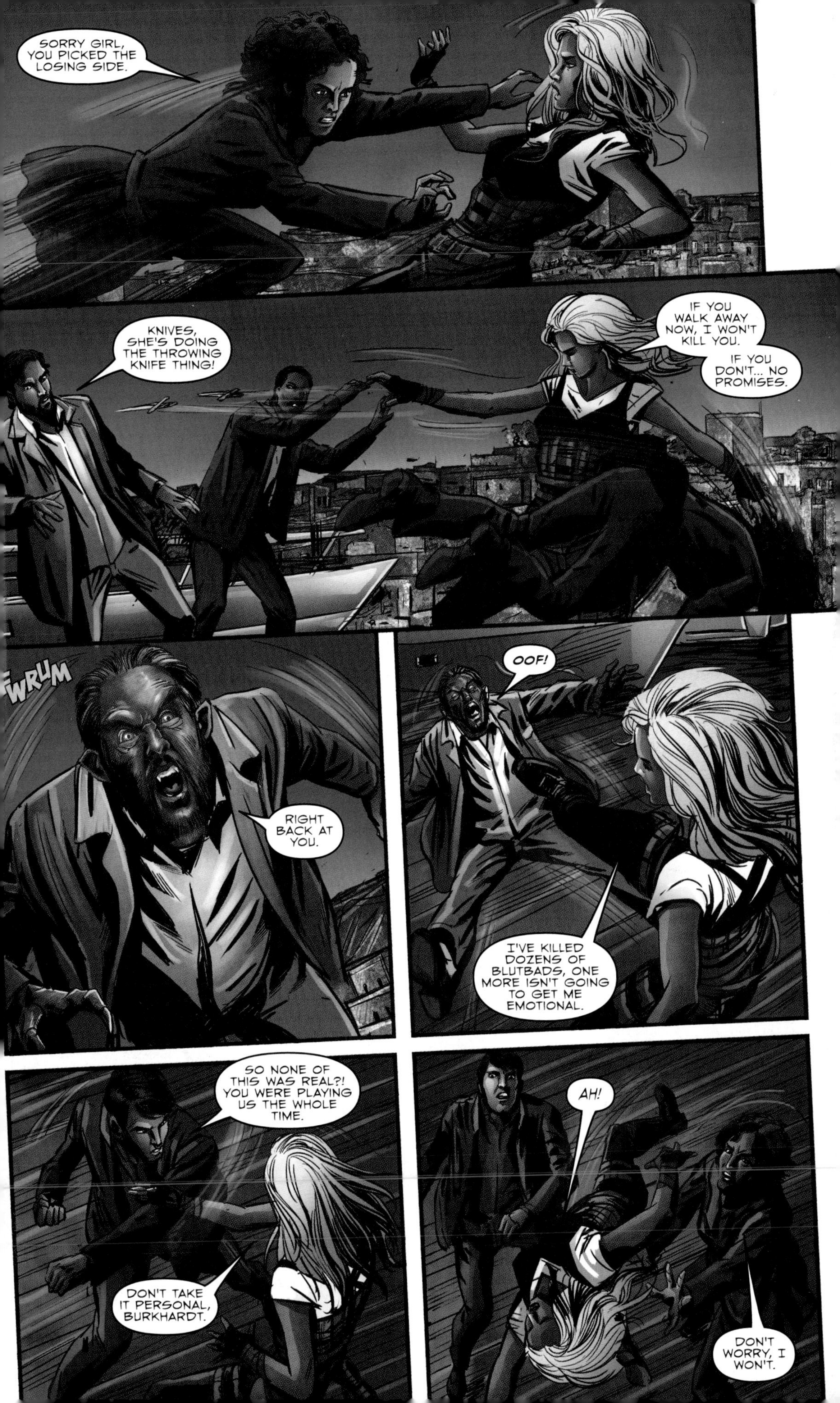
SORRY GIRL, YOU PICKED THE LOSING SIDE.
KNIVES, SHE'S DOING THE THROWING KNIFE THING!
IF YOU WALK AWAY NOW, I WON'T KILL YOU.
IF YOU DON'T... NO PROMISES.
WRUM
RIGHT BACK AT YOU.
OOF!
I'VE KILLED DOZENS OF BLUTBADS, ONE MORE ISN'T GOING TO GET ME EMOTIONAL.
SO NONE OF THIS WAS REAL?! YOU WERE PLAYING US THE WHOLE TIME.
DON'T TAKE IT PERSONAL, BURKHARDT.
AH!
DON'T WORRY, I WON'T.

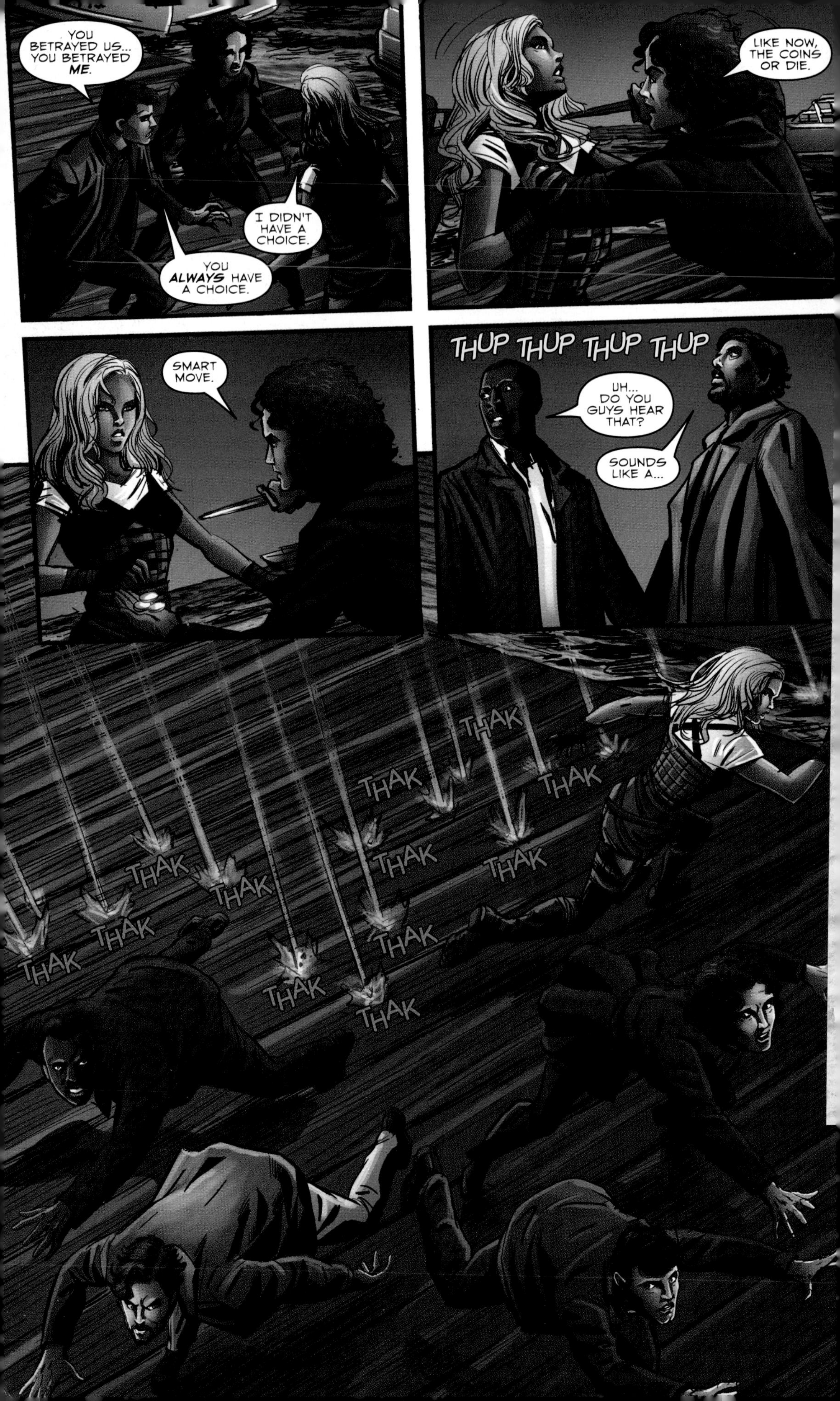
YOU BETRAYED US... YOU BETRAYED ME.
I DIDN'T HAVE A CHOICE.
YOU ALWAYS HAVE A CHOICE.
LIKE NOW, THE COINS OR DIE.
SMART MOVE.
THUP THUP THUP THUP
UH... DO YOU GUYS HEAR THAT?
SOUNDS LIKE A...
THAK
THAK
THAK
THAK
THAK
THAK
THAK
THAK
THAK
THAK
THAK
THAK
THAK

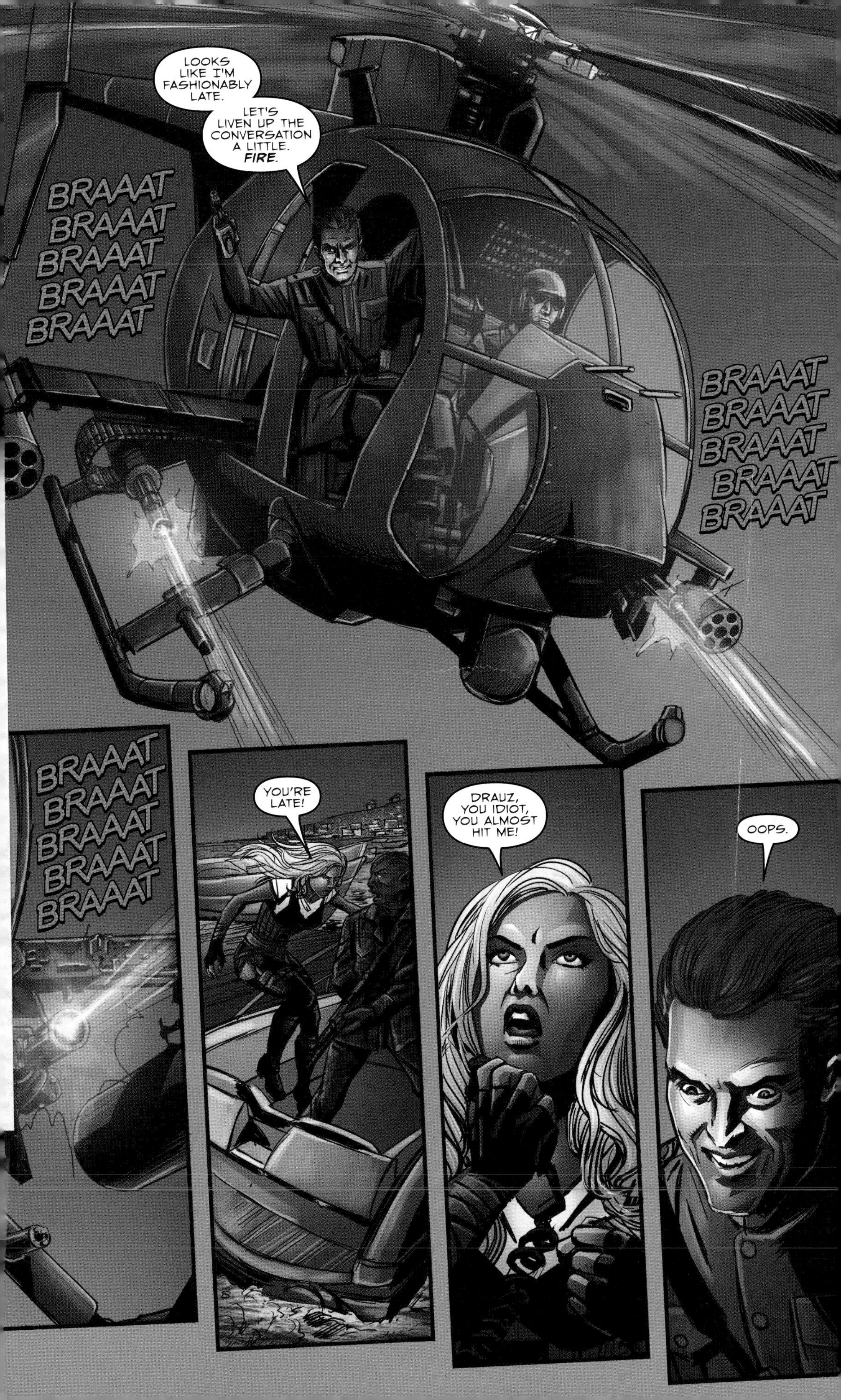
LOOKS LIKE I'M FASHIONABLY LATE.
LET'S LIVEN UP THE CONVERSATION A LITTLE. FIRE.
BRAAAT BRAAAT BRAAAT BRAAAT BRAAAT
BRAAAT BRAAAT BRAAAT BRAAAT BRAAAT
BRAAAT BRAAAT BRAAAT BRAAAT BRAAAT
YOU'RE LATE!
DRAUZ, YOU IDIOT, YOU ALMOST HIT ME!
OOPS.

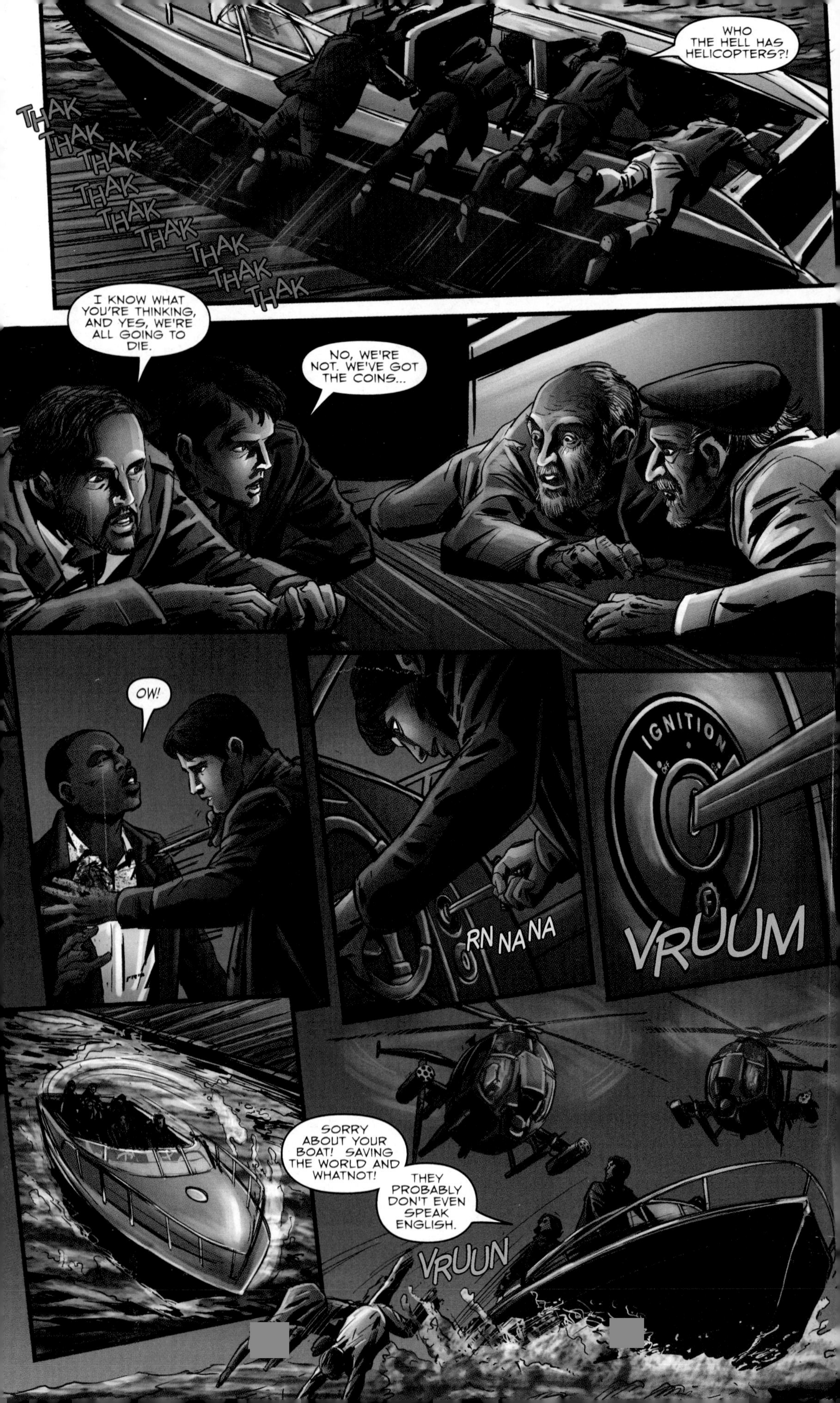
WHO THE HELL HAS HELICOPTERS?!
THAK THAK THAK THAK THAK THAK THAK THAK THAK
I KNOW WHAT YOU'RE THINKING, AND YES, WE'RE ALL GOING TO DIE.
NO, WE'RE NOT. WE'VE GOT THE COINS...
OW!
RN NA NA
IGNITION
VRUUM
SORRY ABOUT YOUR BOAT! SAVING THE WORLD AND WHATNOT!
THEY PROBABLY DON'T EVEN SPEAK ENGLISH.
VRUUN

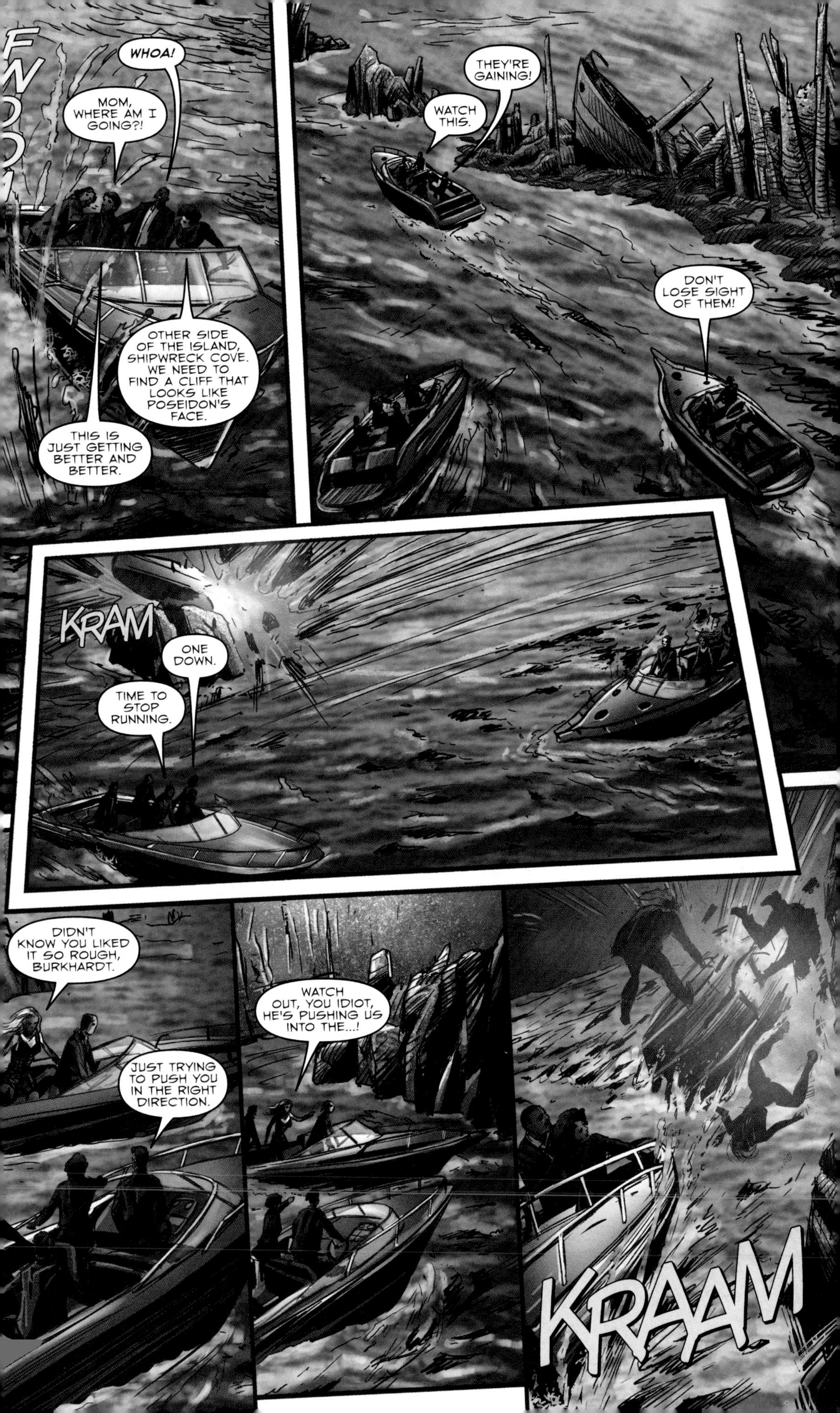
WHOA!
MOM, WHERE AM I GOING?!
OTHER SIDE OF THE ISLAND, SHIPWRECK COVE. WE NEED TO FIND A CLIFF THAT LOOKS LIKE POSEIDON'S FACE.
THIS IS JUST GETTING BETTER AND BETTER.
THEY'RE GAINING!
WATCH THIS.
DON'T LOSE SIGHT OF THEM!
KRAM
ONE DOWN.
TIME TO STOP RUNNING.
DIDN'T KNOW YOU LIKED IT SO ROUGH, BURKHARDT.
JUST TRYING TO PUSH YOU IN THE RIGHT DIRECTION.
WATCH OUT, YOU IDIOT, HE'S PUSHING US INTO THE...!
KRAAM

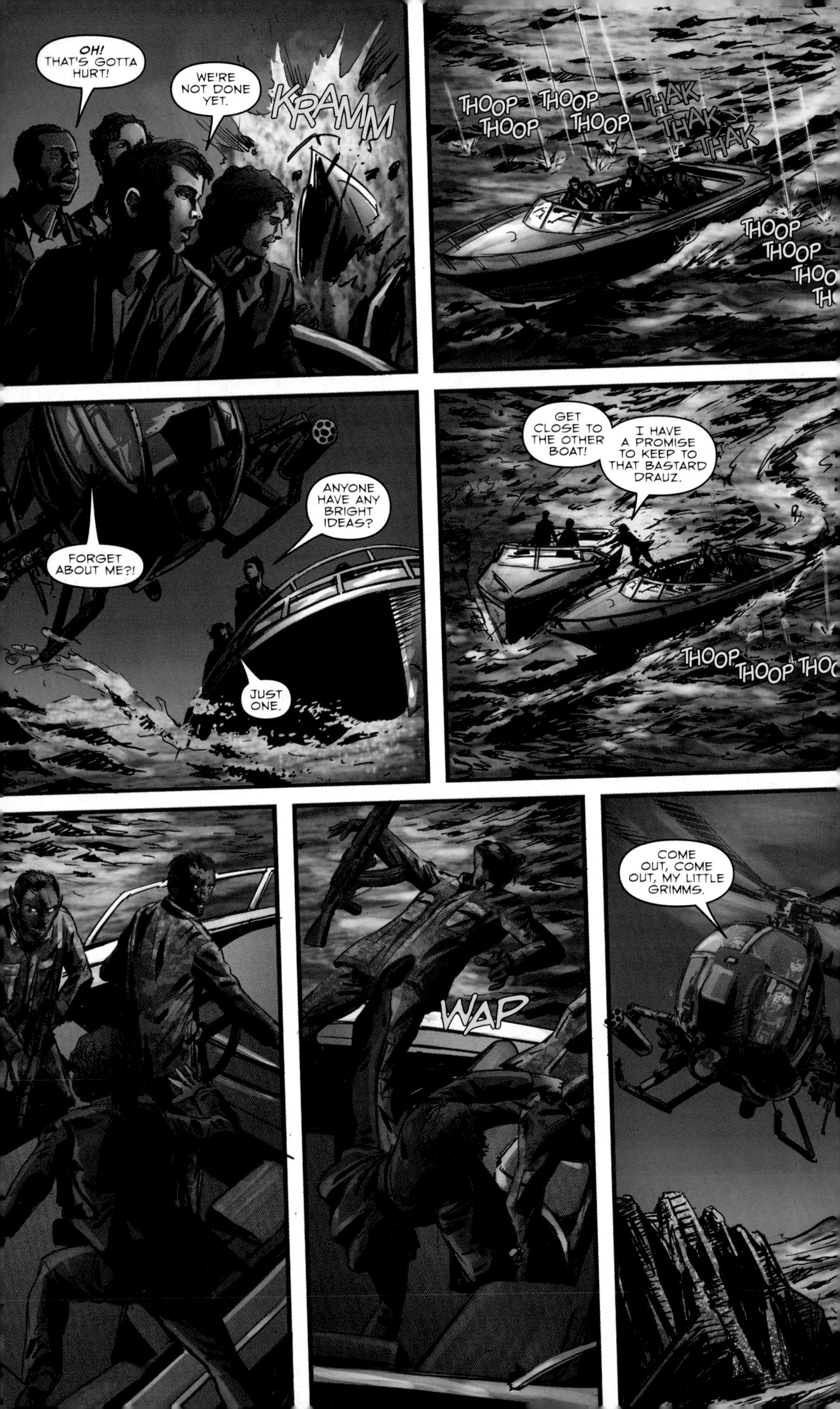
OH! THAT'S GOTTA HURT!
WE'RE NOT DONE YET.
KRAMM
THOOP THOOP
THOOP THOOP
THAK THAK THAK
THOOP THOOP THOO TH
FORGET ABOUT ME?!
ANYONE HAVE ANY BRIGHT IDEAS?
JUST ONE.
GET CLOSE TO THE OTHER BOAT!
I HAVE A PROMISE TO KEEP TO THAT BASTARD DRAUZ.
THOOP THOOP THOO
WAP
COME OUT, COME OUT, MY LITTLE GRIMMS.

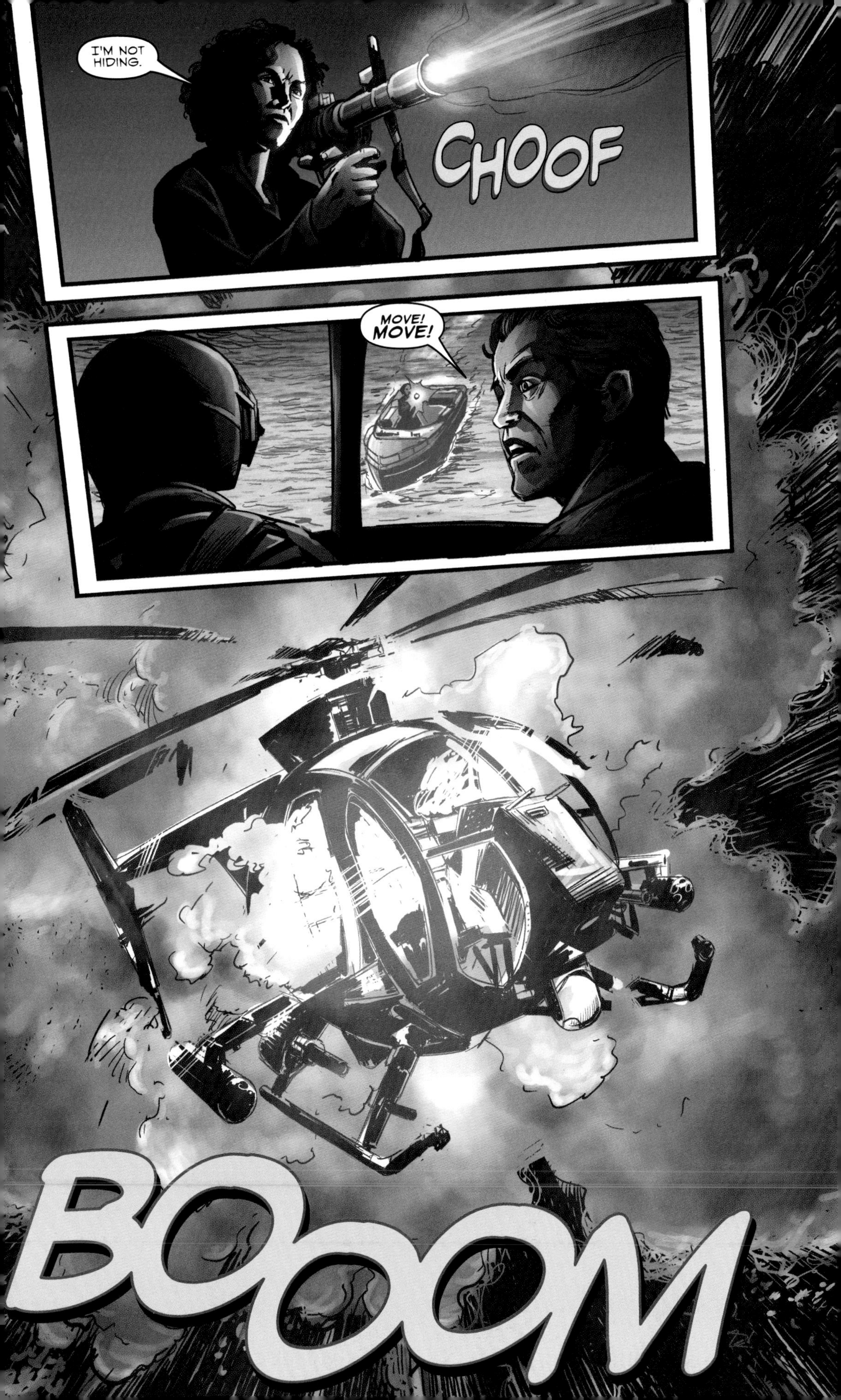
I'M NOT HIDING.
CHOOF
MOVE! MOVE!
BOOOM

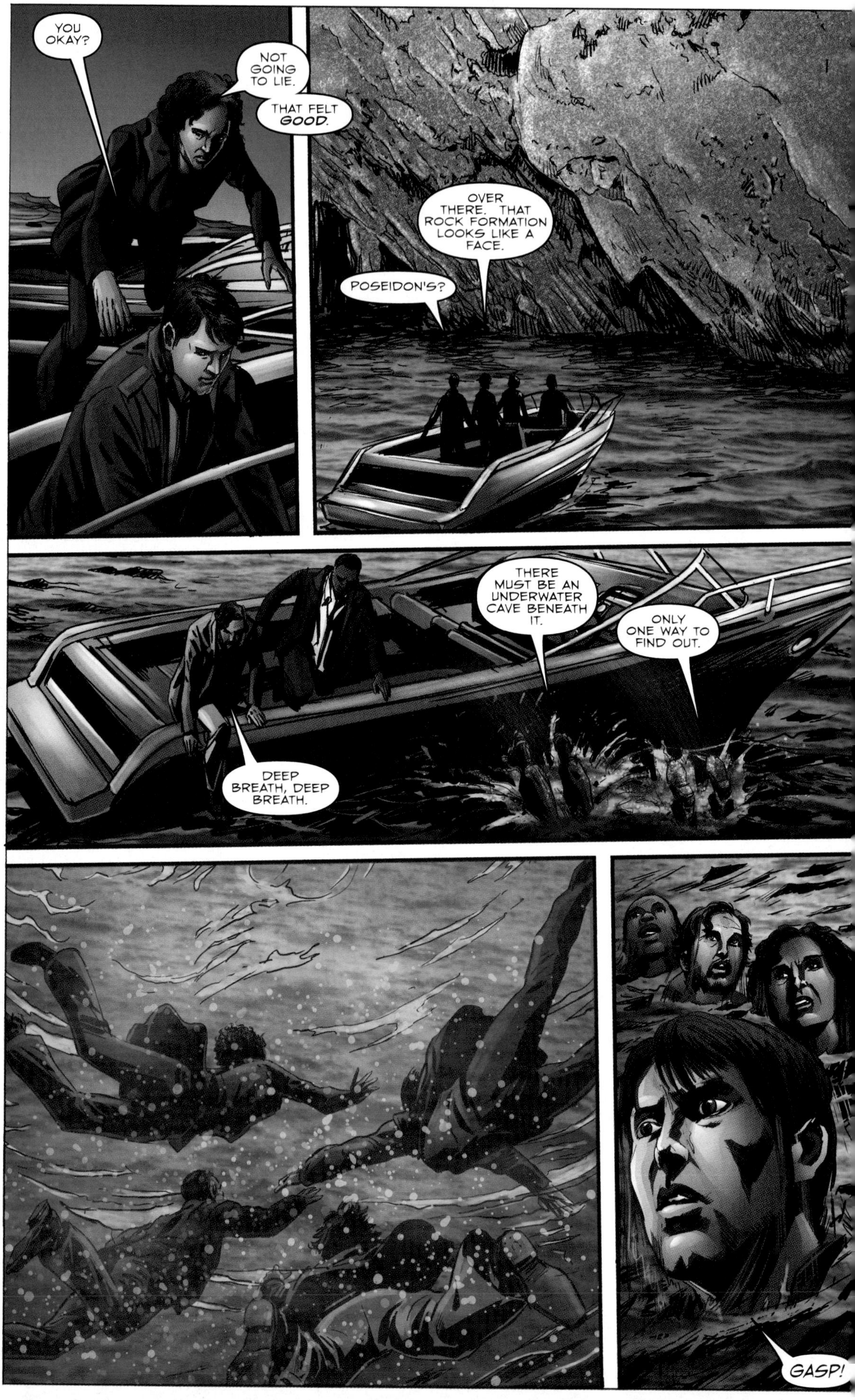

YOU OKAY?
NOT GOING TO LIE.
THAT FELT *GOOD*.
OVER THERE. THAT ROCK FORMATION LOOKS LIKE A FACE.
POSEIDON'S?
THERE MUST BE AN UNDERWATER CAVE BENEATH IT.
ONLY ONE WAY TO FIND OUT.
DEEP BREATH, DEEP BREATH.
GASP!

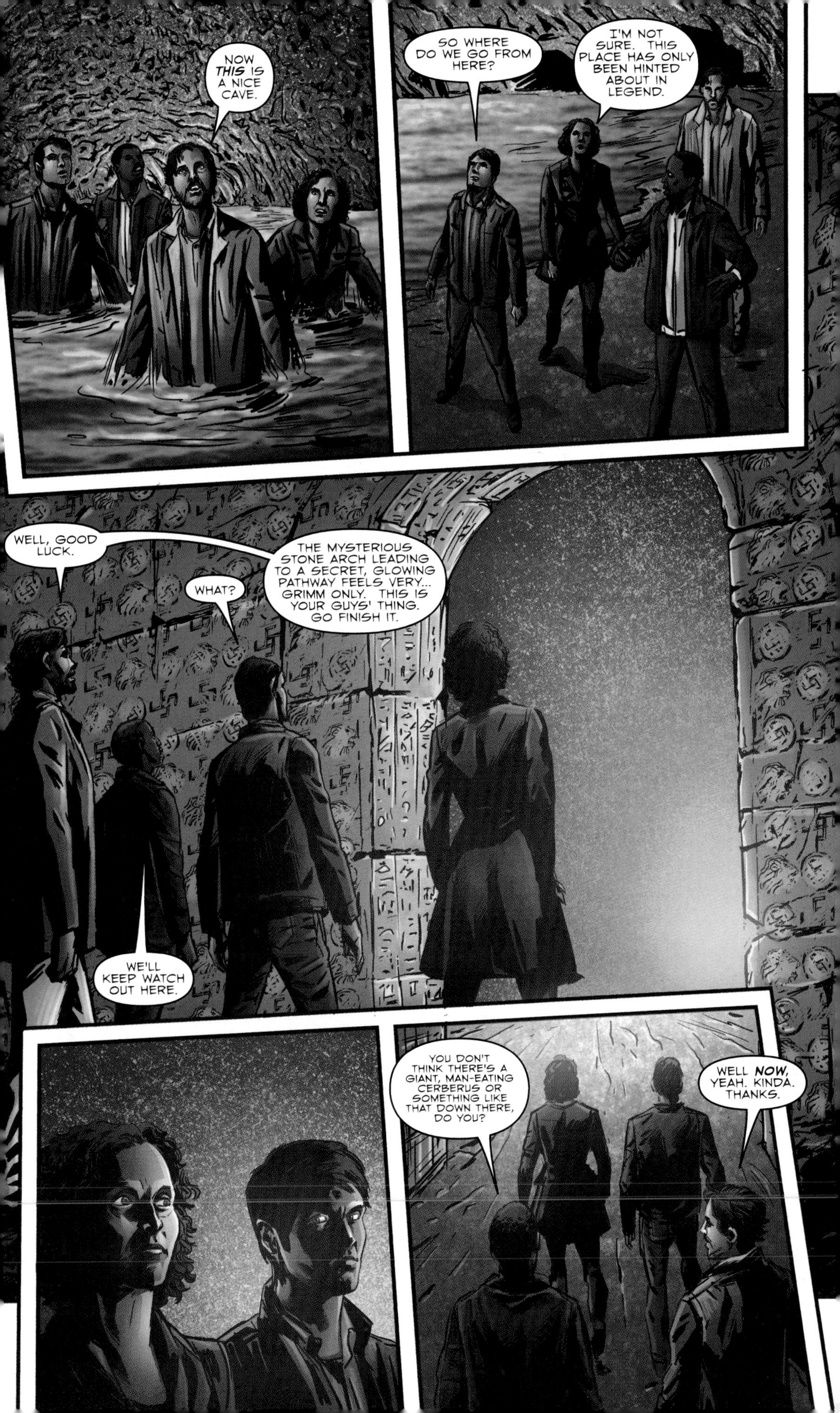
NOW *THIS* IS A NICE CAVE.
SO WHERE DO WE GO FROM HERE?
I'M NOT SURE. THIS PLACE HAS ONLY BEEN HINTED ABOUT IN LEGEND.
WELL, GOOD LUCK.
WHAT?
THE MYSTERIOUS STONE ARCH LEADING TO A SECRET, GLOWING PATHWAY FEELS VERY... GRIMM ONLY. THIS IS YOUR GUYS' THING. GO FINISH IT.
WE'LL KEEP WATCH OUT HERE.
YOU DON'T THINK THERE'S A GIANT, MAN-EATING CERBERUS OR SOMETHING LIKE THAT DOWN THERE, DO YOU?
WELL *NOW,* YEAH. KINDA. THANKS.

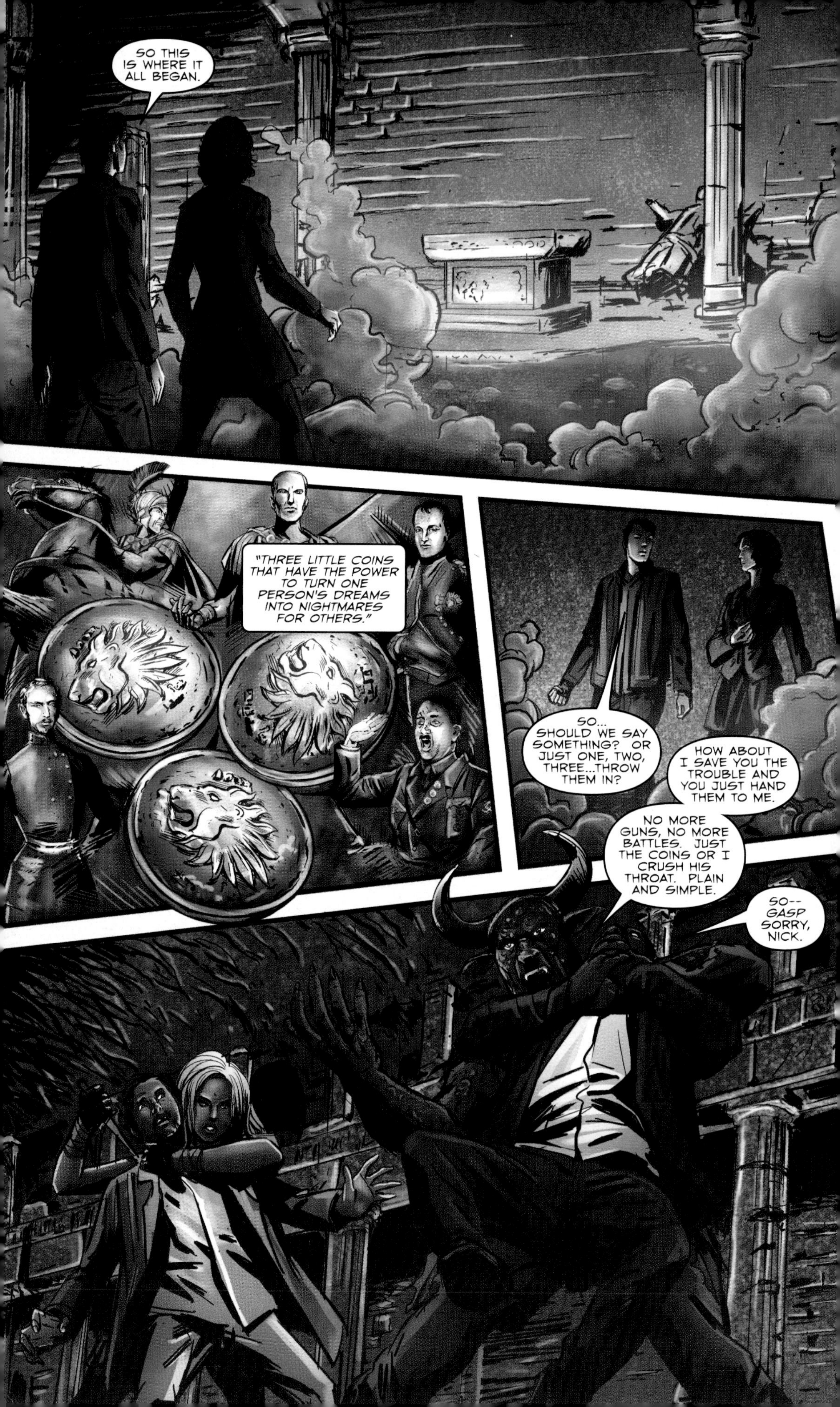
SO THIS IS WHERE IT ALL BEGAN.
"THREE LITTLE COINS THAT HAVE THE POWER TO TURN ONE PERSON'S DREAMS INTO NIGHTMARES FOR OTHERS."
SO... SHOULD WE SAY SOMETHING? OR JUST ONE, TWO, THREE...THROW THEM IN?
HOW ABOUT I SAVE YOU THE TROUBLE AND YOU JUST HAND THEM TO ME.
NO MORE GUNS, NO MORE BATTLES. JUST THE COINS OR I CRUSH HIS THROAT. PLAIN AND SIMPLE.
SO-- GASP SORRY, NICK.

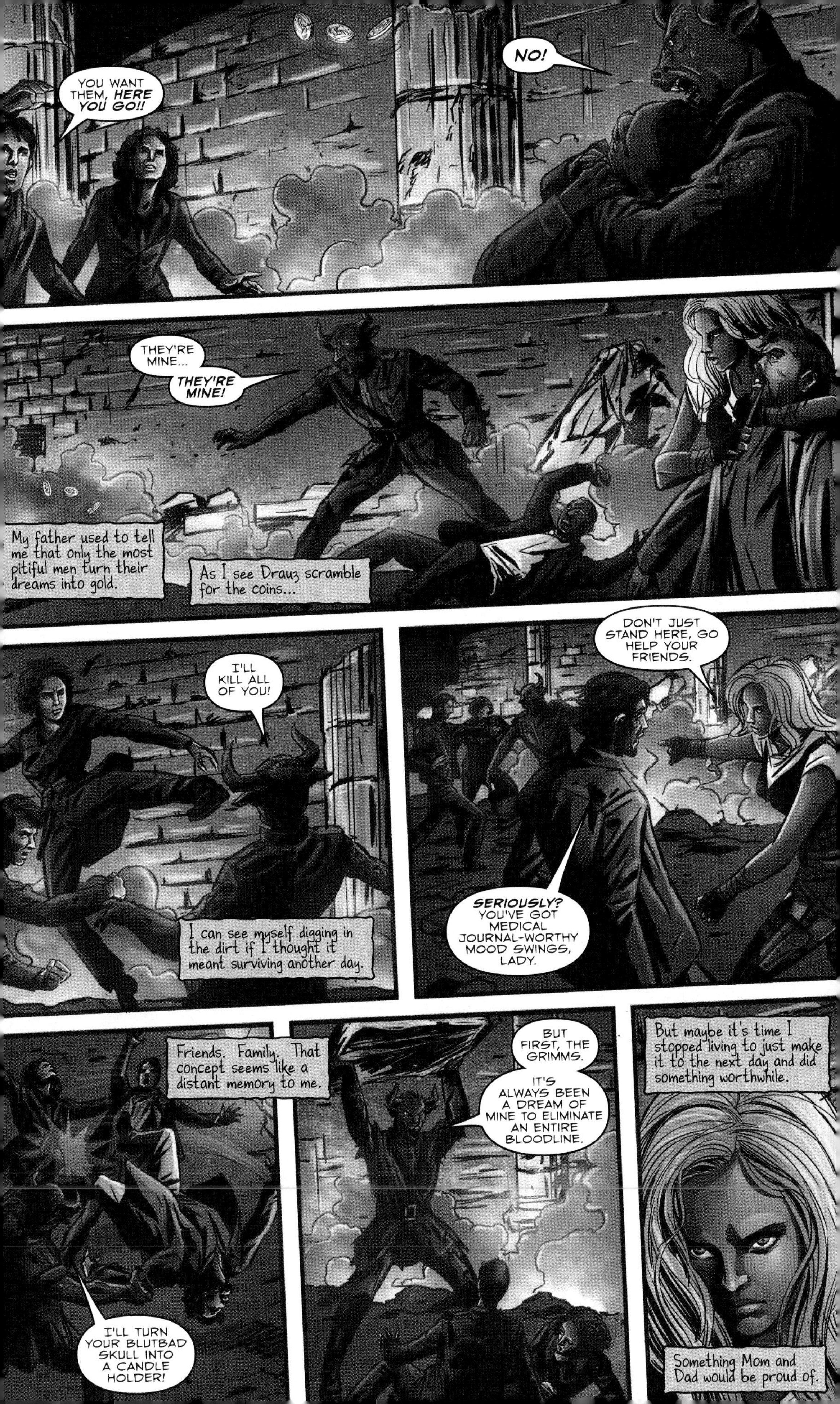
YOU WANT THEM, HERE YOU GO!!
NO!
THEY'RE MINE... THEY'RE MINE!
My father used to tell me that only the most pitiful men turn their dreams into gold.
As I see Drauz scramble for the coins...
I'LL KILL ALL OF YOU!
I can see myself digging in the dirt if I thought it meant surviving another day.
DON'T JUST STAND HERE, GO HELP YOUR FRIENDS.
SERIOUSLY? YOU'VE GOT MEDICAL JOURNAL-WORTHY MOOD SWINGS, LADY.
Friends. Family. That concept seems like a distant memory to me.
I'LL TURN YOUR BLUTBAD SKULL INTO A CANDLE HOLDER!
BUT FIRST, THE GRIMMS.
IT'S ALWAYS BEEN A DREAM OF MINE TO ELIMINATE AN ENTIRE BLOODLINE.
But maybe it's time I stopped living to just make it to the next day and did something worthwhile.
Something Mom and Dad would be proud of.

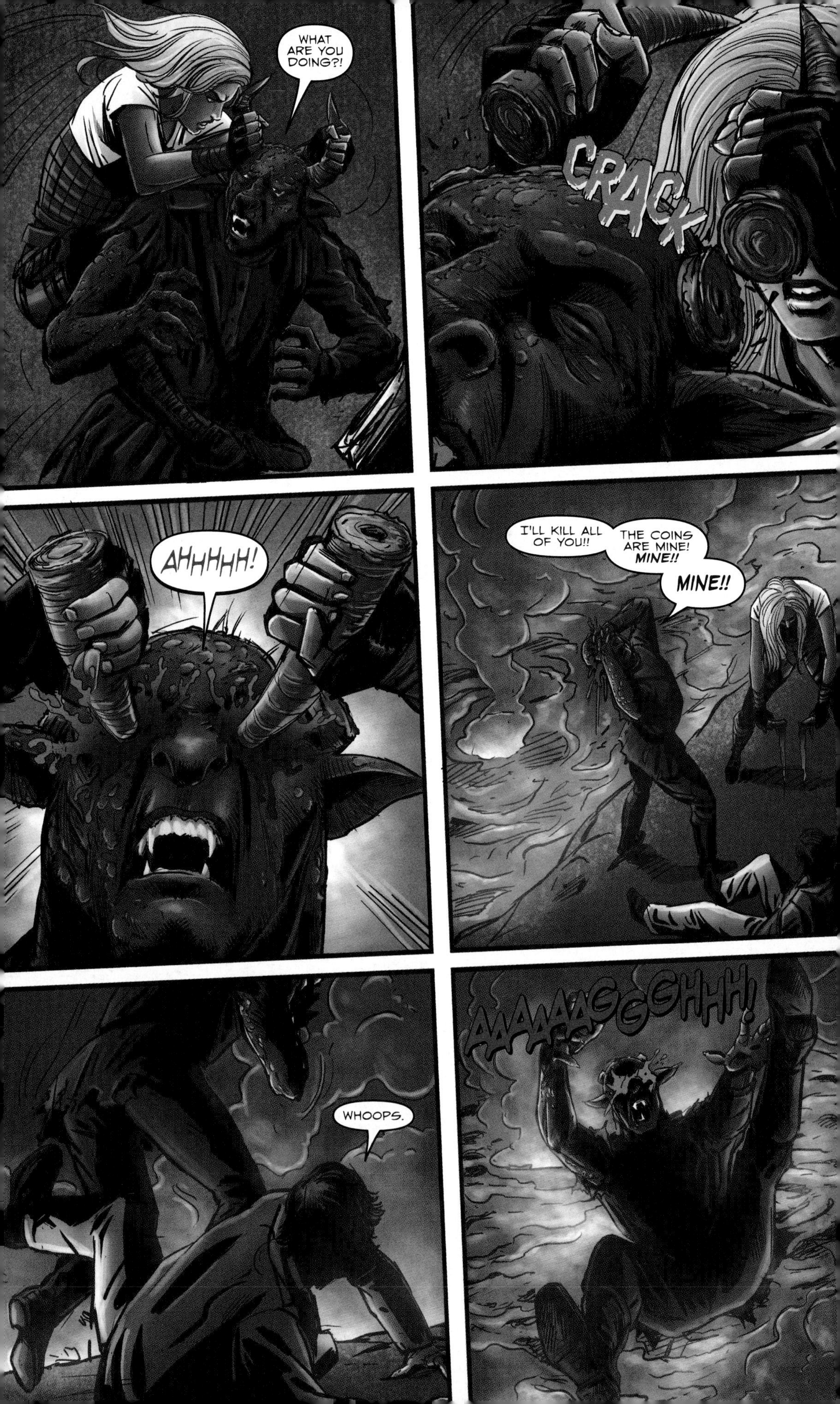
WHAT ARE YOU DOING?!
CRACK
AHHHHH!
I'LL KILL ALL OF YOU!!
THE COINS ARE MINE! MINE!!
MINE!!
WHOOPS.
AAAAAAGGGHHH!

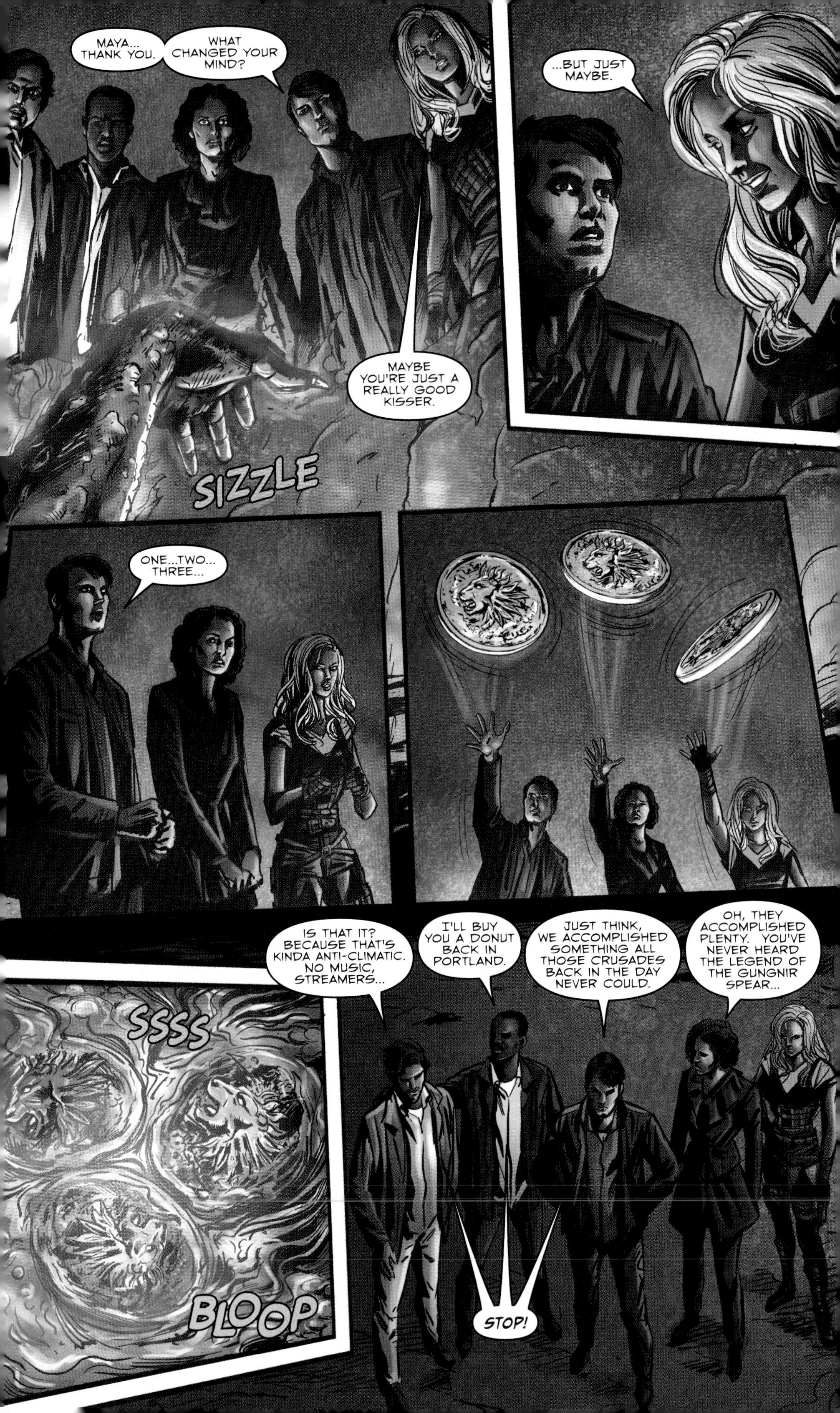
MAYA... THANK YOU.
WHAT CHANGED YOUR MIND?
MAYBE YOU'RE JUST A REALLY GOOD KISSER.
SIZZLE
...BUT JUST MAYBE.
ONE...TWO... THREE...
SSSS
BLOOP
IS THAT IT? BECAUSE THAT'S KINDA ANTI-CLIMATIC. NO MUSIC, STREAMERS...
I'LL BUY YOU A DONUT BACK IN PORTLAND.
JUST THINK, WE ACCOMPLISHED SOMETHING ALL THOSE CRUSADES BACK IN THE DAY NEVER COULD.
OH, THEY ACCOMPLISHED PLENTY. YOU'VE NEVER HEARD THE LEGEND OF THE GUNGNIR SPEAR...
STOP!

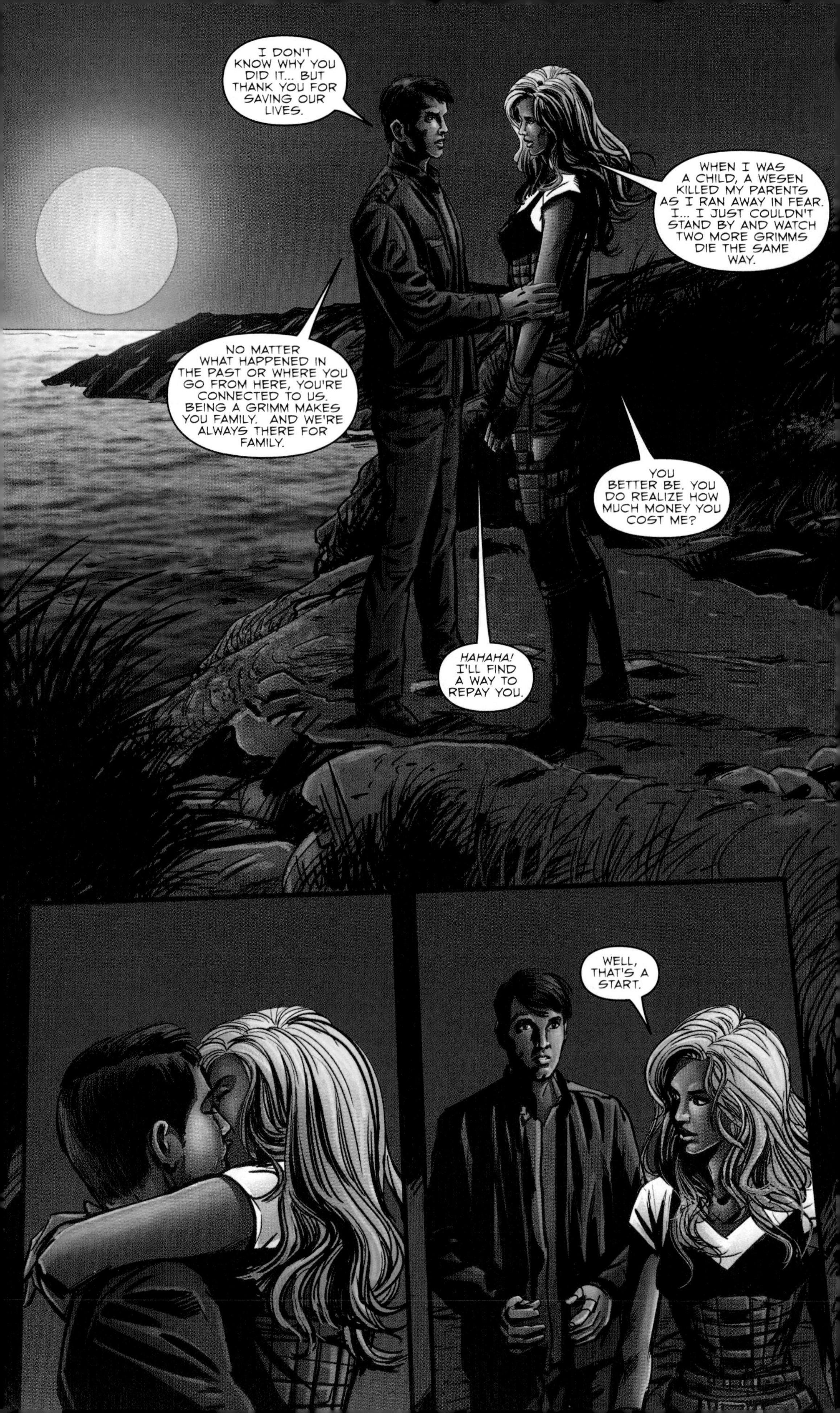
I DON'T KNOW WHY YOU DID IT... BUT THANK YOU FOR SAVING OUR LIVES.
WHEN I WAS A CHILD, A WESEN KILLED MY PARENTS AS I RAN AWAY IN FEAR. I... I JUST COULDN'T STAND BY AND WATCH TWO MORE GRIMMS DIE THE SAME WAY.
NO MATTER WHAT HAPPENED IN THE PAST OR WHERE YOU GO FROM HERE, YOU'RE CONNECTED TO US. BEING A GRIMM MAKES YOU FAMILY. AND WE'RE ALWAYS THERE FOR FAMILY.
YOU BETTER BE. YOU DO REALIZE HOW MUCH MONEY YOU COST ME?
HAHAHA! I'LL FIND A WAY TO REPAY YOU.
WELL, THAT'S A START.

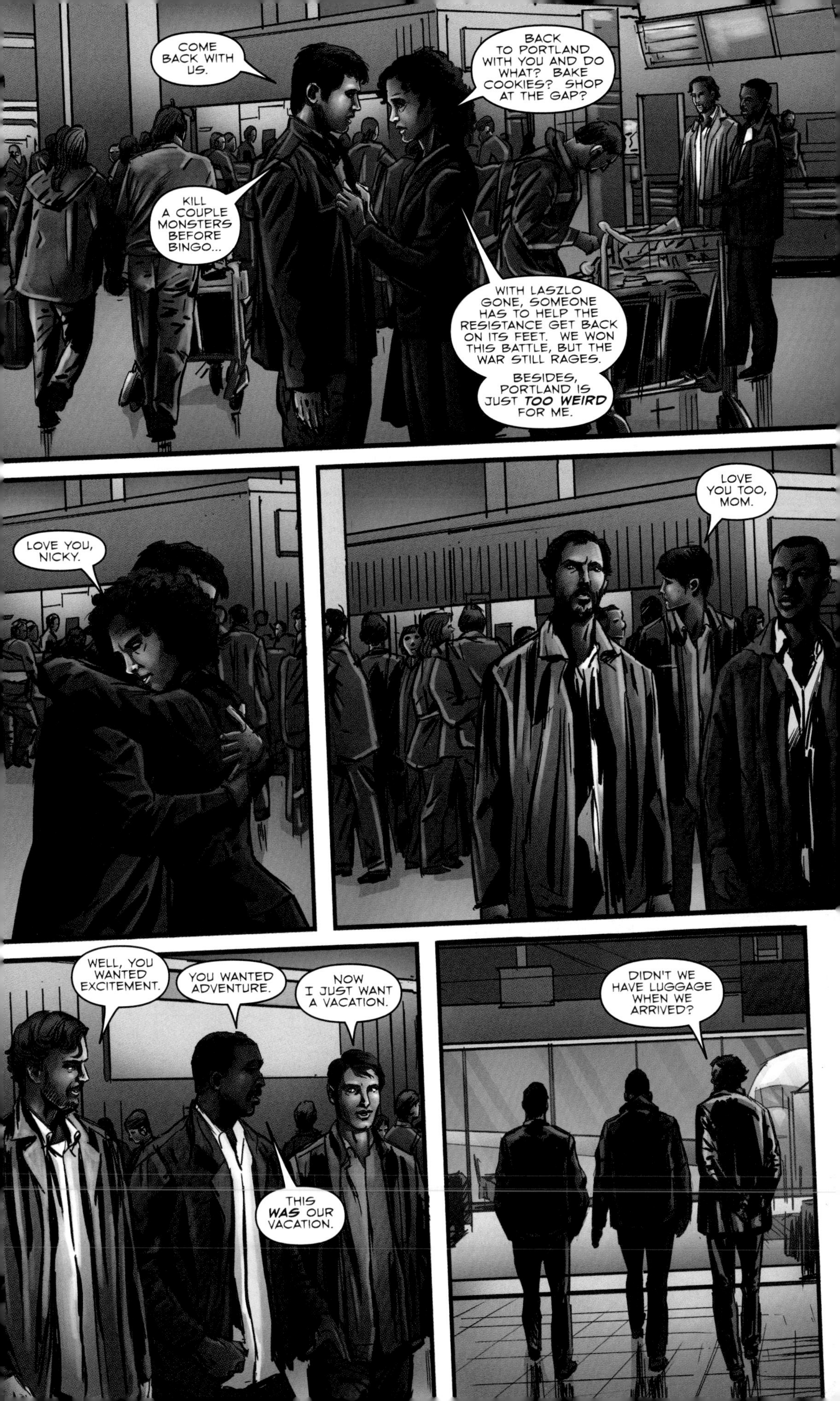

COME BACK WITH US.
BACK TO PORTLAND WITH YOU AND DO WHAT? BAKE COOKIES? SHOP AT THE GAP?
KILL A COUPLE MONSTERS BEFORE BINGO...
WITH LASZLO GONE, SOMEONE HAS TO HELP THE RESISTANCE GET BACK ON ITS FEET. WE WON THIS BATTLE, BUT THE WAR STILL RAGES.
BESIDES, PORTLAND IS JUST **TOO WEIRD** FOR ME.
LOVE YOU, NICKY.
LOVE YOU TOO, MOM.
WELL, YOU WANTED EXCITEMENT.
YOU WANTED ADVENTURE.
NOW I JUST WANT A VACATION.
THIS **WAS** OUR VACATION.
DIDN'T WE HAVE LUGGAGE WHEN WE ARRIVED?

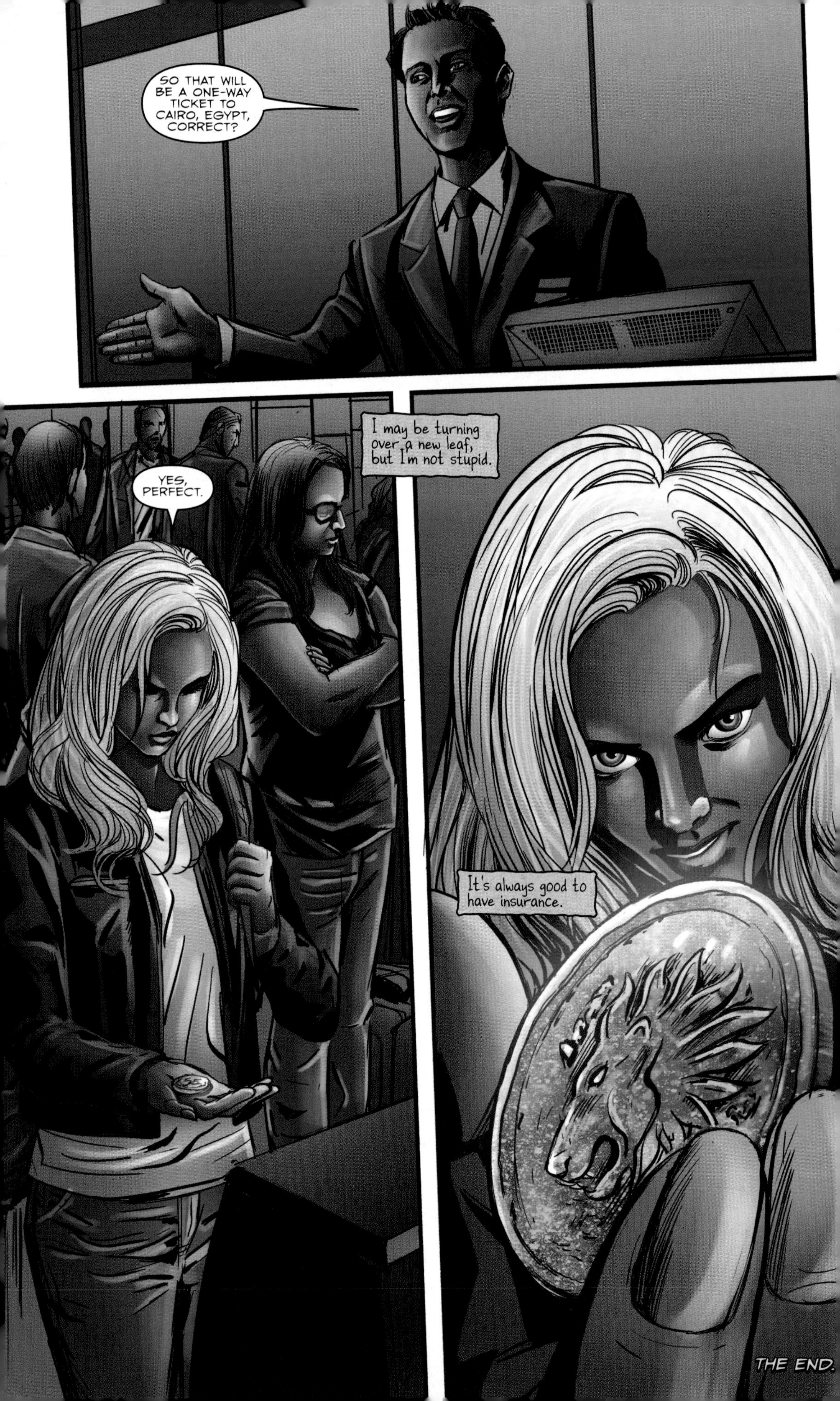
SO THAT WILL BE A ONE-WAY TICKET TO CAIRO, EGYPT, CORRECT?
YES, PERFECT.
I may be turning over a new leaf, but I'm not stupid.
It's always good to have insurance.
THE END.

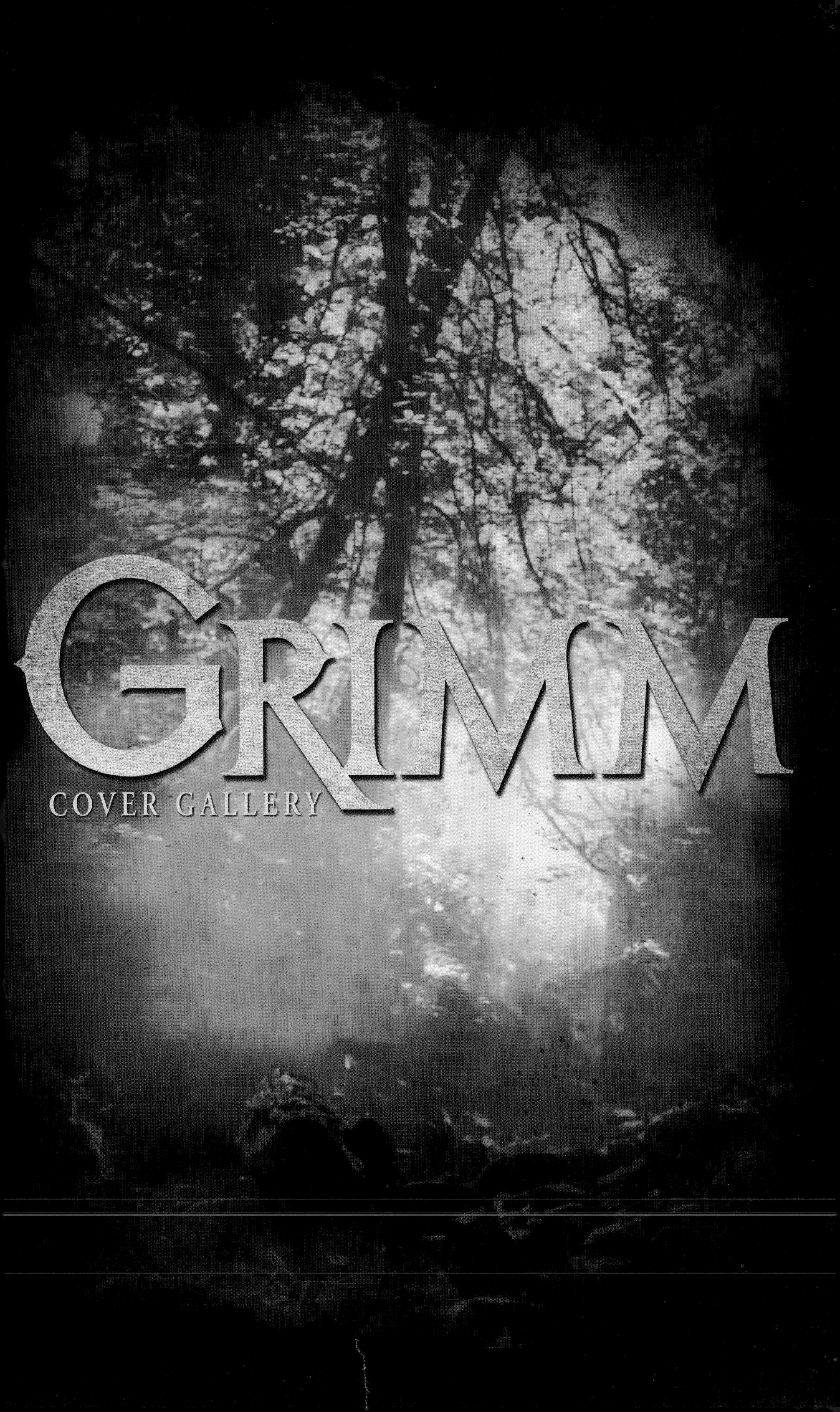
GRIMM
COVER GALLERY

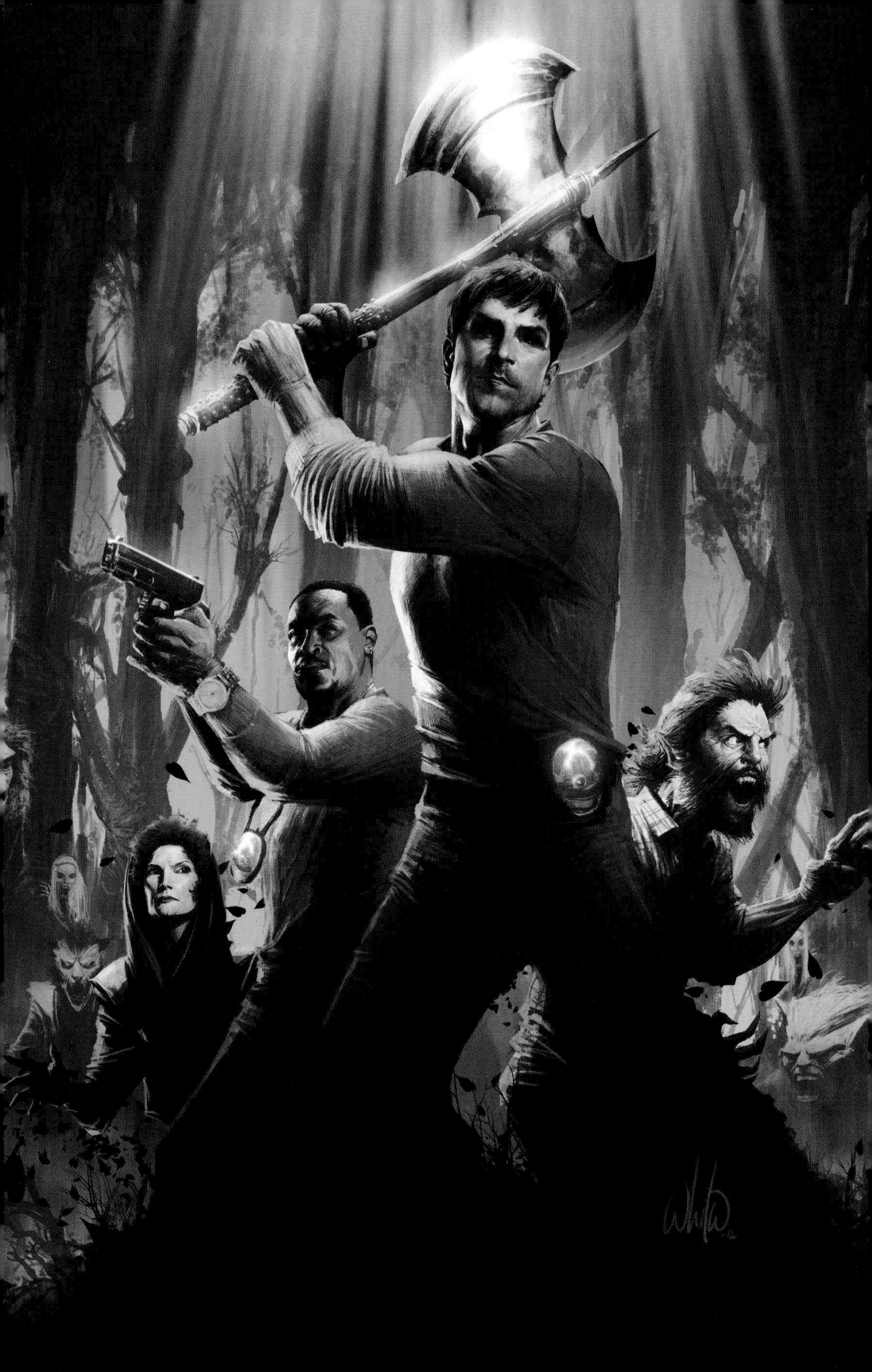

issue #0 cover by WHILCE PORTACIO

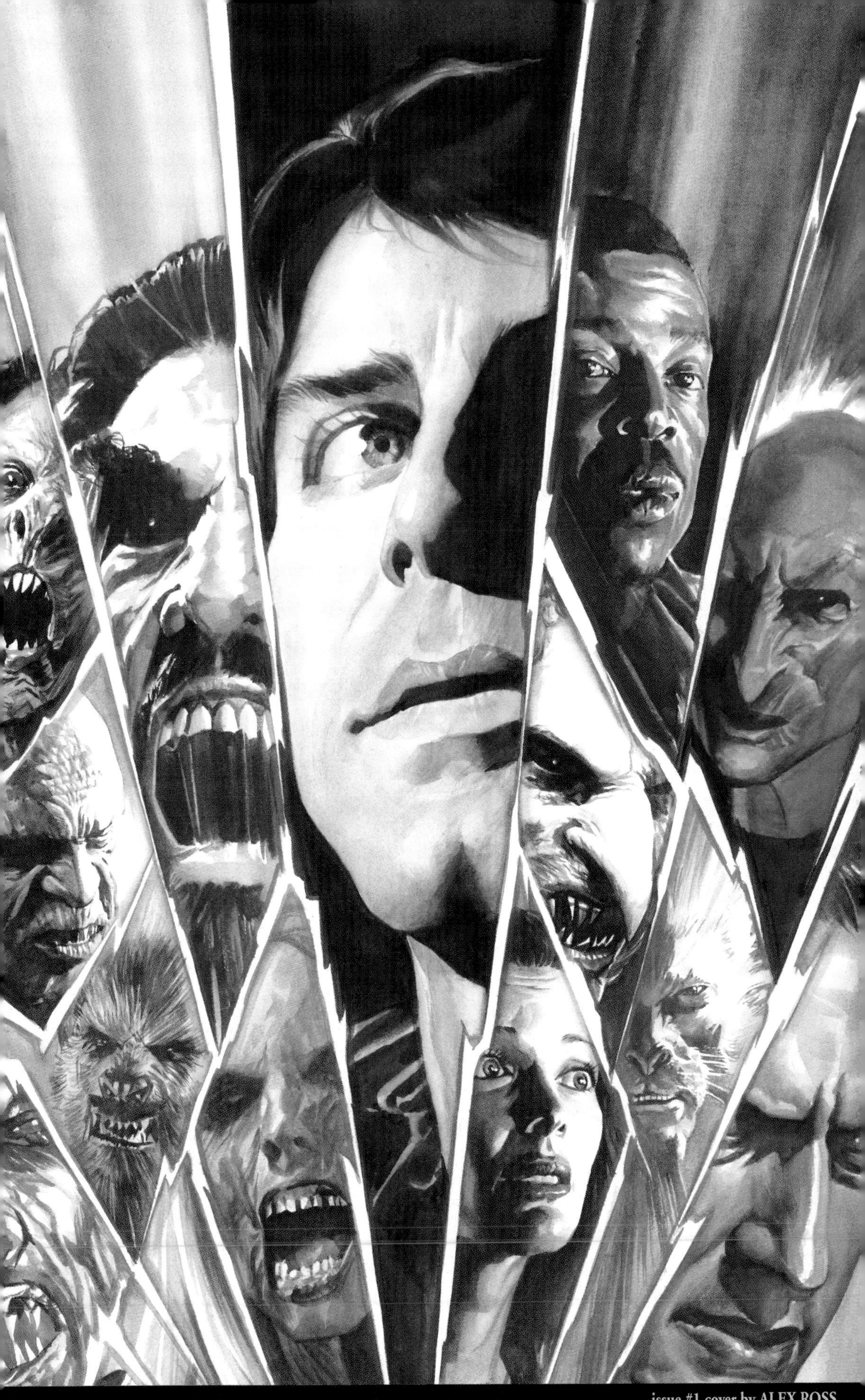

issue #1 cover by ALEX ROSS

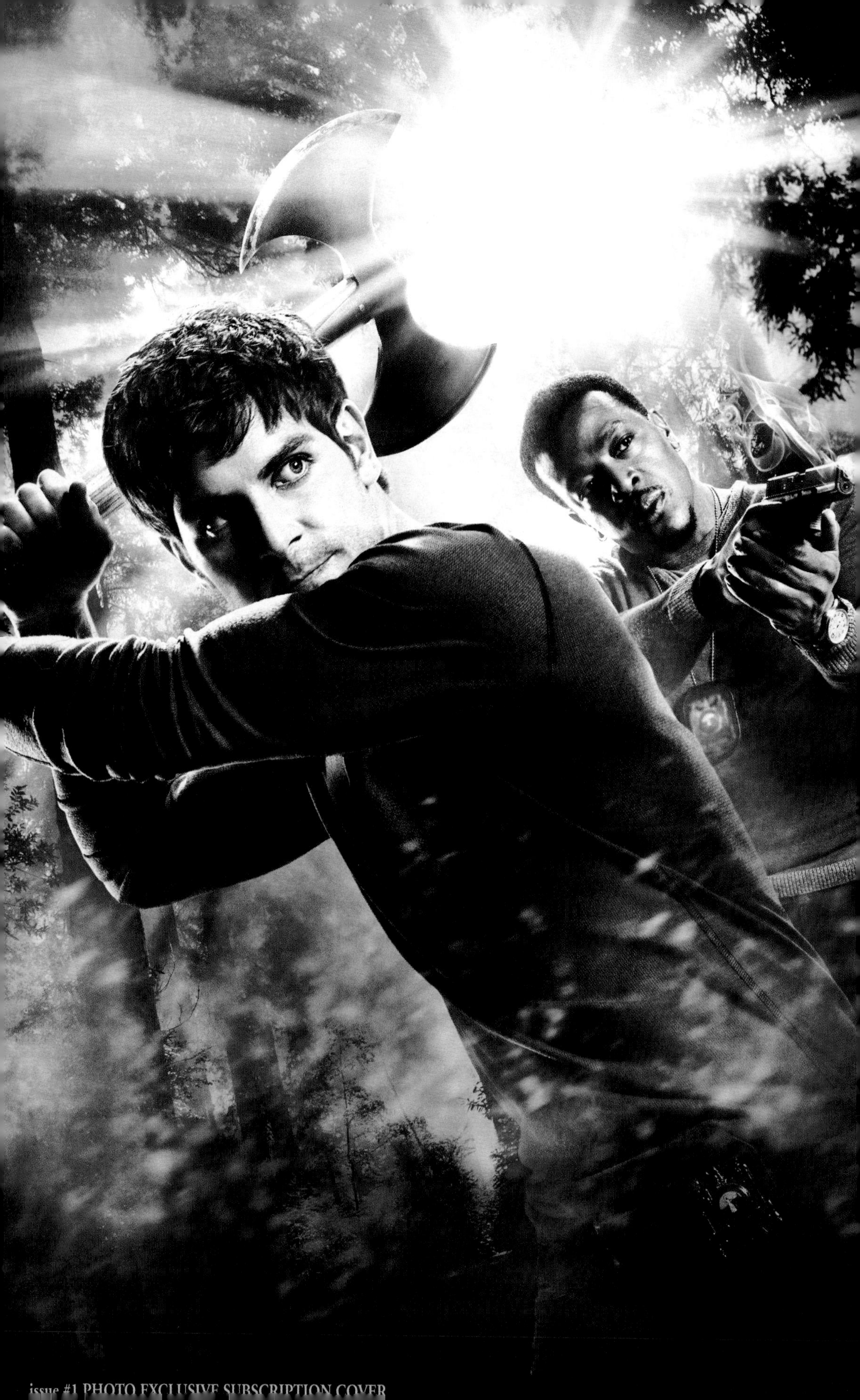

issue #1 PHOTO EXCLUSIVE SUBSCRIPTION COVER

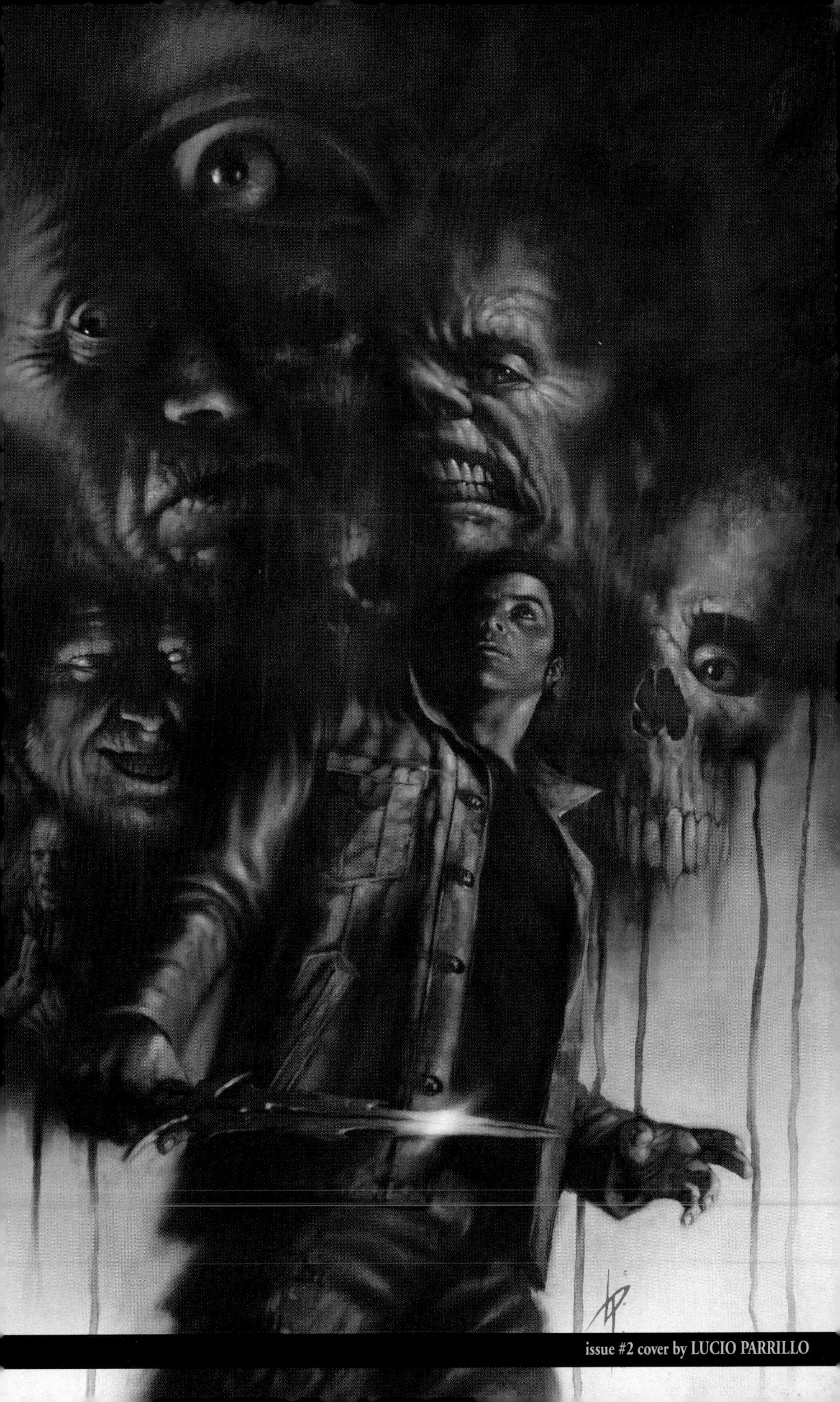

issue #2 cover by LUCIO PARRILLO

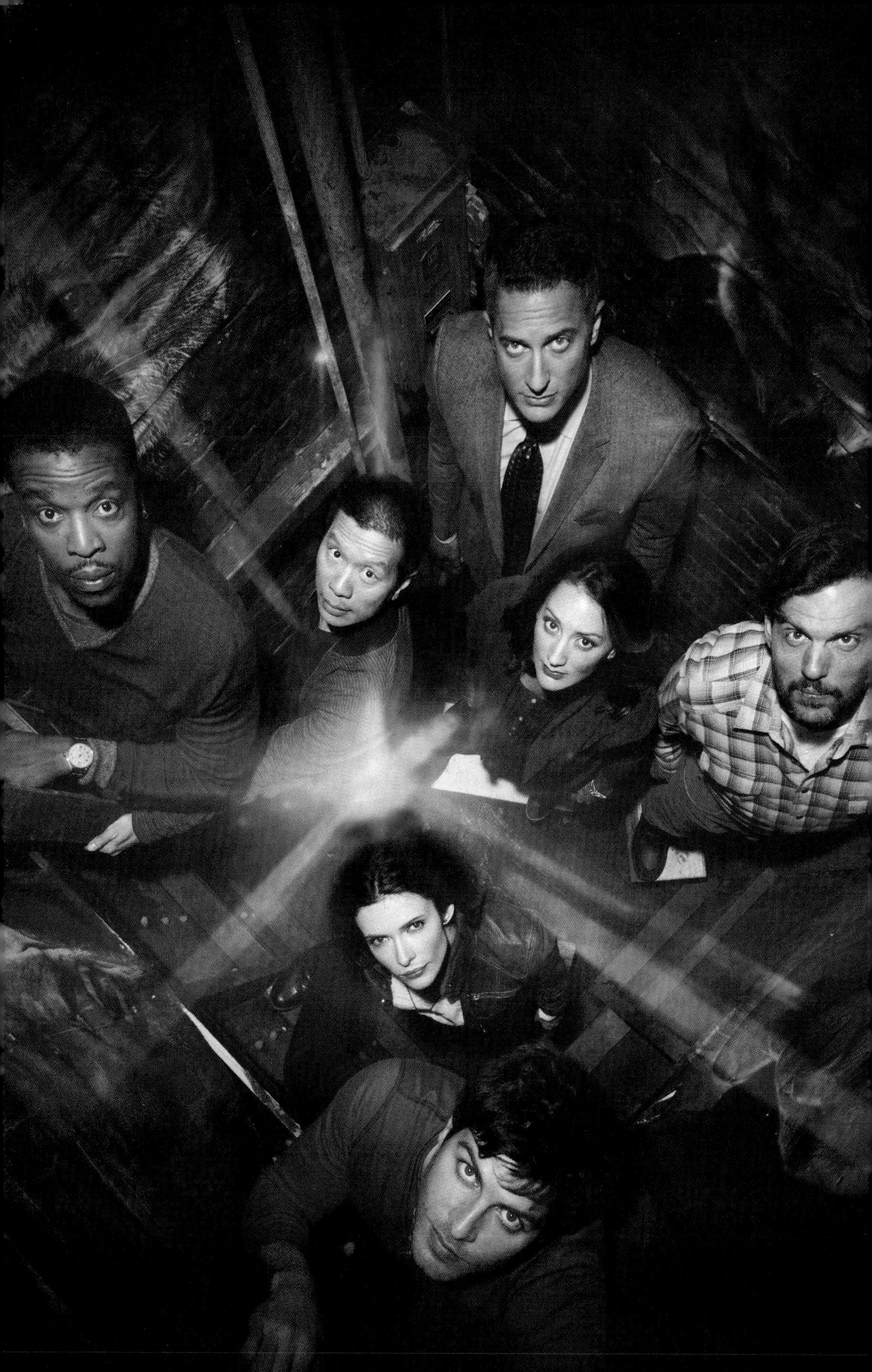

issue #2 PHOTO EXCLUSIVE SUBSCRIPTION COVER

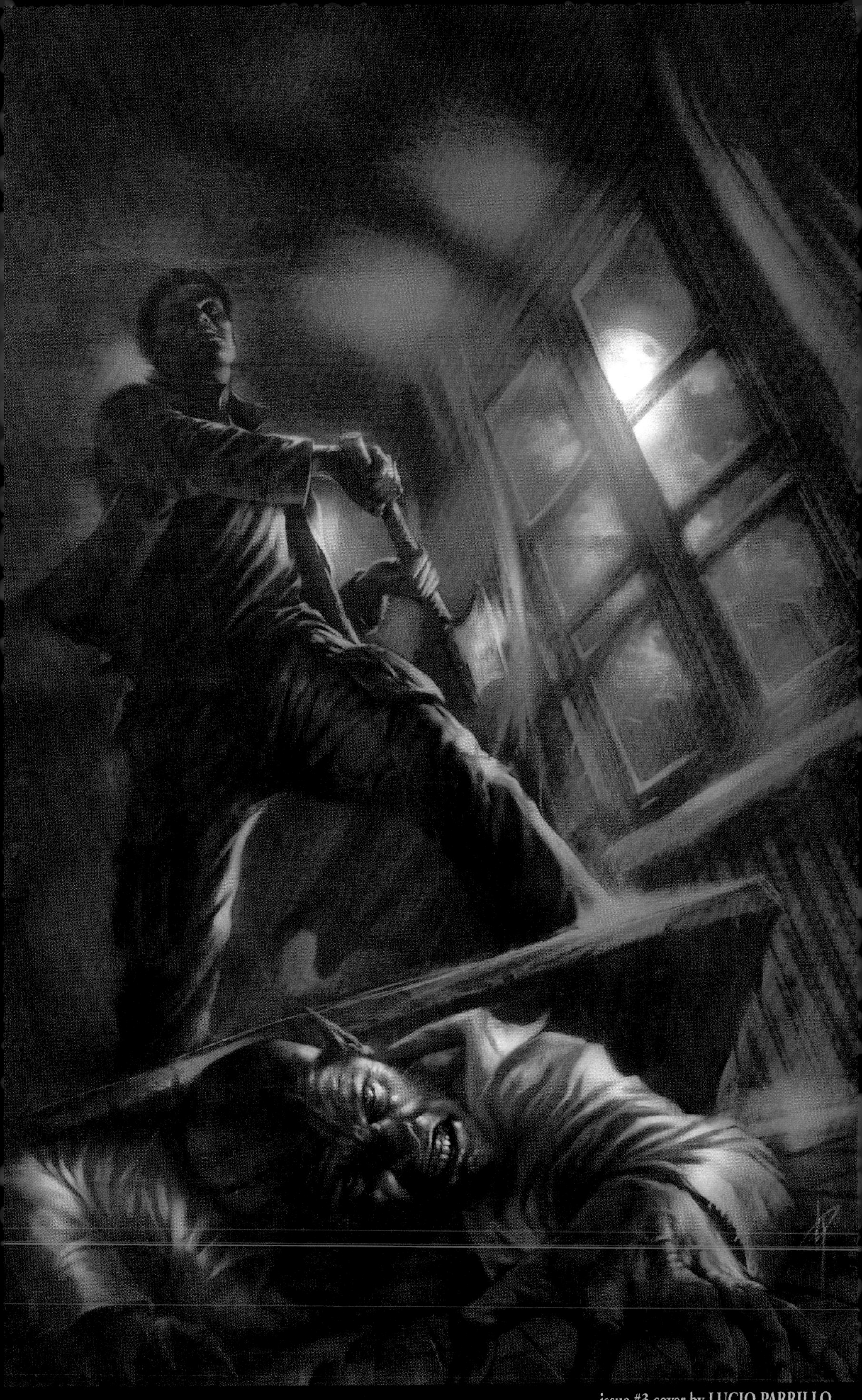

issue #3 cover by LUCIO PARRILLO

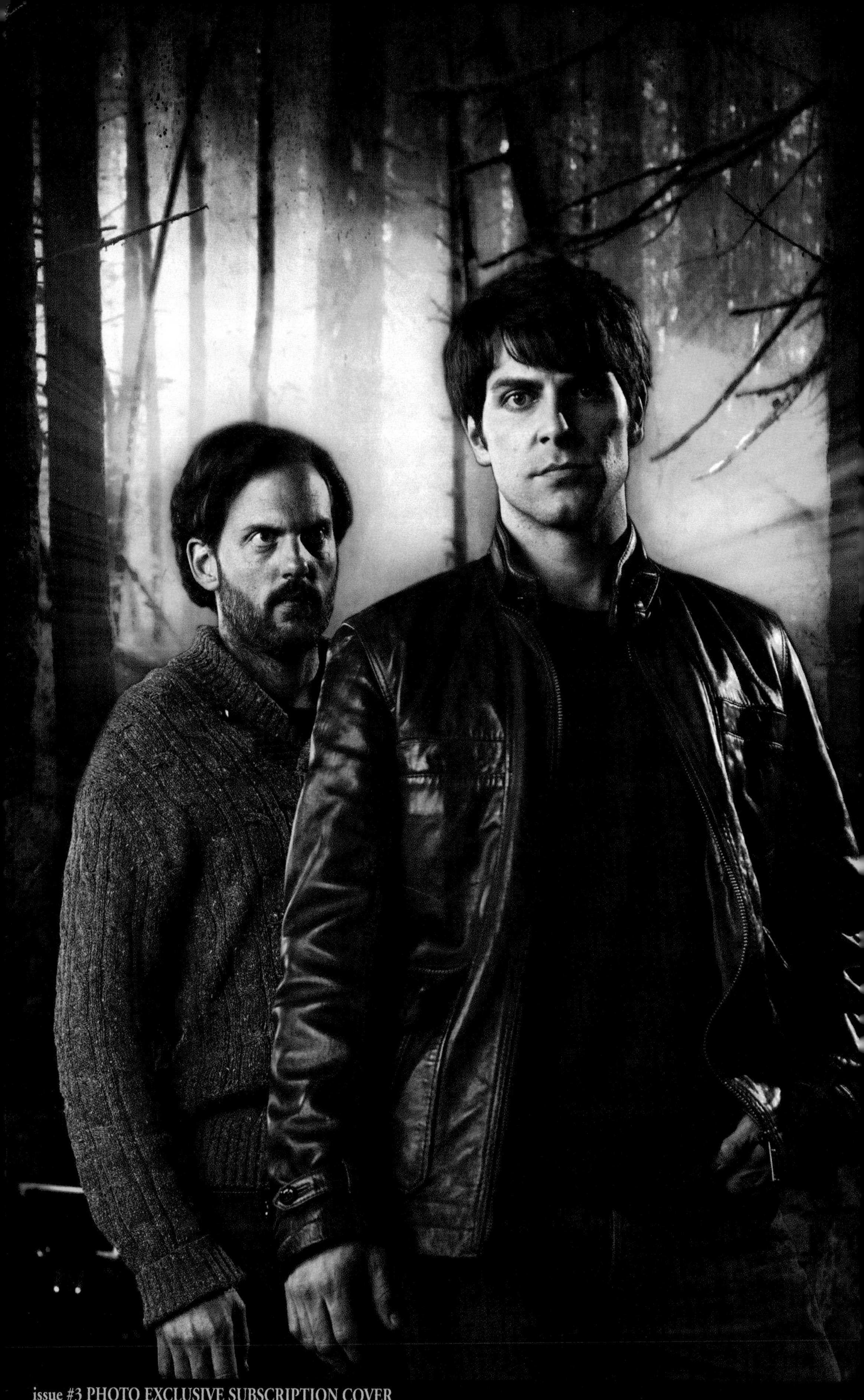

issue #3 PHOTO EXCLUSIVE SUBSCRIPTION COVER

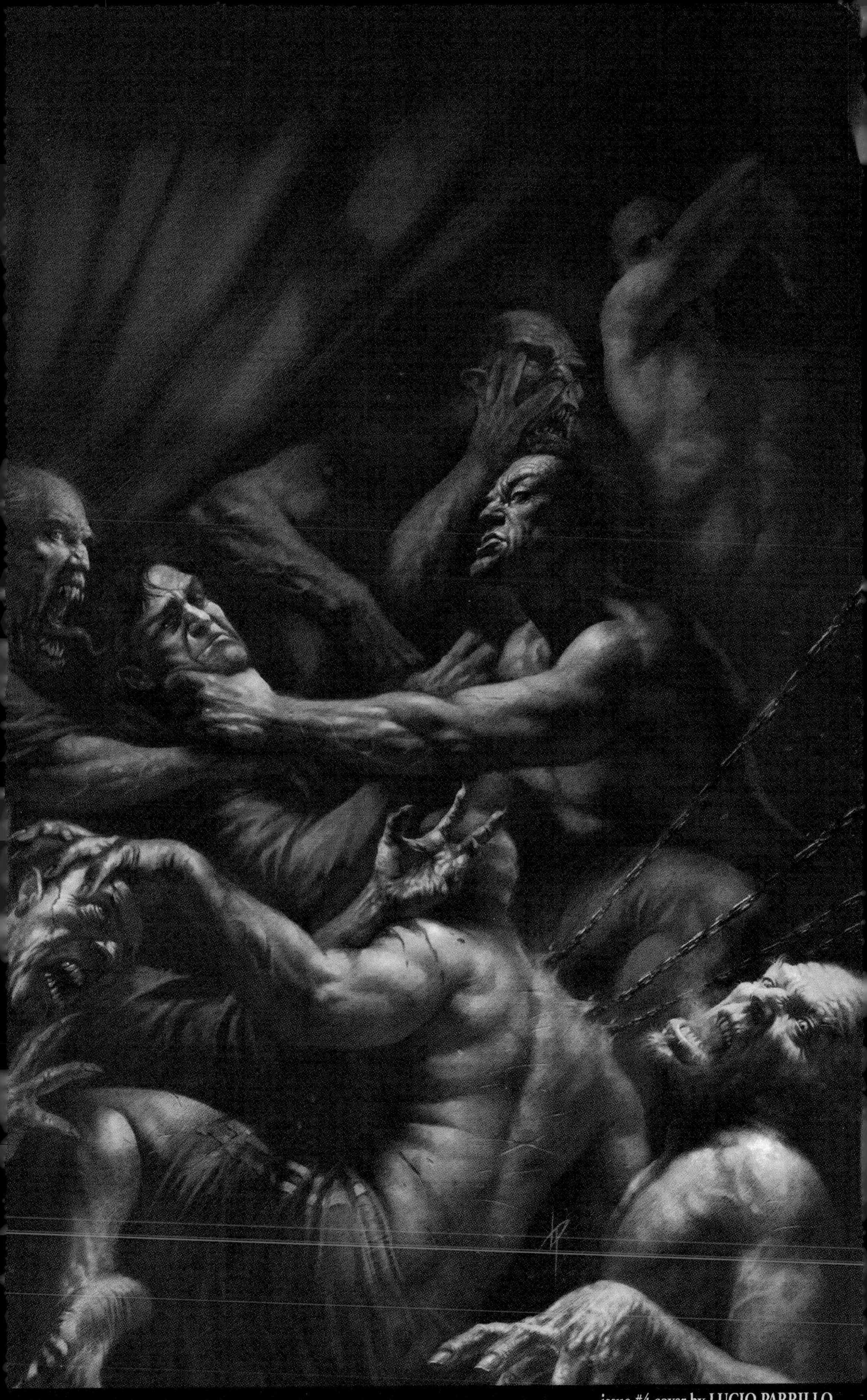

issue #4 cover by LUCIO PARRILLO

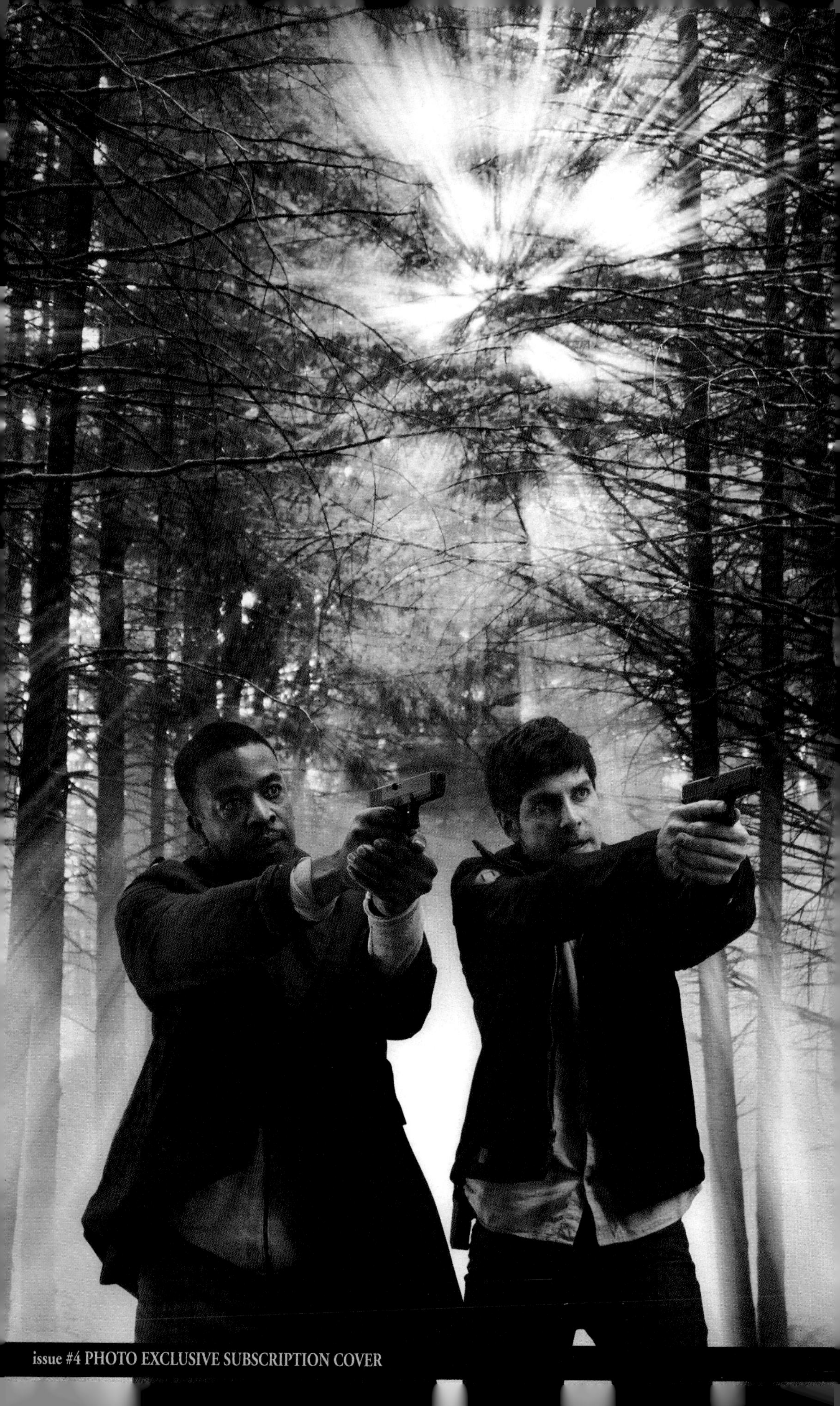

issue #4 PHOTO EXCLUSIVE SUBSCRIPTION COVER